THE DINERS CLUB
DRINK BOOK

HOW TO FIND YOUR WAY AROUND THE BEST BARS IN THE WORLD

Was James Bond right when he insisted his dry vodka martini be *shaked* not stirred?

If you say "Iechyd Da" in Wales do you get a drink or a punch in the mouth?

What is the magic ingredient in a Kiss-in-the-Dark cocktail?

What makes a Dickens martini different from all other martinis?

You'll find the answers to these and many other juice-y questions in THE NEW DINERS CLUB DRINK BOOK. Matty Simmons, who has visited more bars and restaurants in more cities than any ten ordinary men, has collected his findings and presents them to you in a unique volume for tasteful tippling and bravura bartending. So pick up THE NEW DINERS CLUB DRINK BOOK and learn to *skoal* in style!

SIGNET Cook Books

THE NEW DINERS CLUB DRINK BOOK

Revised and Enlarged

Illustrations by
JOHN V. CIOFALO
and RICHARD D. SOMMERS

by Matty Simmons

A SIGNET BOOK

Published by The New American Library

SIGNET TRADEMARK REG. U.S. PAT. OFF. AND FOREIGN COUNTRIES
REGISTERED TRADEMARK—MARCA REGISTRADA
HECHO EN CHICAGO, U.S.A.

SIGNET BOOKS are published by
The New American Library, Inc.,
1301 Avenue of the Americas, New York, New York 10019

FIRST PRINTING, MAY, 1969

PRINTED IN THE UNITED STATES OF AMERICA

Dedicated to:

Lee, Mike, Julie and Andy
My Fifth and Three Half Pints

This book was created by the ~~~~ of The Diners Club Magazine. As the then-Exec~~~~ e Editor of that publication, I would like to than~~~~ fellow editors and other associates for their e~~~~. I leave them with one word: Bicarb.

—M.S.

contents

FOREWORD
by Joe E. Lewis   ix

INTRODUCTION
by Matty Simmons   xi

SOME IMPORTANT QUESTIONS AND ANSWERS ON DRINK   15

Including:
How Experts Mix Drinks   15

Sobering Up   16

Holding your Liquor   17

Calorie Content of Alcoholic Beverages   19

The Compleat Bar   20

Official Bar Measures   20

How to Order Wines   21-23

How to Read a Wine Label   25

DRINK RECIPES   29

THE STORY OF RYE, BOURBON AND BLENDED WHISKEY
by Sam Boal   48

THE WATER OF LIFE (THE STORY OF SCOTCH WHISKY)
by Bernard Landis   79

INTERNATIONAL DRINK TOASTS   100

THE JUNIPER DRINK (THE STORY OF GIN)
by Hunter Barnhall   115

JOHN BARLEYCORN
by Richard Sharpe   135

THERE'S A TOWN CALLED COGNAC
by Myra Waldo   162

IT'S THE FIZZ THAT GETS YOU   186

THE REAL SPIRIT OF '76 (THE STORY OF RUM)
by Michael Fain   191

THE DRINK YOU CANNOT SEE—OR TASTE
(THE STORY OF VODKA)
by Andrew Barton   219

THE DAY THE BEACHCOMBER INVENTED THE ZOMBIE   228

Non-alcoholic "Legal" Recipes as Prepared
by *Weight Watchers*® Magazine   230

SNACK RECIPES   232

GLOSSARY OF DRINK TERMS   258

KING EDWARD'S LIQUOR LAWS ARE STILL WITH US
by Don Simmons   272

DRINK INDEX   275

SNACK INDEX   286

foreword

I'M GLAD I was invited to do the foreword for this book, the history of mankind. I can think of no one the author and publishers of this production could call on who could be more of an expert on the subject at hand than me.

As a matter of fact I started research on this piece many years ago, and today after this intense study I've decided that I've learned nothing—but who the hell cares because I'm the happiest researcher I know.

Personally I'm against drink books. I don't believe in recipes that involve more than one lift and one pour. The best recipe ever created for a drink goes: "Take the juice from one bottle of Scotch—."

I've also other helpful things I can tell you about drinking. For example, the best way to melt ice is to pour Scotch over it.

The perfect hangover remedy? Stay drunk.

And here's a new creation: You mix Scotch and carrot juice. You get just as drunk, but you see better.

But, let Simmons tell you HOW to drink. It's more important that I instill in you the proper philosophy of drink and I'm just the man who can do it. In my circles I'm known as the Albert Schweitzer of the gin mills. My drinking research has helped millions. I cannot count the number of marooned seamen I've helped by emptying the bottles for them to put messages in.

As a matter of fact, I'm seriously considering retiring from the night club business and devoting all my time to helping people—people like Schenley, Haig & Haig, Carstairs. I might even buy my own distillery. What the hell, one customer like me and I'm a millionaire!

Many people have suggested that I give up drinking. My doctor once did put me on the wagon to lose weight. In two weeks I lost nearly 14 days.

But, actually my drinking has been overplayed. I don't drink any more than the man next to me. Of course the man next to me is usually Dean Martin.

Newspaper columnists particularly, tend to exaggerate my drinking. Every time I drink a quart, they say it's a gallon, and when I drink a gallon, they say I'm drunk.

But, I'm glad that I've been given this opportunity to pass along some sound advice about drink. This is a helluva book and I really think you ought to read it from cover to cover. Although if you want me to save you the trouble, I'll tell you right now—the Butler Did It!

It's no little prestige to be asked to write the foreword for the first Diners Club Drink Book and the Author was very wise in selecting a man of letters—letters like B & B, V.O., and XXX.

They originally wanted my photo to go with this, and I sat for my portrait for two hours, but the picture didn't turn out—the bottle moved.

JOE E. LEWIS

introduction

THIS is the second edition of "Booze Who In America."
We've gathered on these pages what we believe to be as large
and comprehensive a collection of drink and snack recipes and
whys, wherefores, yesses and nos on liquors and wines as has
ever been assembled in any book of this kind.

Some people regard liquor as something evil, a sort of potion
of the devil. It can be—but it shouldn't be.

Drinking can be fun and it can be relaxing and convivial and
sociable. Excessive drinking, however, just doesn't make sense.
We're not members of the Temperance League or the Prohibition Party, and Grandma didn't carry a hatchet with Carry
Nation. We simply agree with all the big liquor distillers who
urge people to drink moderately. Do that and you'll enjoy your
drinking.

The preparation of fine liquors and wines is a great art.
Appreciate that art. Enjoying a good drink is very much the
same as relishing good food and a gourmet is never a gour-
mand. End of lecture.

Is there a more logical outfit to sponsor a drink book than
The Diners Club, whose credit card holders charge millions
of dollars each year in the purchase of liquor? This, then, is the
new Diners Club Drink Book.

We've tried to be informative and yet not ponderous. We
hope that we've not only given you a reference book, but one
also that you'll read for the fun of it.

MATTY SIMMONS

THE NEW DINERS CLUB DRINK BOOK

some important
questions and answers
on drink

LIQUOR, aside from being the great equalizer, and aside from adding more to a good time than any other ingredient, and aside from reportedly being excellent for medicinal purposes, and aside from being capable of being turned into all kinds of delightful tastes, is very possibly as great a conversation piece as politics, baseball and sex. People always seem to be talking about it, and like politics, baseball and sex, people are always giving out with facts, figures and instructions that more often reflect opinion than truth. Therefore, in compiling a drink book we felt it advisable to inject a question and answer segment in an effort to straighten out some of the old wives' tales about booze, and also to give you more of an insight into what is called in Gaelic, "The Water of Life." We have, in addition, thrown in the questions asked about the more practical aspects of mixology. For example: What do you mix what with?

QUESTION: *How do the experts mix?*

ANSWER: Here are some tips on mixing best. Drinks, that is. They're yours, courtesy of a drunk we know who got that way writing drink books.

a) Pre-chill your glasses. It's not only a physical edge to start a cold drink with a cold glass, but psychologically it looks better, so in the mind of the beholder it will taste better.

b) When preparing on-the-rocks drinks, crack the ice a little. It will chill the drink better and faster. Before pouring your liquor over the rocks, make sure to drain out all excess water.

c) When mixing a drink in a shaker, again be sure to drain off the water. Use cracked ice and when shaking your drink, really shake it; don't rock it to sleep. If you shake it for about fifteen seconds you will be adding three quarters of an ounce of water per drink, and the longer you shake it the more water you add, so stop after 10 to 15 seconds and have your glasses handy so you can pour as soon as you finish.

d) For Frappes, use very finely shaved ice in the glass. After mixing your drink over cracked ice or ice cubes, again be sure to cool and frost glasses.

e) Blenders are fine but the real mixologist prefers hand oscillating since blending tends to put even more water in the drink via its violent handling of the ice. At any rate, if you do use a blender don't blend too long.

f) When mixing a carbonated highball, put in your ice first, then toss in your liquor and then your soda, cola or ginger ale. Stir vigorously.

g) When using sugar you'll want to use finely granulated sugar and not confectioner's sugar. Dissolve the sugar completely in a bit of liquid in the glass before you add ice.

h) For heaven's sake, whenever you make a Martini, remember *stir*—do not shake.

i) To obtain egg whites, bore a small hole in the egg shell or crack it sharply on the edge of the glass splitting the shell into two parts, passing the yolk from one shell to another allowing the white to slurp through. Whenever you do this, please make sure there's a glass beneath!

j) The only thing worse than a weak drink is one that's too strong. So stick to the measurements and don't try to indulge your guests by giving them more booze than the recipe calls for.

k) Measure jiggers and ponies accurately and make your squirts and dashes just that and not steady streams. If you use too much liquor, shake and stir longer and stretch the ice.

QUESTION: *Will fresh air help sober you?*
ANSWER: According to Dr. Theodore Koppanyi, Professor of Pharmacology at Georgetown University's medical school

in Washington, D. C., fresh air won't help you "sober up." Thus, another facet of hangover lore explodes.

In a paper prepared for the American Association for the Advancement of Science, Dr. Koppanyi dismissed as worthless the deep breathing of fresh air always counted upon to help in the sobering-up process. He said it takes five to six hours for the body to burn up four ounces of whiskey and whether you do your breathing out-of-doors or in a smoke-filled cabaret, the time's still five to six hours.

The Professor did reveal, however, that limited experiments show that injections of fructose, a kind of sugar, do help the body get rid of alcohol at a greater speed. Fructose is obtained from honey and other tests have shown that eating honey will help the sobering up process.

Incidentally, aside from fresh air, the usual hangover and sobering up treatment involves saturating the victim with pots of black coffee. This is probably the worst thing you can do for a person with a load on. Black coffee, of course, is a stimulant, and the best thing that can be done is to go to bed and sleep it off. Try sleeping with 10 cups of black coffee in your stomach.

If your head aches, of course, take a couple of aspirins; they won't sober you up, but they might reduce the clanging in the brain.

QUESTION: *Can some people, because of experience or certain physical capabilities, drink more liquor than others?*

ANSWER: No. Some might be able to handle their liquor better, but this is purely mental and not physical.

All things being equal, it takes just about the same alcoholic content for one man to go blotto as another. Physicians figure that anyone whose blood-alcohol content reaches .15% is drunk. Some people may be able to navigate better than others when drunk and that can come from experience. But let's face it, there is no such thing as a hollow leg.

QUESTION: *Is liquor good for a cold?*

ANSWER: Nothing is "good" for a cold. Liquor, however, is an analgesic, so it's good for aches and pains. Try any of the hot toddies, recipes for which can be found on these pages. If they don't cure your cold, enough of them will get your mind on something else, anyway.

QUESTION: *Can mixing your drinks cause ill effects?*

ANSWER: No, but drinking too much can. When it comes to drinking, it's not *what* you drink but *how much* alcohol you consume that makes you ill. On the other hand, soda used as a mixer will tend to heighten the effect of the drink, and, conversely, if you eat while you're drinking, it will absorb some of the alcohol.

17

Along the same lines, a drink mixed with something that has food value (milk, egg, tomato juice) will have less effect than a straight highball. Incidentally, according to Yale's expert on alcoholic effect, Dr. Leon Greenberg, it's almost impossible to get drunk on beer. Dr. Greenberg contends that the human stomach cannot hold as much beer as contains the necessary amount of alcohol to get you loaded.

QUESTION: *When preparing a mixed drink such as a Collins or an Old Fashioned or something along those lines, what goes in the glass first?*

ANSWER: If sugar is being used in the drink it should always be put in before the liquor. And since alcohol is a poor solvent for sugar, the drink should be muddled with a squirt of soda or a dash of water.

In general, however, your best bet always is to put in the less costly ingredients first. Suppose you were fixing a Brandy eggnog. The recipe calls for 1 jigger of Brandy, 1 teaspoon sugar, 5 oz. milk, 1 whole egg, cracked ice and nutmeg.

First the ice goes in, then the sugar, then the milk (muddled) then the egg, and finally the Brandy. Of course, the nutmeg is a garnish.

QUESTION: *Is liquor fattening?*

ANSWER: Categorically, yes. An ounce of Rye whiskey adds up to about 100 calories which is equal to about six teaspoons of sugar. Like any other relatively fattening food or drink, however, liquor will make you fat only if, when combined with other calories, your regular caloric intake is more than it should be.

The pastry and cream lover will add suet if he also includes some heavy drinking in his diet. On the other hand, the steak and salad man probably has more room calorie-wise for those extra drinks each day.

For the Record: Here are the calorie contents of the most popular types of liquor. Naturally, if you have a chaser or a highball the calorie content goes up. So, if you're really on a diet, you might want to mix your drink with water or take it straight.

The way we see it, you shouldn't think about calories when you're drinking. You drink to relax and relaxing is even more important healthwise than losing weight. Skip the next piece of whipped cream pie if you have to.

See Next Page for Calorie Chart

CALORIE CONTENT OF ALCOHOLIC BEVERAGES

	GLASS SIZE		CALORIES
Ale	8 oz.	Beer	150
Alexander Cocktail, Brandy	3 oz.	Cocktail	185
Beer, Lager	8 oz.	Beer	125
Brandy	1 oz.	Cordial	75
Brandy Sour	6 oz.	Delmonico	155
Canadian Whiskey	1 oz.	Pony	100
Canadian Whiskey Highball	8 oz.	Highball	175
Champagne	6 oz.	Champagne	165
Champagne Cocktail	6 oz.	Deep V	175
Claret Wine	4 oz.	Wine	125
Cognac	1 oz.	Pony	75
Crème de Menthe	1 oz.	Cordial	90
Daiquiri	3 oz.	Cocktail	180
Gin	1½ oz.	Jigger	112
Gin Collins	10 oz.	Tom Collins	155
Horse's Neck	10 oz.	Tom Collins	190
Irish Whiskey	1 oz.	Pony	100
Manhattan	3 oz.	Cocktail	260
Martini (dry)	3 oz.	Cocktail	200
Mint Julep	10 oz.	Tom Collins	355
Port	4 oz.	Wine	135
Rob Roy	3 oz.	Cocktail	230
Rum Collins	10 oz.	Tom Collins	175
Rum, Jamaica	1 oz.	Pony	100
Rye Highball	8 oz.	Highball	175
Rye Whiskey	1 oz.	Pony	100
Sauterne (sweet)	4 oz.	Wine	95
Scotch Manhattan	3 oz.	Cocktail	235
Scotch & Soda	8 oz.	Highball	90
Scotch	1 oz.	Pony	85
Sherry	2½ oz.	Sherry	95
Stinger	3 oz.	Cocktail	185
Tom Collins	10 oz.	Tom Collins	155
Vermouth (Dry or French)	4 oz.	Wine	105
Vermouth (Sweet or Italian)	4 oz.	Wine	175
Vodka	1½ oz.	Jigger	180
Whiskey Cocktail	1⅓ oz.	Whiskey	155
Whiskey Highball	8 oz.	Highball	175
Whiskey Sour	3 oz.	Cocktail	200
Wine	4 oz.	Wine	95
Wine, Sweet	4 oz.	Wine	130
Zombie	14 oz.	Tom Collins	510

QUESTION: *I want to be the Compleat Bartender. What equipment should I have in my home bar?*

ANSWER: The best bar you can own is at the Copacabana. If you can't spring for that, here's what to do, step by step:

1. Since the art of drinking begins logically with opening bottles, you need a good lever-action cork screw and a bottle opener.

2. There are four professional implements for the measuring and mixing of drinks: (a) a graduated measuring glass or double-ended cup (a jigger and a pony); (b) a genuine bar shaker, consisting of a metal and a glass container; (c) a wire strainer; (d) a mixing pitcher and a long-stemmed stirring spoon (known as a barspoon).

3. For the preparation of fruit, you need a cutting board and knife, a juicer (either manual or electric), and a lime squeezer.

4. For icing drinks, you need an adjustable ice shaver and two ice buckets, one for cube ice and one for shaved ice.

5. For the preparation of drinks, you need a bar muddler, a bitters bottle, a bowl of lump sugar and one of confectioner's sugar, and a bar towel.

6. For the serving of drinks, you need the following glasses: Cocktail, Highball, Tom Collins, Delmonico (or Sour), Old Fashioned, Sherry, Champagne, Wine, Liqueur and Brandy, in quantities depending upon your needs. You need individual stirrers or muddlers, small silver spoons, coasters and napkins, short straws and toothpicks. Silver goblets for mint juleps, Tom & Jerry mugs, and Toddy glasses with handles will put you in the top professional category.

QUESTION: *What are the official bar measures?*

ANSWER:

1 Bar Glass = 1½ oz.
1 Barspoon = ⅛ oz.
1 Cup = 8 oz.
1 Dash = 1/6 teaspoon
1 Fifth = 25.6 oz.
1 Jigger = 1½ oz. (equal to a small whiskey or bar glass)
1 Pint = 16 oz.
1 Pony = 1 oz.
1 Quart = 32 oz.
1 Split = 6 oz. (or ½ regular-sized bottle of carbonated water)
1 Teaspoon = ⅛ oz.
1 Wine Glass = 4 oz.

QUESTION: *Is alcohol a stimulant?*

ANSWER: No, alcohol relaxes. It doesn't generate heat in the body but cools everything. It will even eventually cool your skin although at first it gives the illusion of sudden warmth. When you're in the tropics and want to lower the temperature of your body you should drink Rum and not ice water.

QUESTION: *What is the relative potency of the most popular drinks?*

ANSWER: In terms of cooperative alcohol content, this is an easy question to answer. However, variations are wide because of the differences in strengths and in quantities of liquor dispensed by the bartender involved. At any rate, let's say it's Mr. Average Bartender.

When you know the proof of a liquor you can cut that in half and get the alcoholic content. Therefore the highest concentrate of alcohol is in a straight shot of 100-proof Bottled-in-Bond Whiskey or Brandy, which is 50% alcohol; next comes the Gins, Whiskey, Rums, Brandies and Vodkas. They range from 70 to 90 proof and since alcohol content is half of the proof, then in these cases it's 40-45% alcohol content. Cordials are from 25-55% alcohol content; Martinis, 34-40%; Manhattans 30-36%; Old Fashioneds 25-30%; Highballs 9-20%; Dessert Wines and Vermouths 16-20%; Table and Sparkling Wines 9-14%; Beer and Ale—roughly 4-6%.

QUESTION: *How do most people drink liquor?*

ANSWER: Most Rye drinkers take their whiskey in highballs, cocktails and straight.

Most Scotch drinkers prefer highballs, on the rocks, and then straight.

Brandy and Cognac drinkers: straight, in cocktails, in highballs.

Irish Whiskey: straight, in highballs and on the rocks.

Rum: in cocktails, highballs, and straight.

Vodka: in cocktails, highballs, and straight.

Canadian Whiskey: in highballs, straight and on the rocks.

All these preferences are given in their correct order.

QUESTION: *Which wines do I order with what?*

ANSWER: The common rule of thumb is to order red wine with red meat; white wine with white meat. Here are some specific wines you might order with some specific dishes:

Burgundy *with red meats and game.*

Burgundy, White *for white meats and seafood.*

Chablis *with oysters, seafood and white meats.*

Champagne *with anything.*

Chianti, Red *for red meats, pastas, and oily foods.*

Chianti, White *for white meats and seafood.*

Gamay *for red meats and game.*
Graves *for white meats and dessert.*
Madeira, Dry *as an aperitif or with soups.*
Madeira, Sweet *with dessert or after dinner or between meals.*
Muscatel *with dessert, after dinner or between meals.*
Pinot Blanc *with seafood and white meat.*
Pinot Noir *with red meats.*
Port *with desserts and cheese or between meals.*
Rhine Wine *with seafood and white meat.*
Rosé *for luncheons and picnics (light dining).*
Sherry, Dry *before dinner and with soup.*
Sherry, Sweet *with dessert.*
Tokay *with dessert and after dinner.*
Vermouth, French *with appetizer.*
Vermouth, Italian *with dessert and after dinner.*

We've named only a handful of the fine wines available and when they are appropriate for serving. When in doubt, stick to the rule of thumb.

QUESTION: *When ordering wine or champagne, how do I know what year to order?*

ANSWER: Ask the "sommelier," (the wine steward), the captain, or perhaps your waiter (if he's the kind of waiter who really knows his business). Some wine years are very good, others are very bad. You might want to study the chart below to note the years that experts consider outstanding.

This chart was prepared by the Wine and Food Society, 30 Grosvenor Gardens, London, S.W. 1, England.

0—is no good.
1—is bad and so forth up to 7, which is the best. So, when ordering you'll want to order 7, and if you can't get that, you can work your way down.

Year	Port	Claret	Burgundy	Rhone	Rhine & Moselle	Sauternes	White Burgundy	Champagne
1945	7	7	6	7	6	7	6	6
1946	5	3	3	5	3	3	3	3
1947	6	5	6	6	6	6	6	7
1948	7	5	5	4	4	4	5	4
1949	4	6	5	7	7	5	5	6
1950	6	5	4	6	4	4	5	3
1951	3	3	3	4	2	2	3	2
1952	4	6	5	6	5	6	5	7
1953	5	6	6	6	7	5	6	6
1954	5	4	3	7	2	2	3	3
1955	7	6	5	6	5	6	5	6
1956	1	3	2	5	2	2	2	4
1957	5	6	5	7	5	3	5	2
1958	6	5	3	5	4	4	4	5
1959	3	7	7	6	7	4	7	7
1960	7	5	3	6	4	3	3	4
1961	5	7	7	7	5	5	7	7
1962	5	6	5	6	5	6	6	6
1963	7	3	4	5	4	0	5	4
1964	5	7	7	6	6	1	7	7
1965	4	3	3	5	3	2	4	5
1966	6	6	6	6	6	3	6	6

0—no good   7—the best

QUESTION:
how on earth do you read a wine label?

ANSWER: To buy American wines, you don't need a translator, and to buy the greatest of the great French wines, all you need is money. But if you are less pecunious, or more adventurous, you have to know which words on a French wine label are meant to impress and which are working words—words that will tell you, with amazing precison, what's inside the bottle. Suppose you go shopping for a dry white wine to serve with dinner (white because there's chicken on your menu, and you're too chicken to tamper with the experts' view that heartier reds go better with red meats; dry because you're not in the habit of sprinkling sugar on your chicken). "And not too expensive," you say to your dealer. He hands you a bottle. You can *see* that it's white (okay, so it looks green or gold; it's not red!) and you know it's a table wine because it's less than 14 per cent alcohol. But what else can you find out about this wine without biting the neck off the bottle? Follow the system used in reading the fake label on page 26, and you'll be able to cut through the maze on any wine label, from anywhere in the world. Look first to see where the wine was produced. If it comes from California, or New York, or Ohio, say, the rest is easy. The label will tell you right out what type of wine it is, and probably how and when to serve it, besides. No baffling questions about vintages will loom before you, and the most meaningful item on the label, the brand name, will be written in plain English. But if it comes from France, well, you'll have to find out more than *that* about it. . . . For a starter—from where in France? To find out turn the page . . .

1. The seal at the top
And, besides, here's a seal of approval from a reasonably objective person or group (in the case of Bordeaux wines, ADEB). Someone we respect has tasted the wine before us, so we buy.

2. Vin de Château
We're not fooled. Every vineyard in Bordeaux is called a château, whether its center is an old castle or a simple farmhouse. The label mentions no particular château, so it says only that the wine comes from vineyards. (Where else?)

3. Grand Haut Royal Superieur—(also) Fin (and) Special

More pie in the sky. Except for Premier Cru and Classe, indicating that the wine has won official recognition, adjectives on French wine labels are pure salesmanship, only as credible as the salesman who uses them. Who he?

4. Fin Graves Special

Graves. A distinct, identifiable type of white wine: dry, clean, fresh; less fruity than a Rhine or Alsatian wine, more so than a comparable white Burgundy from Chablis. Graves is a district, one of thirty-six separate districts in the region of Bordeaux, and:

5. Appellation Graves Controlee

The name Graves is controlled by law. Grapes, climate, soil and methods vary from one district to the next, and the French government here guarantees us that this wine was grown under the only conditions that can produce a Graves. But where in Graves was this wine grown—in what village area, in which vineyard? A French wine label will always use the most restrictive "address" it's allowed. That this label circles in no more closely than Graves, naming no parish (such as Pessac, Leognan, Gradignan) and no particular château (Carbonnieux, Olivier, etc.) tells us that this is a district wine, a blend, grown all over the district.

6. 1957

A vintage wine, this? Yes, in that the presence of a date means that all the wines in this bottle were harvested the same year. But we know just enough to know how little we know about the complicated vintage question. Our dealer's general vintage chart will show 1957 as a good year. It won't show the specific fact that a 1957 white Bordeaux is not quite ready to drink (it's better when matured for a couple of years).

7. Mis (or mise) en Bouteille d'Origine

Come, come, messieurs! No matter how you phrase it (par le recoltant; dans mes caves), this means that you bottled the wine yourselves. If you don't say Mise (with or without e) en Bouteille au Château, meaning wine was produced and bottled at the same vineyard, do not expect us to think we've found a bargain!

8. Pierre et Andre

Well, we've never heard of them. They may have the skill, taste and knowledge necessary for blending and bottling wine, but then again they may not. Who says that they have?

9. Negociants à Bordeaux, Gironde

Aha! This wine comes from Bordeaux, one of the main wine regions of France, famous for clarets, Sauternes, and yes. . . .

10.   Flanagan & Finnegan, sole agents for the U.S.A.
Voila! Messieurs Flanagan et Finnegan! Surely such good businessmen
would not have chosen to import a real dog. . . .

drink
recipes

ON THE following pages are nearly 1,000 varied drink recipes. Each has been tested by researchers of The Diners Club Magazine after intense study of printed research material and wide canvassing of the country's leading bartenders and restaurant and night club managements. One word of caution offered by the researchers. Don't try to sample more than two pages of drink in one day.

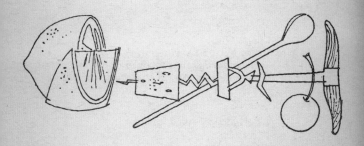

ABBEY COCKTAIL

1½ oz. Dry Gin
Juice of ¼ orange
1 dash orange bitters
Shake well with cracked ice and strain into 3 oz. cocktail glass. Add a maraschino cherry.

ABSINTHE COCKTAIL

1½ oz. Pernod (Absinthe substitute)
¾ oz. water
¼ oz. Anisette
1 dash orange bitters
Shake well with cracked ice and strain into 3 oz. cocktail glass.

ABSINTHE DRIP COCKTAIL

Pour 1½ oz. Pernod (Absinthe substitute) into special drip glass or old fashioned cocktail glass. Place cube of sugar over hole of drip spoon (or in silver tea strainer). Pack spoon or strainer with cracked ice, pour cold water to fill. When water has dripped through, drink is ready.

ABSINTHE SPECIAL COCKTAIL

1½ oz. Pernod (Absinthe substitute)
1 oz. water
¼ teaspoon powdered sugar
1 dash orange bitters
Shake well with cracked ice and strain into 3 oz. cocktail glass.

ACACIA

1 part Benedictine
3 to 4 parts Gin
1 teaspoon Kirsch for each drink
This can be further improved by adding 2 parts of lemon juice and another 3 to 4 parts of gin.

ADAM AND EVE

1 part Forbidden Fruit Liqueur
1 part Cognac
1 part Gin
Shake. Improve by adding a small amount of lemon or lime juice.

ADMIRAL'S TODDY

½ jigger Bourbon
Juice of 1 lemon
1 teaspoon sugar and water
Mix sugar and lemon juice in mug, add Bourbon. Bring water to boil and fill mug. Drink hot. Strawberry and lemon rind may be added for color or taste.

ADONIS COCKTAIL

1 dash orange bitters
¾ oz. Sweet Vermouth
1½ oz. Dry Sherry
Stir well with cracked ice and strain into 3 oz. cocktail glass.

AFFINITY COCKTAIL

¾ oz. Dry Vermouth
¾ oz. Sweet Vermouth
¾ oz. Scotch
2 dashes orange bitters
Stir well with cracked ice and strain into 3 oz. cocktail glass.

AFTER DINNER COCKTAIL

1 oz. Apricot Flavored Brandy
1 oz. Curaçao
Juice of 1 lime
Stir well with cracked ice and strain into 3 oz. cocktail glass. Leave lime in glass.

AFTER SUPPER COCKTAIL

1 oz. Apricot Flavored Brandy
1 oz. Curaçao
½ teaspoon lemon juice
Shake well with cracked ice and strain into 3 oz. cocktail glass.

ALABAMA COCKTAIL

½ oz. lemon juice
1 teaspoon Curaçao
½ teaspoon powdered sugar
1½ oz. Brandy
Shake well with cracked ice and strain into 3 oz. cocktail glass.

ALABAMA FIZZ

Juice of ½ lemon
1 teaspoon powdered sugar
2 oz. Dry Gin
Shake well with cracked ice and strain into 7 oz. high-ball glass. Fill with carbonated water. Add 2 sprigs of fresh mint.

ALASKA COCKTAIL

2 dashes orange bitters
1½ oz. Gin
¾ oz. Yellow Chartreuse
Shake well with cracked ice and strain into 3 oz. cocktail glass.

ALBEMARLE FIZZ

Juice of ½ lemon
1 teaspoon powdered sugar
2 oz. Dry Gin
Shake well with cracked ice and strain into 7 oz. high-ball glass. Fill with carbonated water. Add 1 teaspoon raspberry syrup.

ALEXANDER COCKTAIL NO. 1

1 oz. Dry Gin
1 oz. Crème de Cacao
1 oz. sweet cream
Shake well with cracked ice and strain into 4 oz. cocktail glass.

ALEXANDER COCKTAIL NO. 2

1 oz. Crème de Cacao
1 oz. Brandy
1 oz. sweet cream
Shake well with cracked ice and strain into 4 oz. cocktail glass.

ALEXANDER'S SISTER COCKTAIL

1 oz. Dry Gin
1 oz. Crème de Menthe
1 oz. sweet cream
Shake well with cracked ice and strain into 4 oz. cocktail glass.

ALFONSO XIII

1 part Dubonnet
1 part Dry Sherry
Ice
Stir. Strain into cocktail glass.

ALLEN COCKTAIL

¼ oz. lemon juice
¾ oz. Maraschino Liqueur
1½ oz. Dry Gin
Shake well with cracked ice and strain into 3 oz. cocktail glass.

ALLIES COCKTAIL

1 oz. Dry Vermouth
1 oz. Dry Gin
½ teaspoon Kümmel
Stir well with cracked ice and strain into 3 oz. cocktail glass.

ALPINE GLOW

1 part Cointreau
2 parts lemon juice
4 parts Cognac
4 parts Rum
1 or 2 dashes Grenadine to each drink
Shake with cracked or crushed ice.

AMBROSIA

Soak a small lump of sugar in bitters. Place in a saucer champagne glass, add 1 pony of Cognac, and fill with Champagne.

AMER PICON COCKTAIL

Juice of 1 lime
1 teaspoon Grenadine
1½ oz. Amer Picon
Shake well with cracked ice and strain into 3 oz. cocktail glass.

AMERICAN BEAUTY COCKTAIL

½ oz. orange juice
½ oz. Grenadine
½ oz. Dry Vermouth
½ oz. Brandy
¼ teaspoon Crème de Menthe
Stir well with cracked ice and strain into 3 oz. cocktail glass and top with a little Port.

AMERICAN GROG

1 lump of sugar
Juice of ¼ lemon
1½ oz. Rum
Fill hot whiskey glass with hot water and stir.

ANGEL'S DELIGHT

¼ oz. Grenadine
¼ oz. Triple Sec
¼ oz. Crème de Yvette
¼ oz. fresh cream
Pour carefully, in order given, into Pousse Café glass, so that each ingredient floats on top of preceding one.

ANGEL'S KISS

¼ oz. Crème de Cacao
¼ oz. Crème de Yvette
¼ oz. Brandy
¼ oz. sweet cream
Pour as you do for Angel's Delight.

ANGEL'S TIP

¾ oz. Crème de Cacao
¼ oz. sweet cream
Float cream and insert toothpick in cherry and put on top. Use Pousse Café glass.

ANGEL'S WING

¾ oz. Crème de Cacao
⅓ oz. Brandy
⅓ oz. sweet cream
Again, pour as you do for Angel's Delight.

ANGLER'S

Gin'n'Bitters *with a dash of Grenadine. Serve in a whiskey sour glass filled with crushed ice.*

APPETIZER

1 part orange juice
2 parts Dubonnet
4 parts Gin
1 dash bitters to each drink
Stir.

APPLE BLOW FIZZ

White of 1 egg
Juice of ½ lemon
1 teaspoon powdered sugar
2 oz. Apple Brandy
Shake well with cracked ice and strain in 8 oz. highball glass. Fill with carbonated water.

APPLE BRANDY COCKTAIL

1½ oz. Apple Brandy
1 teaspoon Grenadine
1 teaspoon lemon juice
Shake well with cracked ice and strain into 3 oz. glass.

APPLE BRANDY HIGHBALL

1 cube of ice
2 oz. Apple Brandy
Fill 8 oz. highball glass with ginger ale or carbonated water. Add twist of lemon peel, if desired, and stir.

APPLE BRANDY RICKEY

1 cube of ice
Juice of ½ lime
1½ oz. Apple Brandy
Fill 8 oz. highball glass with carbonated water and stir. Leave lime in glass.

Our pixie friend Joe E. Lewis has come up with a new wonder diet. You open two quarts of Bourbon and drink it from an empty Metrecal can.

Joe E. also told us that he'd recently come from the hospital where he'd offered to donate a pint of blood to an ailing pal, but that his offer was turned down. "We're different blood types," Joe explained. "I'm Haig & Haig and he's Johnnie Walker."

One last note on Joe, who saw a sleepy child dining late with her parents at McGinnis' Restaurant in New York. The elfish one walked over and said to her, "I'll tell you a bedtime story. Once upon a time, there were three bartenders. . . ."

APPLE BRANDY SOUR

Juice of ½ lemon
½ teaspoon powdered sugar
2 oz. Apple Brandy
Shake well with cracked ice and strain into 6 oz. glass. Fill with carbonated water and stir. Decorate with a slice of lemon and a cherry.

APPLE PIE COCKTAIL

¾ oz. Rum
¾ oz. Sweet Vermouth
1 teaspoon Apricot Flavored Brandy
½ teaspoon Grenadine
1 teaspoon lemon juice
Shake well with cracked ice and strain into 3 oz. cocktail glass.

APPLEJACK COCKTAIL

2 oz. Applejack
1 teaspoon sugar
Juice ½ lime
A few drops Curaçao
Shake well with cracked ice and strain into 3 oz. cocktail glass.

APPLEJACK COLLINS

Juice ½ lemon
½ barspoon powdered sugar
1 jigger Applejack
Shake well and strain into Collins glass. Add lump ice and fill glass with carbonated water.

APPLEJACK DAISY

Juice ½ lemon
½ teaspoon powdered sugar
6 dashes Grenadine
1 jigger Applejack
Half fill a highball glass with finely cracked ice. Stir until glass is frosted. Pour ingredients over ice. Fill with soda water. Decorate with sprig of fresh mint, a slice of lemon, and a slice of orange.

APPLEJACK FLIP

1 jigger Applejack
½ teaspoon sugar
1 whole egg
Ice
Shake, strain into goblet. Grate nutmeg on top.

APPLEJACK OLD FASHIONED

1 cube of sugar
1 dash bitters
1½ oz. Applejack
Muddle sugar and bitters in an old fashioned glass with a dash of soda water. Add cracked ice, Applejack and a twist of lemon peel. Stir.

APPLEJACK ON THE ROCKS

1 jigger Applejack
Fill an old fashioned glass with cracked ice. Pour Applejack over ice, add a dash of water or carbonated water. If desired, a twist of lemon peel.

APPLEJACK RICKEY

Juice and rind of ½ lime
1 jigger Applejack
Place lump of ice in Delmonico glass and pour ingredients over it. Fill with soda water.

APPLEJACK SLING

1 lump of sugar dissolved in 1 teaspoon water
1 jigger Applejack
1 piece twisted lemon peel
Add lump of ice and stir. Serve in whiskey glass with small spoon. Top with grated nutmeg.

APPLEJACK SMASH

1 jigger Applejack
2 teaspoons water
½ teaspoon sugar
3 springs fresh mint
Muddle sugar and water in an old fashioned glass, with mint. Add Applejack, cracked ice. Serve with small spoon.

APPLEJACK SOUR

Juice of ½ lemon
½ barspoon powdered sugar
1 jigger Applejack
Ice
Shake well. Strain into Delmonico glass. Add dash of carbonated water, half a slice of orange and a cherry.

APPLEJACK TODDY

1 lump of sugar
3 teaspoons water
1 jigger Applejack
Put the sugar in an old fashioned glass, and dissolve in the water. Add Applejack, lump of ice, dash of nutmeg. Serve with a teaspoon. For a hot apple toddy, leave out the ice and add hot water.

APRICOT BRANDY RICKY

1 cube of ice
Juice of ½ lime
2 oz. Apricot Flavored Brandy
Fill 8 oz. highball glass with carbonated water and stir. Leave lime in glass.

APRICOT COCKTAIL

Juice of ¼ lemon
Juice of ¼ orange
1½ oz. Apricot Flavored Brandy
1 teaspoon Dry Gin
Shake well with cracked ice and strain into 3 oz. cocktail glass.

APRICOT COOLER

½ teaspoon powdered sugar
2 oz. carbonated water
*Pour into 12 oz. Tom Collins glass, stir and fill glass
with cracked ice. Then add:*
2 oz. Apricot Flavored Brandy
*Fill with carbonated water or ginger ale and stir again.
Insert spiral of orange or lemon peel (or both) and
dangle end over rim of glass.*

APRICOT FIZZ

Juice of ½ lemon
Juice of ½ lime
1 teaspoon powdered sugar
2 oz. Apricot Flavored Brandy
*Shake well with cracked ice and strain into 7 oz. high-
ball glass. Fill with carbonated water.*

AUNT EMILY

1 part orange juice
2 drops Grenadine
1 part Applejack
1 part Gin
1 part Apricot Brandy
Shake with cracked ice and serve in cocktail glass.

B & B

½ oz. Benedictine
½ oz. Cognac
*Use cordial glass and carefully float Cognac on top of
Benedictine.*

BACARDI COCKTAIL

1½ oz. Bacardi Rum
Juice of ½ lime
½ teaspoon Grenadine
*Shake well with cracked ice and strain into 3 oz. cock-
tail glass.*

39

BACHELOR'S BAIT COCKTAIL

1½ oz. Dry Gin
White of 1 egg
1 dash orange bitters
½ teaspoon Grenadine
Shake well with cracked ice and strain into 4 oz. cocktail glass.

BALTIMORE BRACER COCKTAIL

1 oz. Anisette
1 oz. Brandy
Shake well with cracked ice and strain into 4 oz. cocktail glass.

BALTIMORE EGGNOG

1 fresh egg
½ tablespoon sugar
1 oz. Brandy
1 oz. Jamaica Rum
1 oz. Madeira
½ pint fresh milk
Break egg into shaker. Add ice and ingredients. Shake well and strain into tall highball glass. Grate a little nutmeg on top.

BAMBOO COCKTAIL

1½ oz. Sherry
¾ oz. Dry Vermouth
1 dash orange bitters
Stir well with cracked ice and strain into 3 oz. cocktail glass.

BANANA PUNCH

2 oz. Vodka
¼ oz. Apricot Flavored Brandy
Juice of ½ lime
Pour into 12 oz. Tom Collins glass filled with crushed ice. Add carbonated water and top with sprigs of mint and banana slices.

BARBADOS COCKTAIL

1 oz. Falernum
Juice of ½ lime
1 jigger Barbados Rum
Shake well with shaved ice.

BARBADOS RUM SWIZZLE

Juice of ½ lime
2 oz. Barbados Rum
1 dash bitters
½ barspoon sugar
Fill 10 oz. glass with shaved ice. Squeeze lime and drop in glass. Add rest of ingredients and swizzle.

BARBARY COAST COCKTAIL

½ oz. Dry Gin
½ oz. Rum
½ oz. Crème de Cacao
½ oz. Scotch
½ oz. sweet cream
Shake well with cracked ice and strain into 4 oz. cocktail glass.

BARON COCKTAIL

½ oz. Dry Vermouth
1½ oz. Dry Gin
1½ teaspoons Curaçao
½ teaspoon Sweet Vermouth
Stir well with cracked ice and strain into 3 oz. cocktail glass. Add twist of lemon peel and drop in glass.

BEADLESTONE COCKTAIL

1¼ oz. Dry Vermouth
1½ oz. Scotch
Stir well with cracked ice and strain into 3 oz. cocktail glass.

BEALS COCKTAIL

1½ oz. Scotch
½ oz. Dry Vermouth
½ oz. Sweet Vermouth
Stir well with cracked ice and strain into 3 oz. cocktail glass.

BEAUTY SPOT COCKTAIL

1 teaspoon orange juice
½ oz. Sweet Vermouth
½ oz. Dry Vermouth
1 oz. Dry Gin
Shake well with cracked ice and strain into 3 oz. cocktail glass with a dash of Grenadine in bottom of glass.

This fellow is sitting in the woods when he see a grasshopper sitting on a log. He goes over and says, "Little grasshopper, do you realize how famous you are? They've named a drink after you." The grasshopper looks up skeptically and says, "Named a drink after me? Who'd name a drink Melvin?"

BEEHIVE

1 part Bourbon
1 part grapefruit juice
1 teaspoon honey
Shake and serve in old fashioned glass.

BEES' KNEES

Juice of ¼ lemon
1 teaspoon honey
½ glass Gin
Dissolve honey in lemon juice, add Gin and ice. Shake well and serve in cocktail glass.

BELMONT COCKTAIL

2 oz. Dry Gin
1 teaspoon raspberry syrup
¾ oz. sweet cream
Shake well with cracked ice and strain into 4 oz. cocktail glass.

BENNETT COCKTAIL

Juice of ½ lime
1½ oz. Dry Gin
½ teaspoon powdered sugar
2 dashes orange bitters
Shake well with cracked ice and strain into 3 oz. cocktail glass.

BERMUDA BOUQUET

Juice of ¼ orange
Juice of ½ lemon
1 teaspoon powdered sugar
1½ oz. Dry Gin
1 oz. Apricot Flavored Brandy
1 teaspoon Grenadine
½ teaspoon Curaçao
Shake well with cracked ice and strain into 8 oz. highball glass.

BERMUDA HIGHBALL

1 cube of ice
¾ oz. Dry Gin
¾ oz. Brandy
¾ oz. Dry Vermouth
Fill 8 oz. highball glass with ginger ale or carbonated water. Add twist of lemon peel, if desired, and stir.

BERMUDA ROSE COCKTAIL

1¼ oz. Dry Gin
¼ oz. Apricot Flavored Brandy
¼ oz. Grenadine
Shake well with cracked ice and strain into 3 oz. cocktail glass.

BETWEEN THE SHEETS COCKTAIL

Juice of ¼ lemon
½ oz. Brandy
½ oz. Rum
½ oz. Triple Sec
Shake well with cracked ice and strain into 3 oz. cocktail glass.

BIFFY COCKTAIL

Juice of ½ lemon
½ oz. Swedish Punch
1½ oz. Dry Gin
Shake well with cracked ice and strain into 3 oz. cocktail glass.

BIG APPLE

The distinguishing characteristic of this drink is the manner in which it is served. Cut a round chunk the size of a silver dollar from the top of a large, preferably red apple and trim off the point of the cone to leave a plug about ½" thick. Scoop out the pulp and core of the apple, leaving a shell about ¾" thick. Chill the shell. In a Waring Blender beat 1 part lemon juice, 2 parts orange juice, and 3 parts Apple Brandy, with a small amount of honey and the pulp from the apple. Strain into the chilled apple and serve with straws.
This is sometimes called the COUNTRY COCKTAIL, but the original Country Cocktail consists of equal parts of lemon juice, Applejack, and Port, with about 1 teaspoonful of sugar syrup and ¼ to ½ an egg to each drink.

44

BIJOU COCKTAIL

¾ oz. Dry Gin
¾ oz. Green Chartreuse
¾ oz. Sweet Vermouth
1 dash orange bitters
Stir well with cracked ice and strain into 3 oz. cocktail glass. Add cherry on top.

BILLY TAYLOR

Juice of ½ lime
2 cubes of ice
2 oz. Dry Gin
Fill 12 oz. Tom Collins glass with carbonated water and stir gently.

BIRD OF PARADISE FIZZ

Juice of ½ lemon
1 teaspoon powdered sugar
White of 1 egg
1 teaspoon Grenadine
2 oz. Dry Gin
Shake well with cracked ice and strain into 8 oz. highball glass. Fill with carbonated water.

BISHOP

Juice of ¼ lemon
Juice of ¼ orange
1 teaspoon powdered sugar
Pour into 8 oz. highball glass. Add cube of ice, fill with Burgundy and stir well. Decorate with fruits.

BITTERS HIGHBALL

1 cube of ice
¾ oz. bitters
Fill 8 oz. highball glass with ginger ale and carbonated water. Add twist of lemon peel, if desired, and stir.

BITTERSWEET

Rye Sour *with 4 parts orange juice in place of 2 parts lemon juice.*

BLACKBERRY JULEP

2 oz. Blackberry Brandy
4 sprigs fresh mint
1 lump of sugar
Fill tall glass with crushed ice and set it aside. In old-fashioned glass crush sugar with a stick. Add mint leaves and bruise lightly. Add Blackberry Brandy and mix together. Pour over the crushed ice in tall glass. Stir until outside of glass is frosted. Decorate with large sprig of mint on top and sprinkle with powdered sugar.

BLACK HAWK COCKTAIL

1¼ oz. Whiskey
1¼ oz. Sloe Gin
Stir well with cracked ice and strain into 3 oz. cocktail glass. Serve with a cherry.

BLACK RUSSIAN

1 part Kahlua
2 parts Vodka
Serve in Pousse Café glass.

BLACK STRIPE COCKTAIL

2 oz. Rum
1 tablespoon molasses
Shake well with cracked ice and strain into 3 oz. cocktail glass.

the story of rye, bourbon and blended whiskey

By SAM BOAL

IT IS interesting to note that the only people on earth who don't regularly drink fermented or distilled beverages in one form or another are the Eskimos. This is because vegetation of some kind is needed to produce fermentation and of course vegetation in the northland is scarce. However, when the Eskimo is given alcoholic liquor, imported from outside his Arctic area, he accepts it just as happily as does your pal on the commuter train.

By far the most popular of the alcoholic beverages is whiskey. It is always made with fermented mash grain, corn, rye, barley or wheat, distilled and then aged in charred barrels. Whiskey, immediately after it is distilled, is tasteless and colorless. It is the aging that gives it its characteristic color, flavor and aroma.

There are four main types of whiskey in the world: Canadian, American, Irish and Scottish. The tourist may want to note that the only proper use of the word Scottish is in connection with whisky. It is literally ungrammatical to say Scotch whisky, just as it would be ungrammatical to say Scottish tweeds. However, this distinction is of interest only to pedagogues.

Straight American whiskey is distilled from grains and not blended with any other neutral spirits or any other whiskey. There are four major types of straight whiskey: Bourbon, Rye, Corn and Bottled-in-Bond whiskey, the last being different from the others in that it is produced under the United States government supervision. The government does not guarantee the quality of bonded whiskey, but it does require that it be at least four years old, that it be bottled at 100 proof, and that it be started and bottled in bonded warehouses under government inspection.

American blended whiskies are a blend of various whiskies which must contain at least 20% or more straight whiskey.

Scottish whisky (you leave off the "e" when you refer to Scottish whisky) is produced only in Scotland and gets its typical flavor from drying malted barley over peat fires. All the Scottish whisky which comes into this country is at least four years old.

Irish whiskey, which is heavier than Scottish whisky, is also prepared over peat fires, but by law, the Irish whiskey that comes into the U.S. is at least seven years old.

TO HEAR them tell it, the exponents of Bourbon believe that this is the only authentic American whiskey and this is certainly not true. Bourbon, if you wish, is a version of corn meal mash, since corn is the principal ingredient of Bourbon. It is fermented and then distilled and, by government order, it is "Whiskey which has been distilled at not exceeding 160 proof fermented mash of not less than 51% corn and stored in charred new oak containers."

Bourbon seems to have been born in 1789. It was the child of a Baptist minister, the Rev. Elijah Craig, in Georgetown, Kentucky, and he was distilling the world's first Bourbon just as the American Constitution was being declared effective in New York city.

Bourbon fanciers make the night resplendent with claims that the drink they serve is six years old; but age is not necessarily a symbol of quality. The fact that Bottled-In-Bond whiskey is six years old is no assurance that six-year-old whiskey is better than the four or eight-year-old variety. The reason for this rather arbitrary restriction on the life of bonded whiskey is that the federal government, which gets its excise taxes from whiskey only when it is released from the warehouse, doesn't want to tie up its revenue by allowing the distiller to keep it for a longer period. This applies to all whiskies. Whiskey is good because it is good whiskey, not because it is old whiskey.

Bourbon, of all the American whiskies, seems to lend itself

most adroitly to legend and myth. The mint julep, for instance, has become almost ritualistic; and Bourbon and branch water (the latter is nothing more than water), has by now become part of our folklore. Southern colonels out of "Gone With The Wind" drink nothing but Bourbon, and even ladies, such as Scarlett O'Hara, were known to partake of it.

After its invention in the limestone hills of Kentucky, Bourbon spread rapidly across the country, thus causing Mark Twain to remark, "Westward the jug of empire flows," and it is now as popular in California as it is in Kentucky. Students of irony may be gratified that Kentucky, the Birthplace of Bourbon, is also the birthplace of Carry Nation, that redoubtable figure who swept across the land, hatchet in hand and stern of mien, chopping up bars and chopping down drinkers. She kept up her labors until 1911.

There are now 170 Bottled-In-Bond Bourbons, 384 straight Bourbons, and 43 blends being marketed. In this listing, there are 105 brand names which begin with "Old," and the word "Kentucky" appears 42 times.

Madison Avenue will be delighted to learn that the term "brand name" stems from the early Bourbon whiskey barrels, on which the name of the owner was burned with a hot iron or brand. This short treatise on Bourbon can end with the information that a famous tavern in Louisville has a sign reading, "Gentlemen imbibing foreign or alien spirits other than Bourbon whiskey may be requested to pay in cash."

IT WILL come as a distinct surprise to Bourbon fanciers to learn that Rye whiskey antedates Bourbon by many years. Rye appears to have been created in early Colonial days and thus is the first whiskey born on American soil. Rye whiskey was originally called Old Monongahela, from the river in Pennsylvania.

When the first settlers came to that new country, soon to be called the United States, they discovered that wheat wasn't a crop suitable to the eastern coast but that rye was. From almost his infancy, man has learned that nearly any agricultural product can be made to ferment, and the early settlers soon discovered that rye, which flourished in the Eastern regions, could be made into whiskey, and so was born Monongahela Rye.

Rye is a strong whiskey, strong both in proof and in flavor and, by government regulation, must contain no less than 51% of rye mash, the way Bourbon, as noted above, must contain no less than 51% of corn mash. Until about the time of the American Revolution, Rye was a farmer's drink, which he made himself. Rum was the commercial drink. But with the revolution, the shipment of Rum to this country became scarce, so that the Monongahela farmers began to distill whiskey from rye not only for their own consumption, but for sale. It turned out to be a profitable undertaking and the southern portion of Pennsylvania used its rye for distillation so extensively that there soon arose a shortage of rye for bread. The elders of the district were appalled by this situation and passed a law prohibiting the use of rye to make whiskey, but people liked whiskey as much as they liked bread and soon the law was modified to allow a mixture of rye and barley, which is what our Rye is made of today.

Just as in the British Navy, white Rum was considered part of one's wages, Rye was considered part of the wages of the early Pennsylvania farm hands. In those days, cash money was as hard to find as the heart of some chorus girl. So Rye began, in a short while, to become a medium of exchange. Farms were bought and sold for Rye whiskey.

There is another economic consideration. Carrying rye in its grown form from the Alleghenies to the East, where there was a market for it (bakers wanted it for their bread) was almost impossibly arduous. In the early nineteenth century, roads were simply murder, but if the rye were distilled and made into whiskey, transporting it became infinitely easier.

Rye whiskey, in a sense, personified the young America. It was a most astonishing beverage. It was raw, bitter, and stinging, and was often drunk completely unaged, and it would appear that having a drink of this young Rye whiskey was like appearing before a firing squad. It was carried east over the mountains on pack animals, shipped west and south by river boat, and Old Monongahela soon was being consumed almost everywhere in the United States. It found most favor, however, on the frontiers, where its harshness was felt to be part of life.

These days, Rye whiskey is aged like any other whiskey, in charred barrels. It is by far the most popular American alcoholic beverage and is used for an infinite variety of modern cocktails, such as the Manhattan or the Old Fashioned.

As one early day Joe E. Lewis once put it, "Somebody asked me why I drink Rye and the answer is, I can't stand Brandy, Scotch, Gin, Champagne, or Wine. Or water."

An American ballad reads, "Rye whiskey, Rye whiskey, Rye whiskey, I cry. If you don't give me Rye whiskey, I surely will die."

THERE seems to be a popular myth that Canadian whiskey is made principally from rye, but this is not true. Canadian whiskey, like Bourbon, is made mainly from corn—plus rye—and is therefore a blended whiskey. It is far more bland, even milder than Bourbon, and for that reason, women like it. (It is not a myth that women like bland drinks. But anybody who believes this too faithfully should take a trip through an English pub and see what the women are drinking there. Gin, that's what.)

Canadian whiskey, being an imported whiskey in the United States, has considerable snob appeal, particularly because it became fashionable during prohibition, when bone-dry Americans, frolicking off to Canada for a drink, found Canadian whiskey palatable and retained their taste for it after repeal. Canadian whiskey is more expensive than domestic because of the import duties. It is taxed the same as any foreign spirit.

Since the end of World War II, the popularity of Canadian whiskey in this country has increased 70% and now 80% of the production of Canadian distilleries is marketed in the United States. It is also, as is well known, marketed all over the world, and one manufacturer of Canadian whiskey is proud to boast that his whiskey is sold in 88 countries, which is only eleven less than the number of nations in the U.N.

Canadian whiskey, it may astonish you to learn, contains a little wine which is added as a smoothing agent, and health faddists who like to drink will be heartened by the knowledge that Canadian whiskey often contains prune juice. Many whiskies contain small amounts of wine, but in this case, it is an integral part of the drink, lending color as well as flavor. (By U.S. law, American distillers of straight whiskey can add nothing in the way of coloring matter. It must get its color solely from the barrel.)

If you remember your last trip to Canada, you will probably recall that the Canadian whiskey you drank in Canada seemed smoother than the Canadian whiskey you drank in the U.S., although they appear to be the same whiskey. The fact is they were not the same. The Canadian whiskey you drank in Canada was 80 proof. To gain favorable customs or import duty privileges, the Canadian whiskey sold here is either 86.8 or 90 proof, which of course makes for a slightly more violent drink. Canadian whiskey, like Scotch, and Irish, for some reason even the distillers don't really know, can stand aging better than American whiskey. This may be because it's stored in second-hand barrels rather than in new ones. Canadian, being a lighter whiskey than American, can stand additional aging. American whiskey of great age tends to taste excessively woody.

BLACK VELVET

5 oz. Stout
5 oz. Champagne
Pour very carefully into 12 oz. glass with cubes of ice.
Stir very gently.

BLACKTHORN COCKTAIL

1½ oz. Sloe Gin
¾ oz. Dry Vermouth
1 dash orange bitters
Stir well with cracked ice and strain into 3 oz. cocktail
glass. Serve with a slice of lemon.

BLARNEY STONE COCKTAIL

2 oz. Irish Whiskey
½ teaspoon Pernod (Absinthe substitute)
½ teaspoon Curaçao
¼ teaspoon Maraschino Liqueur
1 dash of bitters
Shake well with cracked ice and strain into 3 oz. cock-
tail glass. Serve with twist of orange peel and an olive.

BLINKER COCKTAIL

1 part Grenadine
3 parts fresh grapefruit juice
6 to 8 parts Rye or Bourbon
Serve in cocktail glass.

BLOOD AND SAND COCKTAIL

½ oz. orange juice
½ oz. Scotch
½ oz. Wild Cherry Flavored Brandy
½ oz. Sweet Vermouth
Shake well with cracked ice and strain into 3 oz. cock-
tail glass.

BLOOD BRONX COCKTAIL

1½ oz. Dry Gin
¼ oz. Dry Vermouth
Juice of ¼ blood orange
Shake well with cracked ice and strain into 3 oz. cocktail glass.

BLOODHOUND COCKTAIL

½ oz. Dry Vermouth
½ oz. Sweet Vermouth
1 oz. Dry Gin
2 or 3 crushed strawberries
Shake well with cracked ice and strain into 3 oz. cocktail glass.

BLOODY BLOODY MARY COCKTAIL

1½ oz. Vodka
3 oz. tomato juice
Juice of ½ lemon
Pinch of salt, pepper and celery salt
½ teaspoon Worcestershire Sauce
¼ teaspoon powdered sugar
Shake well with cracked ice and strain into 6 oz. old fashioned cocktail glass with cube of ice. Decorate with sprig of fresh mint.

BLOODY DAGMAR COCKTAIL

8 oz. tomato juice
1½ oz. Akvavit
Pour in the shot and pray.

BLOODY MARY COCKTAIL

1½ oz. Vodka
1½ oz. tomato juice
1 dash lemon juice
1 dash Worcestershire Sauce
Shake well with cracked ice and strain into old fashioned cocktail glass with cube of ice.

BLOSSOM

1 part pineapple juice
2 parts lime juice
8 parts Rum
Shake with cracked or crushed ice.

BLUE BLAZER

2½ oz. Whiskey
2½ oz. boiling water
Use two large silver-plated mugs, with handles. Put the whiskey into one mug, and the boiling water into the other. Ignite the Whiskey and, while blazing, mix both ingredients by pouring them four or five times from one mug to the other. If well done, this will have the appearance of a continued stream of liquid fire. Sweeten with 1 teaspoon of powdered sugar and serve with a piece of lemon peel. Serve in 4 oz. heated whiskey glass.

BLUE DEVIL COCKTAIL

1 oz. Dry Gin
Juice of ½ lemon or lime
½ oz. Maraschino Liqueur
½ teaspoon Crème de Yvette
Shake well with cracked ice and strain into 3 oz. cocktail glass.

BLUE MONDAY COCKTAIL

1½ oz. Vodka
¾ oz. Triple Sec
1 dash blue vegetable coloring
Stir well with cracked ice and strain into 3 oz. cocktail glass.

BLUE MOON COCKTAIL

1½ oz. Dry Gin
¾ oz. Crème de Yvette
Stir well with cracked ice and strain into 3 oz. cocktail glass. Add twist of lemon peel and drop in glass.

BOBBY BURNS COCKTAIL

1¼ oz. Sweet Vermouth
1¼ oz. Scotch
1 teaspoon Benedictine
Stir well with cracked ice and strain into 3 oz. cocktail glass. Add twist of lemon peel and drop in glass.

BOLERO COCKTAIL

1½ oz. Rum
¾ oz. Apple Brandy
¼ teaspoon Sweet Vermouth
Stir well with cracked ice and strain into 3 oz. cocktail glass.

BOLO COCKTAIL

2 oz. Rum
Juice of ½ lime
Juice of ¼ orange
1 teaspoon powdered sugar
Shake well with cracked ice and strain into 4 oz. cocktail glass.

BOMBAY COCKTAIL

½ oz. Dry Vermouth
½ oz. Sweet Vermouth
1 oz. Brandy
¼ teaspoon Pernod (Absinthe substitute)
½ teaspoon Curaçao
Stir well with cracked ice and strain into 3 oz. cocktail glass.

BOMBAY PUNCH

Juice of 12 lemons
Add enough powdered sugar to sweeten. Place large block of ice in punch bowl and stir. Then add
1 qt. Brandy
1 qt. Sherry Wine
¼ pt. Maraschino Liqueur
¼ pt. Curaçao
4 qts. Champagne
2 qts. carbonated water
Some prefer to add the strained contents of a pot of tea. Stir well and decorate with fruits in season. Serve in 4 oz. punch glasses.

BOOMERANG

    1 part Passion-Fruit Nectar
    1 part Gin
    1 part Rum
    1 dash each of lemon juice and bitters
       to each drink
Serve in highball glass.

BOOSTER COCKTAIL

    1 teaspoon Curaçao
    White of 1 egg
    2 oz. Brandy
Shake well with cracked ice and strain into 4 oz. cocktail glass. Grate nutmeg on top.

BOSTON COCKTAIL

    ¾ oz. Dry Gin
    ¾ oz. Apricot Flavored Brandy
    Juice of ¼ lemon
    ¼ oz. Grenadine
Shake well with cracked ice and strain into 3 oz. cocktail glass.

BOSTON COOLER

Juice of ½ lemon
1 teaspoon powdered sugar
2 oz. carbonated water
Pour into 12 oz. Tom Collins glass. Stir. Then fill glass with cracked ice and add
2 oz. Rum
Fill with carbonated water or ginger ale and stir again. Insert spiral of orange or lemon peel (or both) and dangle end over rim of glass.

BOSTON SIDE CAR COCKTAIL

¾ oz. Brandy
¾ oz. Rum
¾ oz. Triple Sec
Juice of ½ lime
Shake well with cracked ice and strain into 3 oz. cocktail glass.

BOSTON SOUR

Juice of ½ lemon
1 teaspoon powdered sugar
2 oz. Whiskey
White of 1 egg
Shake well with cracked ice and strain into 8 oz. highball glass. Then add cube of ice, fill with carbonated water and decorate with half-slice of lemon and a cherry.

BOURBON COLLINS

Pour 1 jigger of Bourbon *over ice cubes in glass. Fill glass with Collins mix, garnish and serve.*

BOURBON CRÈME

2 parts Bourbon
1 part cream
Shake with shaved ice and strain into glass.

BOURBON EGGNOG

1 egg
1 teaspoon sugar
2 oz. Bourbon
8 oz. milk
Shake with cracked ice, strain into glass and serve with dash of nutmeg over the top.

BOURBON FRUIT

Drop one slice lime, lemon and orange each into old fashioned glass, over ice. Fill with Bourbon.

BOURBON HIGHBALL

1 cube of ice
2 oz. Bourbon
Fill 8 oz. highball glass with ginger ale or carbonated water. Add twist of lemon peel, if desired, and stir.

BOURBON OLD FASHIONED

1 lump of sugar
Dash of bitters
Bourbon
Place sugar in an old fashioned glass and sprinkle with bitters. Add ice cubes, twist of lemon and maraschino cherry.

BOURBON SHAKE

2 teaspoons sugar syrup
3 teaspoons lemon juice
3 oz. Bourbon
Mix ingredients with shaved ice and strain. Garnish with mint leaves and serve in water goblet.

BOURBON SOUR

1 part sugar syrup
2 parts lemon juice
8 parts Bourbon
1 maraschino cherry
Shake well with ice and strain into sour glasses. Serve with slice of orange and maraschino cherry.

BOURBON AND COKE

1 jigger of Bourbon in glass of coke
Pour both over ice cubes.

BOURBON AND EGG (for hangovers)

Break raw egg into glass, add Bourbon.
Stir and drink.

BOURBON AND ICED TEA

1 jigger Bourbon
Fill 8 oz. glass with iced tea, add lemon peel and sugar to taste. Add ice cubes.

BOURBON AND SODA

1 jigger Bourbon
Fill large highball glass with ice and soda water.

BRANDY AND SODA

2 cubes of ice
2 oz. Brandy
6 oz. carbonated water
Serve in 12 oz. Tom Collins glass and stir.

BRANDY BLAZER

1 lump of sugar
1 piece orange peel
1 piece lemon peel
2 oz. Brandy
Use old fashioned glass. Light with a match, stir with long spoon for a few seconds and strain into a hot whiskey glass.

BRANDY COBBLER

Dissolve 1 teaspoon powdered sugar in 2 oz. carbonated water; then fill 10 oz. goblet with shaved ice. Add 2 oz. Brandy.
Stir well and decorate with fruits in season. Serve with straws.

BRANDY COCKTAIL

2 oz. Brandy
¼ teaspoon simple syrup
2 dashes bitters
Twist of lemon peel
Stir well with cracked ice and strain into 3 oz. cocktail glass.

BRANDY COLLINS

Juice of ½ lemon
1 teaspoon powdered sugar
2 oz. Brandy
Shake well with cracked ice and strain into 12 oz. Tom Collins glass. Add several cubes of ice, fill with carbonated water and stir. Decorate with slice of orange, lemon and a cherry. Serve with straws.

This car stops on a lonely road and a hitchhiker climbs in. "Thanks a lot, buddy," he says to the driver. With this he pulls an unlabeled bottle out of his hip pocket and says, "Have a drink?" "Thanks, no," says the driver politely. Suddenly, the hitchhiker's hand darts into another pocket and he pulls out a gun. "I think," he growls menacingly, "that you'd better have a drink." The driver gulps a swig, sputtering wildly as the burning liquid runs down his throat. He shudders violently then slowly recovers. The hitchhiker grabs the bottle from his hand. "Now," he says cheerfully, "You hold the gun and make *me* take a drink!"

BRANDY DAISY

Juice of ½ lemon
½ teaspoon powdered sugar
1 teaspoon raspberry syrup or Grenadine
2 oz. Brandy
Shake well with cracked ice and strain into stein or 8 oz. metal cup. Add cube of ice and decorate with fruit.

BRANDY EGGNOG

1 egg
1 teaspoon powdered sugar
2 oz. Brandy
Fill glass with milk
Shake well with cracked ice and strain into 12 oz. Tom Collins glass. Grate nutmeg on top.

BRANDY FIX

Juice of ½ lemon
1 teaspoon powdered sugar
1 teaspoon water
Stir. Then fill glass with shaved ice.
Add 2½ oz. Brandy.
Use 8 oz. highball glass. Stir well. Add slice of lemon. Serve with straws.

BRANDY FIZZ

Juice of ½ lemon
1 teaspoon powdered sugar
2 oz. Brandy
Shake well with cracked ice and strain into 7 oz. highball glass. Fill with carbonated water.

BRANDY FLIP

1 egg
1 teaspoon powdered sugar
1½ oz. Brandy
2 teaspoons sweet cream (if desired)
Shake well with cracked ice and strain into 5 oz. flip glass. Grate a little nutmeg on top.

BRANDY GUMP COCKTAIL

1½ oz. Brandy
Juice of ½ lemon
½ teaspoon Grenadine
Shake well with cracked ice and strain into 3 oz. cocktail glass.

BRANDY HIGHBALL

1 cube of ice
2 oz. Brandy
Fill 8 oz. highball glass with ginger ale or carbonated water. Add twist of lemon peel, if desired, and stir gently.

BRANDY JULEP

1 teaspoon powdered sugar
5 or 6 sprigs fresh mint
2½ oz. Brandy
Then fill 12 oz. Tom Collins glass with finely shaved ice, and stir until mint rises to top, being careful not to bruise mint. (Do not hold glass with hand while stirring.) Decorate with slice of pineapple, orange, lemon and a cherry. Serve with straws.

BRANDY MILK PUNCH

1 teaspoon powdered sugar
2 oz. Brandy
½ pint milk
Shake well with cracked ice, strain into 12 oz. Tom Collins glass and grate nutmeg on top.

BRANDY PUNCH

Juice of 12 lemons
Juice of 4 oranges
Add enough sugar to sweeten.
8 oz. Grenadine
1 qt. carbonated water
Place large block of ice in punch bowl and stir well. Then add
½ pint Curaçao
2 qts. Brandy
Some prefer to add the strained contents of a pot of tea. Stir well and decorate with fruits in season. Serve in 4 oz. punch glasses.

BRANDY SANGAREE

½ teaspoon powdered sugar dissolved in 1 teaspoon of water.
2 oz. Brandy
2 cubes of ice
Serve in 8 oz. highball glass. Fill balance with soda water. Stir, leaving enough room on which to float a tablespoon of Port Wine. Sprinkle lightly with nutmeg.

BRANDY SLING

1 teaspoon powdered sugar dissolved in teaspoon of water and juice of ½ lemon.
2 oz. Brandy
2 cubes of ice
Serve in old fashioned cocktail glass and stir. Twist of lemon peel and drop in glass.

BRANDY SMASH

1 lump of sugar muddled with 1 oz. carbonated water and 4 sprigs of green mint.
2 oz. Brandy
Add a cube of ice. Stir and decorate with a slice of orange and a cherry. Twist lemon peel on top. Use old fashioned cocktail glass.

BRANDY SOUR

Juice of ½ lemon
½ teaspoon powdered sugar
2 oz. Brandy
Shake well with cracked ice and strain into 8 oz. sour glass. Fill with carbonated water. Decorate with a half-slice of lemon and a cherry.

BRANDY SQUIRT

1½ oz. Brandy
1 tablespoon powdered sugar
1 teaspoon raspberry syrup or Grenadine
Shake well with cracked ice and strain into 8 oz. highball glass and fill with carbonated water. Decorate with cubes of pineapple and strawberries.

BRANDY TODDY

½ teaspoon powdered sugar
2 teaspoons water *and stir*
2 oz. Brandy
1 lump of ice.
Stir again and twist lemon peel on top. Use old fashioned cocktail glass.

BRANDY TODDY (Hot)

Put lump of sugar into hot whiskey glass and fill two-thirds with boiling water. Add 2 oz. Brandy. Stir and decorate with slice of lemon. Grate nutmeg on top.

BRANDY VERMOUTH COCKTAIL

½ oz. Sweet Vermouth
2 oz. Brandy
1 dash bitters
Stir well with cracked ice and strain into 3 oz. cocktail glass.

BRAZIL COCKTAIL

1¼ oz. Dry Vermouth
1¼ oz. Sherry Wine
1 dash bitters
¼ teaspoon Pernod (Absinthe substitute)
Stir well with cracked ice and strain into 3 oz. cocktail glass.

BREAKFAST EGGNOG

1 egg
½ oz. Curaçao
2 oz. Brandy
Fill glass with milk. Shake well with cracked ice and strain into 12 oz. Tom Collins glass. Grate nutmeg on top.

BRIGHTON PUNCH

¾ oz. Whiskey
¾ oz. Cognac
¾ oz. Benedictine
Juice of ½ orange
Juice of ½ lemon
*Shake well and pour into 12 oz. Tom Collins glass
filled with shaved ice. Then fill with carbonated water
and stir gently. Serve with straws.*

BROKEN SPUR COCKTAIL

¾ oz. Sweet Vermouth
1½ oz. Port Wine
¼ teaspoon Curaçao
*Stir well with cracked ice and strain into 3 oz. cocktail
glass.*

BRONX COCKTAIL

1 oz. Dry Gin
½ oz. Dry Vermouth
½ oz. Sweet Vermouth
Juice of ¼ orange
*Shake well with cracked ice and strain into 3 oz. cock-
tail glass. Serve with slice of orange.*

BRONX COCKTAIL

1 oz. Dry Gin
1 oz. Dry Vermouth
Juice of ¼ orange
*Shake well with cracked ice and strain into 3 oz. cock-
tail glass. Serve with slice of orange.*

BRONX SILVER COCKTAIL

Juice of ¼ orange
White of 1 egg
½ oz. Dry Vermouth
1 oz. Dry Gin
*Shake well with cracked ice and strain into 4 oz. cock-
tail glass.*

BRONX TERRACE COCKTAIL

1½ oz. Dry Gin
1½ oz. Dry Vermouth
Juice of ½ lime
Shake well with cracked ice and strain into 3 oz. cocktail glass. Add a cherry.

BROWN COCKTAIL

¾ oz. Dry Gin
¾ oz. Rum
¾ oz. Dry Vermouth
Stir well with cracked ice and strain into 3 oz. cocktail glass.

BUCKS FIZZ

¼ glass orange juice
Fill with Champagne. *Use 12 oz. Tom Collins glass and stir very gently.*

BULLDOG COCKTAIL

1¼ oz. Wild Cherry Flavored Brandy
¾ oz. Dry Gin
Juice of ½ lime
Shake well with cracked ice and strain into 3 oz. cocktail glass.

BULLDOG HIGHBALL

1 cube of ice
Juice of ½ orange
2 oz. Dry Gin
Fill 8 oz. highball glass with ginger ale and stir.

BULLFROG

An Apricot Brandy Sour but with no sugar. This drink is also sometimes called the HOP TOAD. Some recipes call for equal parts of Apricot Brandy and Jamaica Rum.

BULL'S EYE

1 oz. Brandy
2 oz. Hard Cider
1 cube of ice
Fill 8 oz. highball glass with ginger ale and stir.

BULL SHOT

3 oz. cold bouillon
1 oz. Vodka or Gin
*Pour bouillon over ice cubes in Old Fashioned glass.
Add Vodka or Gin.*

BULL'S MILK

1 teaspoon powdered sugar
1 oz. Rum
1½ oz. Brandy
½ pint milk
*Shake well with cracked ice and strain into 12 oz.
Tom Collins glass. Grate nutmeg and pinch of cinnamon on top.*

BURGUNDY BISHOP

Juice of ¼ lemon
1 teaspoon powdered sugar
1 oz. Rum
*Shake well and strain into 8 oz. highball glass and
fill with Burgundy and stir. Decorate with fruits.*

BUTTON HOOK COCKTAIL

½ oz. Crème de Menthe (White)
½ oz. Apricot Flavored Brandy
½ oz. Pernod (Absinthe substitute)
½ oz. Brandy
*Shake well with cracked ice and strain into 3 oz.
cocktail glass.*

CABARET COCKTAIL

1½ oz. Dry Gin
2 dashes bitters
½ teaspoon Dry Vermouth
¼ teaspoon Benedictine
*Stir well with cracked ice and strain into 3 oz. cock-
tail glass. Serve with a cherry.*

CABLEGRAM HIGHBALL

Juice of ½ lemon
1 teaspoon powdered sugar
2 oz. Whiskey
*Stir well with cracked ice and fill with ginger ale.
Use 8 oz. highball glass.*

CAFÉ DE PARIS COCKTAIL

White of 1 egg
1 teaspoon Pernod (Absinthe substitute)
1 teaspoon sweet cream
1½ oz. Dry Gin
Shake well with cracked ice and strain into 4 oz. cocktail glass.

CAFÉ ROYALE

1 cup hot black coffee
Put cube of sugar, well soaked with Brandy, in teaspoon and hold so that it will rest on top of coffee and ignite and hold until flame burns out. Drop contents in coffee.

CALIFORNIA LEMONADE

Juice of 1 lemon
Juice of 1 lime
3 teaspoons powdered sugar
2 oz. Whiskey
¼ teaspoon Grenadine
Shake well with cracked ice and strain into Tom Collins glass filled with shaved ice. Fill with carbonated water and decorate with slice of orange, lemon, and a cherry. Serve with straws.

CAMERON'S KICK COCKTAIL

¾ oz. Scotch
¾ oz. Irish Whiskey
Juice of ¼ lemon
2 dashes orange bitters
Shake well with cracked ice and strain into 3 oz. cocktail glass.

CANADIAN COCKTAIL

1½ oz. Canadian Whiskey
¼ teaspoon Curaçao
2 dashes bitters
1 teaspoon powdered sugar
Shake well with cracked ice and strain into 3 oz. cocktail glass.

CANASTA

1 part lemon juice
2 parts Southern Comfort
Shake well with cracked ice.

CAPTAIN'S BLOOD

1 part lime juice
2 to 3 parts Jamaica Rum
2 or 3 dashes bitters to each drink
Shake with finely cracked ice.

CARACAS

1 part sweet cream
1 part Crème de Cacao
4 parts Bourbon
Mix cream, Crème de Cacao, Bourbon with crushed ice and strain into 7 oz. wine glass.

A friend of ours comes from a small town in the midwest—the typical kind of country hamlet with its own town drunk. This one used to wander off to nearby towns and wind up in every conceivable kind of jam. Finally, the local citizenry made up a small tag which they fastened to his coat lapel. It read: "Attention Members of the Medical Profession. I am not in a coma. I am not suffering from any rare diseases. Please do not remove my appendix or examine me for brain concussion. I am merely drunk. Let me sleep."

CARDINAL PUNCH

Juice of 12 lemons
Add enough powdered sugar to sweeten. Place large block of ice in punch bowl and stir well. Then add
1 pt. Brandy
1 pt. Rum
1 pt. Champagne
2 qts. Claret
1 qt. carbonated water
½ pt. Sweet Vermouth
Some prefer to add the strained contents of a pot of tea. Stir well and decorate with fruits in season. Serve in 4 oz. punch glasses.

CARIOCA

Juice of ½ lime
1½ oz. Carioca Rum
1 barspoon sugar
Dash Maraschino Liqueur
*Shake with finely shaved ice and serve in cocktail
glass.*

CARIOCA COLLINS

Juice of ½ lime
½ barspoon powdered sugar
1 jigger Carioca Rum
*Shake well and strain into Collins glass. Add lump of
ice and fill glass with soda water.*

CARIOCA EGGNOG

1 egg
1 tablespoon powdered sugar
1 jigger Carioca Rum
1 glass milk
*Break egg into shaker. Add ice and ingredients. Shake
well and strain into tall highball glass. Grate a little
nutmeg on top.*

CARROL COCKTAIL

1½ oz. Brandy
¾ oz. Sweet Vermouth
*Stir well with cracked ice and strain into 3 oz. cocktail
glass. Serve with a cherry.*

CASINO COCKTAIL

2 dashes orange bitters
¼ teaspoon Maraschino Liqueur
¼ teaspoon lemon juice
2 oz. Dry Gin
*Shake well with cracked ice and strain into 3 oz. cock-
tail glass. Serve with a cherry.*

CHAMPAGNE COCKTAIL

Spiral rind of ½ lemon
1 lump of sugar
2 dashes bitters
Use 6 oz. champagne glass. Fill with Champagne.

CHAMPAGNE CUP

4 teaspoons powdered sugar
6 oz. carbonated water
½ oz. Triple Sec
½ oz. Curaçao
2 oz. Brandy
Fill large glass pitcher with cubes of ice. Add 1 pint of Champagne. Stir well and decorate with as many fruits as available and also rind of cucumber inserted on each side of pitcher. Top with small bunch of mint sprigs. Serve in 5 oz. claret glass.

CHAMPAGNE PUNCH

1 qt. Champagne
1 qt. Sauterne
1 pt. soda water
6 teaspoons powdered sugar
1 sliced orange
1 sliced lemon
Scoop out center of large ice block. Place in bowl and decorate with maraschino cherries and sprigs of fresh mint. Serve in 4 oz. punch glasses.

CHAMPERELLE (or SHAMPARELLE)

This is a large Pousse Café served in a sherry glass instead of the regular Pousse Café glass. Kirsch, Goldwasser or some other very dry liqueur is frequently used instead of Cognac. Care must be taken to prevent the different liquors from running together.
Any combination of liqueurs and spirits that will remain separate can be used.

CHAMPS ÉLYSÉES COCKTAIL

1 oz. Cognac
½ oz. Yellow Chartreuse
Juice of ¼ lemon
½ teaspoon powdered sugar
1 dash bitters
Shake well with cracked ice and strain into 3 oz. cocktail glass.

CHARLES COCKTAIL

1¼ oz. Sweet Vermouth
1¼ oz. Brandy
1 dash bitters
Stir well with cracked ice and strain into 3 oz. cocktail glass.

CHARLIE CHAPLIN

2 parts lime juice
3 parts Sloe Gin
3 parts Apricot Brandy
Shake with crushed or cracked ice. The original recipe for this drink calls for three times as much Sloe Gin as Brandy, but this may be too sweet.

CHARLOTTE RUSSE

One half teaspoon sugar syrup, 1 dash each bitters and orange bitters to each drink of Gin. Shake with cracked or crushed ice. Rinse pre-chilled cocktail glass with a few drops of Absinthe (or Pernod) and strain the Gin mixture into it.

CHELSEA SIDE CAR COCKTAIL

Juice of ¼ lemon
¾ oz. Triple Sec
¼ oz. Dry Gin
Shake well with cracked ice and strain into 3 oz. cocktail glass.

CHERRY BLOSSOM COCKTAIL

1 oz. Wild Cherry Flavored Brandy
1 oz. Brandy
¼ teaspoon Curaçao
¼ teaspoon lemon juice
¼ teaspoon Grenadine
Shake well with cracked ice and strain into 3 oz. cocktail glass.

CHERRY FIZZ

Juice ½ of lemon
2 oz. Wild Cherry Flavored Brandy
Shake well with cracked ice and strain into 7 oz. highball glass. Fill with carbonated water and decorate with a cherry.

CHERRY FLIP

1 egg
1 teaspoon powdered sugar
1½ oz. Wild Cherry Flavored Brandy
2 teaspoons sweet cream (if desired)
Shake well with cracked ice and strain into 5 oz. flip glass. Grate a little nutmeg on top.

CHERRY SLING

2 cubes of ice
2 oz. Wild Cherry Flavored Brandy
Juice of ½ lemon
Serve in old fashioned cocktail glass and stir. Twist of lemon peel and drop in glass.

CHEZ ASCH

3 parts Vodka
1 part Cherry Heering
1 part lemon or lime juice
Shake with finely crushed ice and strain into chilled cocktail glass.

CHICAGO COCKTAIL

2 oz. Brandy
1 dash bitters
¼ teaspoon Curaçao
Stir well with cracked ice and strain into 3 oz. cocktail glass. Frost glass by rubbing slice of lemon around rim and then dip in powdered sugar.

CHICAGO FIZZ

Juice of ½ lemon
1 teaspoon powdered sugar
White of 1 egg
1 oz. Port Wine
1 oz. Imported Rum
Shake well with cracked ice and strain into 7 oz. highball glass. Fill with carbonated water and stir.

CHINESE COCKTAIL

½ oz. Grenadine
1½ oz. Jamaica Rum
1 dash bitters
1 teaspoon Maraschino Liqueur
1 teaspoon Curaçao
Shake well with cracked ice and strain into 3 oz. cocktail glass.

CHOCOLATE COCKTAIL

1½ oz. Port Wine
¼ oz. Yellow Chartreuse
Yolk of 1 egg
1 teaspoon powdered sugar
Shake well with cracked ice and strain into 4 oz. cocktail glass.

CHOCOLATE DAISY

Juice of ½ lemon
½ teaspoon powdered sugar
1 teaspoon raspberry syrup or Grenadine
1½ oz. Brandy
1½ oz. Port Wine
Shake well with cracked ice and strain into stein or 8 oz. metal cup. Add cube of ice and decorate with fruit.

CHOCOLATE FLIP

1 egg
1 teaspoon powdered sugar
¾ oz. Sloe Gin
¾ oz. Brandy
2 teaspoons sweet cream (if desired)
Shake well with cracked ice and strain into 5 oz. flip glass. Grate a little nutmeg on top.

CHOCOLATE SOLDIER COCKTAIL

Juice of ½ lime
¾ oz. Dubonnet
1½ oz. Dry Gin
Shake well with cracked ice and strain into 3 oz. cocktail glass.

CHRISTMAS YULE EGGNOG

Beat the yolks and whites of 12 eggs separately and then pour together and add
1 pinch baking soda
6 oz. Rum
2 lbs. granulated sugar
Beat into stiff batter. Then add
1 qt. milk
1 qt. sweet cream
2 qts. Whiskey
Stir. Set in refrigerator over night. Before serving, stir again, and serve in 4 oz. punch glasses, and grate nutmeg on top.

the water of life

By BERNARD LANDIS

AT THE east end of Edinburgh's Rose Street—a narrow, cobbled, 17th century byway—is situated a typical Scottish pub, the steady haunt of the city's better-known fishermen, farmers, poets, and politicians. One recent, typically-misty Friday evening some cronies were gathered together commencing their weekend with a little Scotch whisky and the traditional Gaelic toast.

"Slawn Givah," proclaimed greybearded Ian MacCaig, the eldest of the group. With a broad smile he raised his glass containing that golden distillation of good Scottish barley, crystal clear water, and fragrant peat; then suddenly he stopped short. His face reddened, and Ian gasped for breath.

Turning about, his friends perceived immediately the reason for Ian's shock. At a corner of the rectangular bar, an American tourist was drinking Scotch on the rocks!

"Och, the puir sinner, what is he doing?" cried Callum Dickson, an old-time journalist. "Doesn't he know that the sin of putting ice in Scotch will send him surely straight to Hell?"

Sandy MacDiarmid nodded solemnly. "Next to adding soda water to Scotch whisky, the most certain way to ruin the taste is to drink it with ice."

"Ruin the taste? Aye, devastate it entirely," wailed Ian. "Och, my evening is spoiled for sure. I'm happy that whisky is Britain's greatest dollar earner, but why, oh why, don't the Americans learn to drink it properly?"

The American, realizing that he was the object of outrageous consternation, garnered courage and approached the three Scotsmen. Directly he asked them what seemed to be the trouble and, with an accompaniment of sighs and groans, they duly informed him of his horrendous crime.

"I still don't see what's wrong with mixing my drink with ice," the American persisted.

"The lower temperature," interrupted the bartender, "kills the flavor. If you must mix your Scotch with anything then take a wee bit of Scottish water. And then, the only good water is from the same stream that furnished the water for the making of that particular whisky."

"The trouble with you Americans," declared Sandy, "is that you drink for kicks. Waal, when you drink Uisgebeatha, you should drink for the ays-thet-ick pleasure."

The American looked puzzled at hearing the strange word and Ian explained. "Uisgebeatha is the Gaelic term from which *Uisge* means water, and *beatha* means of life. Whisky comes from the first half of the word."

"Tell him the story of Uisgebeatha, Ian," urged Callum. "When he knows the history of the water of life, then he'll drink it differently . . . with respect, yea, even with reverence."

"Please do," requested the American, and thus encouraged, Ian MacCaig told the story.

Uisgebeatha was probably discovered, somewhere in Scotland or Ireland, about 2,000 years ago. It was doubtless discovered by accident, one of the most tremendous accidents in our history. It may have been a bitter cold day when one of our shivering Celtic ancestors, warming himself by his cave fire, decided also to warm his beer, for they already had beer then.

Soon he noticed that the vapor from the boiling beer was condensing in watery drops on an overhanging cold rock. Just for fun, this curious forebear tasted one of these drops and found that it didn't resemble water in the slightest. You understand, he couldn't have known that it was the alcohol in the beer that had first come to a boil and condensed. But he couldn't have cared less, for the more he tasted, the peppier he felt and he quickly named this remarkable fluid the Water of Life.

Before long every crofter in the land heard of this discovery and was soon distilling his own whisky in his own pot. But all good things come to an end. And so, starting around the 17th century the English government started passing all kinds of laws on the making of whisky. Some lawmakers wanted heavy duties to raise revenue; others wanted restrictions to control the excesses of drink that appeared as a direct result of the industrial revolution and the factory slums. (Before the time of factories and squalor, our ancestors rarely drank to excess; they treated Uisgebeatha with respect and sipped it like a Liqueur —the way it should be drunk.)

Anyway, in 1823 the government forbade the use of stills under the 40-gallon size. That about finished the small fellow and ushered in the commercial age of whisky. Naturally some folks kept up illicit small pot stills and did us all a big favor. It was they who kept alive the true art of distillation for they didn't have to sacrifice quality for quantity.

"Tell him how whisky is made today, Ian," Sandy said.

"I'm coming to that," Ian replied. "I'm going to explain just how the soil and soul of guid auld Scotland is converted into the most romantic drink in the world. But first, you Americans should know that the true Scotch whisky can only be made in Scotland. Sure they tried to make it in many lands from Japan, France, and Russia, but all those experiments failed.

"Just why they failed is hard to say. Some people, like Callum here, will tell you the rare flavor of Scotland's peat can't be duplicated; others insist the secret lies in Scotland's water; still others say it's in the barley. But let's continue with the present day process."

Imagine one of the many small distilleries along the green and heathered valley of the River Spey. There, a family with hundreds of years of know-how behind it will be practicing the art of distillation with the love possessed only by those born and raised in the tradition.

The initial step takes place in the malt barn where a large floor is covered with water-soaked barley. The barley is turned and churned by men with wooden shovels in order to keep separate the grains as they germinate. You see, as the barley germinates, or sprouts, a chemical change occurs and the starch in the barley is converted to sugar. When this happens, we call the barley "malt."

When the sprouting has gone on long enough, usually about three days (though it takes a trained expert to know just when), it has to be dried on a kiln to stop further germinating. It's in this drying process that Scotch whisky gets it unique flavor.

The drying takes place in a small two-story building. The peat fire is on the ground floor. The barley sets on the second floor which is made like a metal sieve that lets the peat smoke get to the barley.

"Ye have to be darned careful," said Callum, "not to let too much peat smoke in. A good man can tell, a dozen years later, if a bottle of whisky is too peaty. It's little things like this that

81

explain why whisky from two stills not 50 meters apart will taste differently."

The American shook his head in wonderment and Ian went on.

Next, the dried malted barley is ground up and mixed with hot water. Later, the sweetened water . . . it's then called the "wort" . . . is cooled. Temperature control is important every inch of the way. After cooling, the wort is piped into big wooden tubs where, with the help of some yeast, it begins to ferment and change into alcohol. There's a lot of frothing at the top and the good distiller makes sure that none of the froth is lost.

Anyhow, the solution ferments and thins at the same time. If it thins too much, the whisky will be ruined. The specific gravity has to be just under that for water when this process is stopped. At this point, the fermented or alcoholic "wort" is called the "wash" and it has now to be distilled.

The wash is put into giant, round, long-necked pots that are heated by a furnace underneath. As the spirit vapor rises, it exits through the neck into a pipe that's cooled by water on the outside. At the end of the pipe, out comes the distilled spirit, the diamond dew, the Water of Life.

Of course, the distillation is very complicated because the strength has to be just right. Sometimes, at the end of a run the wash has to be redistilled. After everything is checked and rechecked, then the whisky is put into casks and warehoused for years while it matures.

"When you look at whisky in that way . . .", began the American.

"Oh, there's more to it than that," said Sandy. "There's the coloring. Where do you think the golden hue comes from?"

"I never thought about that," replied the American.

"Well, mon, I'll tell ye. The color comes from the spirit being stored in used sherry casks that we get from Spain. The distilled whisky is colorless. It takes its hue during the aging process when it absorbs the sherry color from the wood. Course, if the spirit stays too long in the barrel it may take on a woody flavor. Takes an expert to know."

"Aye, a Scottish expert," interjected Callum. "It also takes a keen Scottish palate to do the blending. You Americans don't drink our whisky right from the still as it's a little too heavy for most palates. So it has to be blended skillfully with lighter spirits made from a raw or unmalted grain."

"Like the unmalted maize used in Bourbon?" asked the American.

"Aye, that's it," answered Callum. "Though personally I prefer the spirit straight from the pot still."

"That's because you're an unregenerated Highland rebel," said the bartender.

"After hearing all this," the American stated, "I've got to have another shot . . . without ice, without anything. Let me buy this round."

With cheers and backslapping, Sandy, Ian, and Callum accepted the invitation and they called for the house's best twelve-year-old Scotch. And they sipped it straight and slow.

"Easy now," said Ian. "Remember it's liquid gold from the heart of Scotland."

"A trifle peaty," said Callum, as the others hemmed and hawed skeptically.

Sandy added a little water and apologized: "My stomach isn't what she used to be, puir thing."

"I don't know what it is," the American said ecstatically, "but this drink tastes different than any other Scotch I've ever tasted. Perhaps it's the story you told me. Perhaps for the first time I'm actually *tasting* the whisky. I tell you this drink is the best I've ever known. No wonder they call it the Water of Life."

Reprinted from The Diners Club Magazine

CIDER CUP

4 teaspoons powdered sugar
6 oz. carbonated water
½ oz. Triple Sec
½ oz. Curaçao
2 oz. Brandy
Fill large glass pitcher with cubes of ice. Add 1 pint of Cider. Stir well and decorate with as many fruits as available and also rind of cucumber inserted on each side of pitcher. Top with small bunch of mint sprigs. Serve in 5 oz. claret glasses.

CIDER EGGNOG

1 egg
1 teaspoon powdered sugar
¼ pt. milk
Shake well with cracked ice and strain into Tom Collins glass. Then fill glass with Sweet Cider and stir. Grate nutmeg on top.

CIRCUS RICKEY

1 cube of ice
Juice of ½ lime
½ teaspoon Grenadine
1½ oz. Dry Gin
Fill 8 oz. highball glass with carbonated water and stir. Leave lime in glass.

CLARET COBBLER

Dissolve 1 teaspoon powdered sugar in 2 oz. carbonated water; then add 3 oz. Claret. Fill 10 oz. goblet with shaved ice and stir. Decorate with fruits in season. Serve with straws.

CLARET CUP

4 teaspoons powdered sugar
6 oz. carbonated water
½ oz. Triple Sec
½ oz. Curaçao
2 oz. Brandy
Fill large glass pitcher with cubes of ice. Add 1 pint of Claret. Stir well and decorate with as many fruits as available and also rind of cucumber inserted on each side of pitcher. Top with small bunch of mint sprigs. Serve in 5 oz. claret glass.

CLARET PUNCH

Juice of 12 lemons
Add enough powdered sugar to sweeten. Place large block of ice in punch bowl and stir well. Then add
½ pt. Curaçao
1 pt. Brandy
3 qts. Claret
1 qt. carbonated water
Some prefer to add the strained contents of a pot of tea. Stir well and decorate with fruits in season. Serve in 4 oz. punch glasses.

CLARIDGE COCKTAIL

¾ oz. Dry Gin
¾ oz. Dry Vermouth
½ oz. Apricot Flavored Brandy
½ oz. Triple Sec
Stir well with cracked ice and strain into 3 oz. cocktail glass.

CLASSIC

1 part Curaçao
1 part Maraschino Liqueur
4 parts lemon juice
8 parts Cognac
Shake with cracked ice. Serve with twist of lemon over each drink.

CLASSIC COCKTAIL

Juice of ¼ lemon
¼ oz. Curaçao
¼ oz. Maraschino Liqueur
1 oz. Brandy
Shake well with cracked ice and strain into 3 oz. cocktail glass. Frost rim of glass by rubbing with lemon and dipping in powdered sugar.

CLOVE COCKTAIL

1 oz. Sweet Vermouth
½ oz. Sloe Gin
½ oz. Muscatel
Stir well with cracked ice and strain into 3 oz. cocktail glass.

CLOVER CLUB COCKTAIL

Juice of ½ lemon
2 teaspoons Grenadine
White of 1 egg
1½ oz. Dry Gin
Shake well with cracked ice and strain into 4 oz. cocktail glass.

CLOVER LEAF COCKTAIL

Juice of 1 lime
2 teaspoons Grenadine
White of 1 egg
1½ oz. Dry Gin
Shake well with cracked ice and strain into 4 oz. cocktail glass. Serve with mint leaf on top.

CLUB

Perhaps it would not be too much of an exaggeration to say that there are as many CLUB COCKTAILS as there are clubs . . . Here are a few examples:

#1—Equal parts of Dry Sherry and Tawny Port with a dash of orange bitters to each drink. Stir.

#2—Gin with 2 dashes each of orange bitters, Chartreuse, and Jamaica Rum to each drink. Stir. Decorate with stuffed olive.

#3—Rye with 1 or 2 dashes each of bitters and Grenadine to each drink. Decorate with a cherry.

#4—Cognac with 2 dashes each of Maraschino Liqueur, Crème d'Ananas, and orange bitters to each drink. Stir. A twist of lemon over each glass.

CLUB COCKTAIL

1½ oz. Dry Gin
¾ oz. Sweet Vermouth
Stir well with cracked ice and strain into 3 oz. cocktail glass. Add a cherry or olive.

So this fellow comes home four sheets to the wind one night and hands his wife what was left of his pay for the week. She's furious. "You've spent almost half of it," she screams. "What did you buy?"

"Something for the house," he snaps back defensively.

"Oh," she retreats with. "What was it?"

"A round of drinks."

COBBLER

3 oz. your favorite Spirit or Wine
1 teaspoon sugar
Fill wine goblet ¼ full with cracked ice. Add ingredients and fill glass with water. Stir well. Decorate with half slice of orange, a maraschino cherry, and a pineapple stick. (Typical Cobblers are: Bourbon, Brandy, Claret, Cuban Rum, Gin, Jamaica Rum, Port, Rye, Sauterne, Sherry.)

COFFEE COCKTAIL

1 egg
1 teaspoon powdered sugar
1 oz. Port Wine
1 oz. Brandy
Shake well with cracked ice and strain into 5 oz. cocktail glass. Grate nutmeg on top.

COFFEE FLIP

1 egg
1 teaspoon powdered sugar
1 oz. Brandy
1 oz. Port Wine
2 teaspoons sweet cream (if desired)
Shake well with cracked ice and strain into 5 oz. flip glass. Grate a little nutmeg on top.

COGNAC HIGHBALL

1 cube of ice
2 oz. Cognac
Fill 8 oz. highball glass with ginger ale or carbonated water. Add twist of lemon peel, if desired, and stir gently.

COLD DECK COCKTAIL

½ oz. Crème de Menthe (White)
½ oz. Sweet Vermouth
Stir well with cracked ice and strain into 3 oz. cocktail glass.

COLLINS

1 tablespoon sugar
Juice of 1 medium-sized lemon or lime
3 oz. Whiskey
Stir together in Collins glass, add 4 large ice cubes, fill glass with carbonated water, stir again quickly and serve. (Popular Collins are: Brandy Collins, John Collins, Mint Collins, Orange Gin Collins, Rum Collins, Sloe Gin Collins, Tequila Collins, Tom Collins [Gin], Vodka Collins, Whiskey Collins.)

COLONIAL COCKTAIL

½ oz. grapefruit juice
1 teaspoon Maraschino Liqueur
1½ oz. Dry Gin
Shake well with cracked ice and strain into 3 oz. cocktail glass. Serve with an olive.

COMMANDO

1 part Cointreau
2 parts lime juice
8 parts Bourbon
3 dashes Pernod
Mix ingredients with ice, strain and pour into glass. Plain wine glass may be substituted for tulip-shaped glass, shown on cover.

COMMODORE COCKTAIL

Juice of ½ lime or ¼ lemon
1 teaspoon powdered sugar
2 dashes orange bitters
1½ oz. Whiskey
Shake well with cracked ice and strain into 3 oz. cocktail glass.

CONTINENTAL

1 part sweet cream
2 parts lemon juice
8 parts Bourbon
1 dash Jamaican Rum
Combine ingredients and mix with shaved ice. Strain and pour into glass.

COOLERS

Juice of ½ lemon
¼ teaspoon sugar
1 jigger Spirits
Carbonated water
Ice
(Popular Cooler drinks are made with Claret, Dubonnet, Port, Sherry, Vermouth, or other wines; Applejack, Bourbon, Brandy, Gin, Rum, Rye, Sloe Gin, Southern Comfort or Vodka.)

COOPERSTOWN COCKTAIL

½ oz. Dry Vermouth
½ oz. Sweet Vermouth
1 oz. Dry Gin
2 sprigs fresh mint
Shake well with cracked ice and strain into 3 oz. cocktail glass.

CORNELL COCKTAIL

½ teaspoon lemon juice
1 teaspoon Maraschino Liqueur
White of 1 egg
1½ oz. Dry Gin
Shake well with cracked ice and strain into 4 oz. cocktail glass.

CORONATION COCKTAIL

¾ oz. Dry Gin
¾ oz. Dubonnet
¾ oz. Dry Vermouth
Stir well with cracked ice and strain into 3 oz. cocktail glass.

COUNTRY CLUB COOLER

½ teaspoon Grenadine
2 oz. carbonated water *and stir.*
Fill 12 oz. Tom Collins glass with cracked ice and add
2 oz. Dry Vermouth
Fill with carbonated water or ginger ale and stir again. Insert spiral of orange or lemon peel (or both) and dangle end over rim of glass.

COUNTRY COCKTAIL (see Big Apple)

COWBOY COCKTAIL

1½ oz. Whiskey
½ oz. sweet cream
Shake well with cracked ice and strain into 3 oz. cocktail glass.

CREAM FIZZ

Juice of ½ lemon
1 teaspoon powdered sugar
2 oz. Dry Gin
1 teaspoon fresh cream
Shake well with cracked ice and strain into 8 oz. highball glass. Fill with carbonated water and stir.

CREAM PUFF

2 oz. Rum
1 oz. sweet cream
½ teaspoon powdered sugar
Shake well with cracked ice and strain into 8 oz. highball glass. Fill with carbonated water and stir.

CRÈME DE GIN COCKTAIL

1½ oz. Dry Gin
½ oz. Crème de Menthe
White of 1 egg
2 teaspoons lemon juice
2 teaspoons orange juice
Shake well with cracked ice and strain into 4 oz. cocktail glass.

CRÈME DE MENTHE FRAPPE

Fill cocktail glass up to brim with shaved ice. Add Crème de Menthe (Green). *slowly float in 1 oz.* Brandy *on back of inserted spoon. Serve with two short straws.*

CRÉOLE LADY COCKTAIL

1¼ oz. Whiskey
1¼ oz. Madeira Wine
1 teaspoon Grenadine
Stir well with cracked ice and strain into 3 oz. cocktail glass. Serve with 1 green and 1 red cherry.

CRIMSON COCKTAIL

1½ oz. Dry Gin
2 teaspoons lemon juice
1 teaspoon Grenadine
Shake well with cracked ice and strain into 3 oz. cocktail glass, leaving enough room on top to float ¾ oz. Port Wine.

CRUSTAS

Take a large lemon or a small orange of a size approximating that of the glass (preferably a wine or old fashioned glass) to be used. Cut off both ends and peel the remainder in spiral fashion so as to keep the peel all in one piece. Line the inside of the glass with this peel, wet the edge of the glass, and dip in powdered sugar to frost the edge of both peel and glass. In a bar glass, mix 1 part sugar syrup, 2 parts lemon juice and 8 parts Brandy with 1 or 2 dashes each of Maraschino Liqueur and bitters to each drink. Shake with finely crushed ice and strain into the prepared glass.
Substitution of a different liquor will give you a Gin Crusta, a Rum Crusta, an Applejack Crusta, a Whiskey Crusta, etc.

CRYSTAL SLIPPER COCKTAIL

½ oz. Crème de Yvette
2 dashes orange bitters
1½ oz. Dry Gin
Stir well with cracked ice and strain into 3 oz. cocktail glass.

CUBA LIBRE

Juice of ½ lime
2 oz. Rum
2 cubes of ice
Drop lime rind in 10 oz. glass and fill with any cola.
Stir well.

CUBAN COCKTAIL NO. 1

Juice of ½ lime
½ teaspoon powdered sugar
2 oz. Rum
Shake well with cracked ice and strain into 3 oz.
cocktail glass.

CUBAN COCKTAIL NO. 2

Juice of ½ lime or ¼ lemon
½ oz. Apricot Flavored Brandy
1½ oz. Brandy
1 teaspoon Rum
Shake well with cracked ice and strain into 3 oz.
cocktail glass.

CUBAN SPECIAL COCKTAIL

½ oz. pineapple juice
Juice of ½ lime
1 oz. Rum
½ teaspoon Curaçao
Shake well with cracked ice and strain into 3 oz.
cocktail glass. Decorate with stick of pineapple and
a cherry.

CUP

This is a beverage made of Wine, usually iced, and with flavoring herbs and fruits, served in garnished pitchers, to be poured at table.

1½ ponies Brandy
1 pony Cointreau
1 pony Maraschino Liqueur
1 quart bottle Wine
1 large piece ice

Pour ingredients into large glass pitcher. Decorate with slices of orange, lemon, maraschino cherry, fresh pineapple sticks or slices, strawberries (when in season), and sprig of fresh mint. Top the cup with half a bottle of soda water.

DAIQUIRI COCKTAIL

Juice of 1 lime
1 teaspoon powdered sugar
1½ oz. Rum

Shake well with cracked ice and strain into 3 oz. cocktail glass.

DAISY

1 part Grenadine
2 parts lemon or lime juice
8 parts Whiskey (or Applejack, Brandy, or Rum)

Mix and pour into a goblet filled with fine ice. Muddle with a long spoon until outside of the glass or mug becomes frosted. Serve with straws. Float 1 or 2 teaspoonful Yellow Chartreuse on top. Decorate with pineapple, orange or whatever fruit may be available.

DAMN-THE-WEATHER COCKTAIL

1 teaspoon Curaçao
½ oz. orange juice
½ oz. Sweet Vermouth
1 oz. Dry Gin

Shake well with cracked ice and strain into 3 oz. cocktail glass.

DARB COCKTAIL

1 teaspoon lemon juice
¾ oz. Dry Vermouth
¾ oz. Dry Gin
¾ oz. Apricot Flavored Brandy
Shake well with cracked ice and strain into 3 oz. cocktail glass.

DEAUVILLE COCKTAIL

Juice of ¼ lemon
½ oz. Brandy
½ oz. Apple Brandy
½ oz. Triple Sec
Shake well with cracked ice and strain into 3 oz. cocktail glass.

DEEP SEA COCKTAIL

1 oz. Dry Vermouth
¼ teaspoon Pernod (Absinthe substitute)
1 dash orange bitters
1 oz. Dry Gin
Stir well with cracked ice and strain into 3 oz. cocktail glass.

DEMPSEY COCKTAIL

1 oz. Dry Gin
1 oz. Apple Brandy
½ teaspoon Pernod (Asinthe substitute)
½ teaspoon Grenadine
Stir well with cracked ice and strain into 3 oz. cocktail glass.

DERBY

1 part Peach Brandy
4 parts Gin
Crush 1 small sprig of mint to each drink in bar glass or shaker; add the liquor and shake well with crushed ice. This drink is improved by the addition of a small quantity of sugar syrup (not over 1 teaspoonful to each drink).

There is also another cocktail called the Derby, consisting of straight Cognac *with 1 or 2 dashes each of* Curaçao, *pineapple syrup, and bitters. Fill cocktail glass about ½ to ⅔ full with this mixture and then add* Champagne *to the top.*

DERBY FIZZ

Juice of ½ lemon
1 teaspoon powdered sugar
1 egg
2 oz. Scotch
1 teaspoon Curaçao
Shake well with cracked ice and strain into 8 oz. highball glass. Fill with carbonated water and stir.

DEVIL'S COCKTAIL

½ teaspoon lemon juice
1¼ oz. Port Wine
1¼ oz. Dry Vermouth
Stir well with cracked ice and strain into 3 oz. cocktail glass.

DIAMOND FIZZ

Juice of ½ lemon
1 teaspoon powdered sugar
2 oz. Dry Gin
Shake well with cracked ice and strain into 7 oz. highball glass. Fill with Champagne *and stir gently.*

DIANA COCKTAIL

Fill 3 oz. cocktail glass with shaved ice, then fill ¾ full with Crème de Menthe (white) *and float* Brandy *on top.*

DICKENS' MARTINI COCKTAIL

Same as a regular Martini except no olive or lemon twist is added.

DINAH COCKTAIL

Juice of ¼ lemon
½ teaspoon powdered sugar
1½ oz. Whiskey
2 or 3 sprigs fresh mint
Shake well with cracked ice and strain into 3 oz. cocktail glass. Serve with a mint leaf.

DINERS' CLUB COCKTAILS:
DINERFLO

1½ oz. Southern Comfort
¾ oz. Dry Vermouth
1 dash Cointreau
Stir with ice, strain into cocktail glass and top with twist of lemon peel.

DINERMITE

¼ oz. Sherry
1 oz. Vodka or Gin
Serve over the rocks in old fashioned glass with carbonated water and top with twist of lemon peel.

DINERMO

1 jigger Vodka
3 drops Cointreau
Fill with Champagne. Serve over rocks in champagne glass, with orange slice.

DIPLOMAT COCKTAIL

1½ oz. Dry Vermouth
½ oz. Sweet Vermouth
2 dashes bitters
½ teaspoon Maraschino Liqueur
Stir well with cracked ice and strain into 3 oz. cocktail glass. Serve with ½ slice of lemon and a cherry.

DIVAN (pronounced dee-vahn)

Equal parts lemon juice, orange juice, and Rye, with 1 teaspoonful Grenadine to each drink. This drink can be improved by increasing the proportion of whiskey to 2 or 3 parts.

DIXIE COCKTAIL

Juice of ¼ orange
½ oz. Pernod (Absinthe substitute)
½ oz. Dry Vermouth
1 oz. Dry Gin
Shake well with cracked ice and strain into 4 oz. cocktail glass.

DIXIE JULEP

4 sprigs of mint
1 teaspoon powdered sugar
2½ oz. Bourbon
Fill a 12 oz. Tom Collins glass with shaved ice and stir gently until glass is frosted. Decorate with sprigs of mint. Serve with straws.

DIXIE WHISKEY COCKTAIL

½ lump of sugar
1 dash bitters
¼ teaspoon Curaçao
½ teaspoon Crème de Menthe
2 oz. Whiskey
Shake well with cracked ice and strain into 3 oz. cocktail glass.

DOUBLE STANDARD SOUR

Juice of ½ lemon or 1 lime
½ teaspoon powdered sugar
¾ oz. Whiskey
¾ oz. Dry Gin
½ teaspoon raspberry syrup or Grenadine
Shake well with cracked ice and strain into 6 oz. sour glass. Fill with carbonated water. Decorate with a half-slice of lemon and a cherry.

DOUGLAS FAIRBANKS

2 parts Gin
1 part Apricot Brandy
Juice of 1 lime
1 egg white
Shake with cracked ice, and serve in tall glass.

DREAM COCKTAIL

¾ oz. Curaçao
1½ oz. Brandy
¼ teaspoon Anisette
Shake well with cracked ice and strain into 3 oz. cocktail glass.

DRY MARTINI

See Martini Section on pages 157–158.

DU BARRY COCKTAIL

1 dash bitters
¾ oz. Dry Vermouth
½ teaspoon Pernod (Absinthe substitute)
1½ oz. Dry Gin
Stir well with cracked ice and strain into 3 oz. cocktail glass. Add slice of orange.

DUBONNET COCKTAIL

1½ oz. Dubonnet
¾ oz. Dry Gin
1 dash orange bitters *if desired*
Stir well with cracked ice and strain into 3 oz. cocktail glass. Twist of lemon peel on top and drop in glass.

DUBONNET FIZZ

Juice of ½ orange
Juice of ¼ lemon
1 teaspoon Wild Cherry Flavored Brandy
2 oz. Dubonnet
Shake well with cracked ice and strain into 7 oz. high-ball glass. Fill with carbonated water and stir.

DUBONNET HIGHBALL

1 cube ice
2 oz. Dubonnet
Fill 8 oz. highball glass with ginger ale or carbonated water. Add twist of lemon peel, if desired, and stir.

DUCHESS COCKTAIL

¾ oz. Dry Vermouth
¾ oz. Sweet Vermouth
¾ oz. Pernod (Absinthe substitute)
Stir well with cracked ice and strain into 3 oz. cocktail glass.

DUKE COCKTAIL

½ oz. Triple Sec
1 teaspoon orange juice
2 teaspoons lemon juice
½ teaspoon Maraschino Liqueur
1 egg
Shake well with cracked ice and strain into 8 oz. stem glass. Fill with Champagne *and stir very gently.*

EAST INDIA COCKTAIL NO. 1

1½ oz. Brandy
½ teaspoon pineapple juice
½ teaspoon Curaçao
1 teaspoon Jamaica Rum
1 dash bitters
Shake well with cracked ice and strain into 3 oz. cocktail glass. Twist of lemon peel and add a cherry.

EAST INDIA COCKTAIL NO. 2

1¼ oz. Dry Vermouth
1¼ oz. Sherry Wine
1 dash orange bitters
Stir well with cracked ice and strain tnto 3 oz. cocktail glass.

international drink toasts

American	Bottoms Up	
	Here's How	
	Happy Days	
Australian	Cheers	
Austrian	Prosit	*Proh'zit*
Bohemian	Naz Dar	*Naz-Dar'*
Brazilian	Saúde	*Sah oo' Day*
Canadian	Cheers	
Chinese	Nien Nien Ju E	*Nyen-Nyen Zhu Ee'*
French Canadian	Santé	*Sahn-tay'*
Czechoslovakian	Na Zdravi	*Nah Zdrah'vee*
Danish	Skaal	*Skohl*
Dutch	Proost	*Prohst*
Ecuadorian	Salud	*Sa-lood'*
Egyptian	Fee sihetak	*Fee Say'-tok*
English	Cheers	
Estonian	Tervist	*Ter'vist*
Finnish	Kippis	*Kee'pees*
French	A votre santé	*A vuhtr sahn'tay*
German	Prosit	*Proh'zit*
Greek	Eis Igian	*Ees igee' an*
Hawaiian	Okole Maluna	*Okoh'lay Mah-loo'na*
	Hauoli Maoli	*Hah-oh'-lay*
	Oe	*Mah-oh'-lay-oy*

100

international drink toasts

		Pronunciation Key
Hebrew	Lehayim	*Leh-hah'-yim*
Hungarian	Kedves Egeszsegere	*Ked'vesh Eh-gay-say-gay-reh'*
Irish	Sláinte	*Slahn'cha*
Italian	A la Salute	*Ah lah Sa-loo'-tay*
Japanese	Kampai	*Kahm-pah'-ee*
Luxembourg	Prost	*Prusht*
Norwegian	Skål	*Skohl*
Polish	Na Zdrowie	*Nah Zdruh'vyeh*
Portuguese	A sua saude	*Ah soo'-ah sah-ood'*
Romanian	Pentru Sanatatea Dunneavoastra	*Pen'troo Sah-nah-tah-tee'-ah Doo-nee-ah-vah'-trah*
Russian	Na Zdorovia	*Nah Zdroh-vee-'uh*
Scotch	Shlante	*Shlahn'-tay*
Spanish	Salud	*Sa-lood'*
Swedish	Skol	*Skohl*
Thai	Sawasdi	*Sa-wah-dee'*
Turkish	Serese	*Sheh-reh'-say*
Welsh	Iechyd Da	*Yeh'-hid Dah*
Yiddish	Lechaim	*L'hah'-yim*
Yugoslavian	Na Zdravje	*Nah Zdrah'-vee-yeh*

ECLIPSE COCKTAIL

1 oz. Dry Gin
2 oz. Sloe Gin
½ teaspoon lemon juice

Put enough Grenadine into 4 oz. cocktail glass to cover a ripe olive. Mix the above ingredients with ice and pour gently onto the Grenadine so that they do not mix.

EGGNOG

A drink of American origin, it enjoys world-wide popularity, especially around Christmas and the holiday season.

1 egg
1 tablespoon powdered sugar
1 jigger (1½ oz.) any liquor
1 glass of milk (or part milk and part sweet cream)

All the ingredients are shaken together with ice. Serve in large highball glass, with grated nutmeg on top. See page 62 for Brandy Eggnog.

EGG SOUR

1 egg
1 teaspoon powdered sugar
Juice of ½ lemon
2 oz. Brandy
¼ teaspoon Curaçao

Shake well with cracked ice and strain into 8 oz. highball glass.

EL PRESIDENTE COCKTAIL NO. 1

Juice of 1 lime
1 teaspoon pineapple juice
1 teaspoon Grenadine

Shake well with cracked ice and strain into 3 oz. cocktail glass.

EL PRESIDENTE COCKTAIL NO. 2

¾ oz. Dry Vermouth
1½ oz. Rum
1 dash bitters

Stir well with cracked ice and strain into 3 oz. cocktail glass.

These two well-to-do middle-aged businessmen were at the bar at The Blue Fox in San Francisco. "I have a new son-in-law," revealed one, "but he's not much good." "Howcum?" returned the other. "Well," complained the first, "he can't drink and he can't play cards."

"So, he can't drink and he can't play cards," defended the friend. "Does that mean that he's not much good?" "Yeah," came the reply. "He can't drink but he drinks, and he can't play cards but he plays cards!"

ELK'S OWN COCKTAIL

White of 1 egg
1½ oz. Whiskey
¾ oz. Port Wine
Juice of ¼ lemon
1 teaspoon powdered sugar
Shake well with cracked ice and strain into 4 oz. cocktail glass. Add a strip of pineapple.

EMERALD ISLE COCKTAIL

2 oz. Dry Gin
1 teaspoon Crème de Menthe (Green)
3 dashes bitters
Stir well with cracked ice and strain into 3 oz. cocktail glass.

ENGLISH HIGHBALL

1 cube of ice
¾ oz. Dry Gin
¾ oz. Brandy
¾ oz. Sweet Vermouth
Fill 8 oz. highball glass with ginger ale or carbonated water. Add twist of lemon peel, if desired, and stir.

ENGLISH ROSE COCKTAIL

1¼ oz. Dry Gin
¾ oz. Apricot Flavored Brandy
¾ oz. Dry Vermouth
1 teaspoon Grenadine
¼ teaspoon lemon juice
Shake well with cracked ice and strain into 4 oz. cocktail glass. Frost rim of glass by rubbing with lemon and dipping in sugar. Serve with a cherry.

EPICUREAN

1 part Kümmel
2 parts French Vermouth
4 parts Cognac
1 dash bitters to each drink
Stir.

ETHEL DUFFY COCKTAIL

¾ oz. Apricot Flavored Brandy
¾ oz. Crème de Menthe (White)
¾ oz. Curaçao
Stir well with cracked ice and strain into 3 oz. cocktail glass.

EVERYBODY'S IRISH COCKTAIL

1 teaspoon Crème de Menthe (Green)
1 teaspoon Green Chartreuse
2 oz. Irish Whiskey
Stir well with cracked ice and strain into 3 oz. cocktail glass. Serve with green olive.

EYE-OPENER COCKTAIL

Yolk of 1 egg
½ teaspoon powdered sugar
1 teaspoon Pernod (Absinthe substitute)
1 teaspoon Curaçao
1 teaspoon Crème de Cacao
2 oz. Rum
Shake well with cracked ice and strain into 4 oz. cocktail glass.

FAIR AND WARMER COCKTAIL

¾ oz. Sweet Vermouth
1½ oz. Rum
½ teaspoon Curaçao
Stir well with cracked ice and strain into 3 oz. cocktail glass.

FAIRY BELLE COCKTAIL

White of 1 egg
1 teaspoon Grenadine
¾ oz. Apricot Flavored Brandy
1½ oz. Dry Gin
Shake well with cracked ice and strain into 4 oz. cocktail glass.

FALERNUM RUM COLLINS

2 barspoons Falernum
1 jigger Barbados Rum
Juice of ½ lemon
Serve in Collins glass with cracked ice. Fill with carbonated water.

FALERNUM TOM COLLINS

2 barspoons Falernum
1 jigger Dry Gin
Juice of ½ lemon
Serve in Collins glass with cracked ice. Fill with carbonated water.

FALLEN ANGEL COCKTAIL

Juice of 1 lemon or ½ lime
1½ oz. Dry Gin
1 dash bitters
½ teaspoon Crème de Menthe
Shake well with cracked ice and strain into 3 oz. cocktail glass. Serve with a cherry.

FANCY BRANDY COCKTAIL

2 oz. Brandy
1 dash bitters
¼ teaspoon Curaçao
¼ teaspoon powdered sugar
Shake well with cracked ice and strain into 3 oz. cocktail glass. Twist of lemon peel and drop in glass.

FANCY GIN COCKTAIL

Same as FANCY BRANDY COCKTAIL except substitute:
2 oz. Dry Gin

FANCY WHISKEY COCKTAIL

Same as FANCY BRANDY COCKTAIL except substitute:
2 oz. Whiskey

FANTASIO COCKTAIL

1 teaspoon Crème de Menthe (White)
1 teaspoon Maraschino Liqueur
1 oz. Brandy
¾ oz. Dry Vermouth
Stir well with cracked ice and strain into 3 oz. cocktail glass.

FARMER'S COCKTAIL

1 oz. Dry Gin
½ oz. Dry Vermouth
½ oz. Sweet Vermouth
2 dashes bitters
Stir well with cracked ice and strain into 3 oz. cocktail glass.

FAVOURITE COCKTAIL

¾ oz. Apricot Flavored Brandy
¾ oz. Dry Vermouth
¾ oz. Dry Gin
¼ teaspoon lemon juice
Shake well with cracked ice and strain into 3 oz. cocktail glass.

FIFTH AVENUE

⅓ oz. Crème de Cacao
⅓ oz. Apricot Flavored Brandy
⅓ oz. sweet cream
Pour carefully, in order given, into Pousse Café glass, so that each ingredient floats on preceding one.

FIFTY-FIFTY COCKTAIL

1¼ oz. Dry Gin
1¼ oz. Dry Vermouth
Stir well with cracked ice and strain into 3 oz. cocktail glass.

FINE AND DANDY COCKTAIL

Juice of ¼ lemon
½ oz. Triple Sec
1¼ oz. Dry Gin
1 dash bitters
Shake well with cracked ice and strain into 3 oz. cocktail glass. Serve with a cherry.

FIREMAN'S SOUR

Juice of 2 limes
½ teaspoon powdered sugar
½ oz. Grenadine
2 oz. Rum
Shake well with cracked ice and strain into Delmonico glass. Fill with corbonated water, if desired. Decorate with a half-slice of lemon and a cherry.

FISH HOUSE PUNCH

Juice of 12 lemons
Add enough powdered sugar to sweeten. Place large block of ice in punch bowl and stir well. Then add
1½ qts. Brandy
1 pt. Peach Flavored Brandy
1 pt. Rum
1 qt. carbonated water
Some prefer to add the strained contents of a pot of tea. Stir well and decorate with fruits in season. Serve in 4 oz. punch glasses.

FIX

1 part pineapple syrup
2 parts lime or lemon juice
8 parts Gin (or Applejack, Brandy, Rum or Whiskey)
Mix and pour into a goblet filled with fine ice. Muddle with a long spoon until outside of glass or mug becomes frosted. Serve with straws. Cointreau *or* Maraschino Liqueur *may be substituted for the pineapple syrup. A spoonful of* Green Chartreuse *may be floated on top.*

FIZZ

Juice of ½ lemon
½ teaspoon sugar
Fruit syrup
Spirits
Ice
Carbonated water
This is an effervescent drink usually made of the above ingredients. The most popular Fizzes are the Gin Fizz, Golden Fizz, Silver Fizz, Royal Fizz, New Orleans Fizz, and Whisky Fizz.

FLAMINGO COCKTAIL

Juice of ½ lime
½ oz. Apricot Flavored Brandy
1¼ oz. Dry Gin
1 teaspoon Grenadine
Shake well with cracked ice and strain into 3 oz. cocktail glass.

FLIP

This is a drink made with liquor and sugar, mixed with an egg, and spiced. Among the most popular Flips are the Applejack, Brandy, Port, Sherry, and Whiskey Flips.
1 teaspoonful sugar or sugar syrup
1 whole egg
2 oz. Liquor
Shake with cracked or finely crushed ice and strain into a small sour or Delmonico glass. Decorate with a dash of grated nutmeg.
CHOCOLATE FLIP *is made with equal parts of* Cognac *and* Sloe Gin.
COFFEE FLIP *is made with equal parts of* Cognac *and* Port.

FLORADORA COOLER

Juice of 1 lime
½ teaspoon powdered sugar
½ oz. raspberry syrup or Grenadine
2 oz. carbonated water, *and stir.*
Fill a 12 oz. Tom Collins glass with cracked ice and add
2 oz. Dry Gin
Fill with carbonated water or ginger ale and stir again.

FLYING GRASSHOPPER COCKTAIL

¾ oz. Crème de Menthe (Green)
¾ oz. Crème de Cacao (White)
¾ oz. Vodka
Stir well with cracked ice and strain into 3 oz. cocktail glass.

So this fellow is standing at a bar watching the guy next to him who keeps ordering Martinis, and after downing each one, reaches into the glass and pulls out the olive. Then he takes a jar out of his coat pocket and drops the olive into the jar. This routine goes on through a dozen cocktails when finally the onlooker is overwhelmed with curiosity. He calls the bartender over. "What's with this guy?" he asks. "Is he some kind of nut?"

"He's no nut," returns the bartender. "His wife sent him out for a jar of olives!"

FLYING SCOTCHMAN COCKTAIL

1 oz. Sweet Vermouth
1 oz. Scotch
1 dash bitters
¼ teaspoon simple syrup
Stir well with cracked ice and strain into 3 oz. cocktail glass.

FOG HORN

1 cube of ice
Juice of ½ lime
1½ oz. Dry Gin
Fill 8 oz. highball glass with ginger ale and stir. Leave lime in glass.

FOUR W

1 part Jamaican Rum or Cuban Rum
1 part unsweetened grapefruit juice
1 dash bitters
1 dash maple syrup
Stir well with cracked ice and strain into 3 oz. cocktail glass.

FOX RIVER COCKTAIL

½ oz. Crème de Cacao
2 oz. Whiskey
4 dashes bitters
Stir well with cracked ice and strain into 3 oz. cocktail glass.

FRANKENJACK COCKTAIL

1 oz. Dry Gin
¾ oz. Dry Vermouth
½ oz. Apricot Flavored Brandy
1 teaspoon Triple Sec
Stir well with cracked ice and strain into 3 oz. cocktail glass. Serve with a cherry.

FRENCH "75"

Juice of 1 lemon
2 teaspoons powdered sugar
Stir well in 12 oz. Tom Collins glass. Then add 1 cube of ice, 2 oz. Dry Gin, fill with Champagne, and stir gently. Decorate with slice of lemon, orange and a cherry. Serve with straws.

FRESCO

1 part sugar syrup
2 parts lime juice
8 parts Rum
Crush a small piece of pineapple for each drink with a muddler. Add ingredients. Shake with crushed ice and strain into pre-chilled and frosted glasses.

FRISCO SOUR

Juice of ¼ lemon
Juice of ½ lime
½ oz. raspberry syrup or Grenadine
2 oz. Whiskey
Shake well with cracked ice and strain into 6 oz. sour glass. Fill with carbonated water and stir. Decorate with slices of lemon and lime.

FROTH BLOWER COCKTAIL

White of 1 egg
1 teaspoon Grenadine
2 oz. Dry Gin
Shake well with cracked ice and strain into 4 oz. cocktail glass.

FROUPE COCKTAIL

1¼ oz. Sweet Vermouth
1¼ oz. Brandy
1 teaspoon Benedictine
Stir well with cracked ice and strain into 3 oz. cocktail glass.

FROZEN DAIQUIRI

Juice of ½ lime
½ teaspoon sugar
1 jigger White Bacardi Rum
Place in electric mixer with shaved ice. Serve in saucer champagne glass, with 2 short straws.

FROZEN DAIQUIRI COCKTAIL

Juice of 1 lime
1 teaspoon powdered sugar
2 oz. Rum
Put in electric mixer filled with shaved ice for about 2 minutes. Strain through coarse meshed strainer into 6 oz. champagne glass.

FROZEN SCOTCH EL BORRACHO

Juice of ½ lemon
½ teaspoon sugar
Dash Cointreau
Dash bitters
1 thin slice fresh pineapple
1 jigger Scotch
Place ingredients in electric mixer with shaved ice. Mix well. Serve in old fashioned glass and garnish with a thin stick of fresh pineapple.

FRUIT CUP (a popular non-alcoholic summer drink)

2 oz. raspberry syrup
2 oz. strawberry syrup
2 oz. pineapple syrup
    or
6 oz. grenadine syrup
Juice of 1 lemon
Juice of 1 orange
Cracked ice
Use one of syrups listed. Add lemon and orange juice, ice. Fill remainder of pitcher with soda water. Decorate with maraschino cherry, orange slice, lemon slice and sprig of fresh mint.

FUTURITY

1 part Sweet Vermouth
1 part Sloe Gin
3 dashes bitters
2 dashes Grenadine
Shake well with cracked ice and strain into cocktail glass.

111

GASLIGHT

⅓ oz. Dry Vermouth
⅓ oz. Dry Gin
⅓ oz. Scotch
Serve on the rocks with a twist of lemon.

GATSBY'S COLLINS

Juice of ½ lemon
Dash Cointreau
Equal amount of orange juice
1½ oz. gin
Shake well. Pour into tall frosted glass, garnish with fresh fruit.

GENERAL HARRISON'S EGGNOG

1 egg
1 teaspoon powdered sugar
Shake well with cracked ice and strain into Tom Collins glass. Fill glass with Claret or Sweet Cider and stir gently. Grate nutmeg on top.

GEORGIAN

3 parts Bourbon
1 part orange juice
1 part Crème de Cacao
Mix Bourbon, orange juice and Crème de Cacao with crushed ice. Strain and serve.

GIBSON

A dry or extra Dry Martini with a twist of lemon peel and served with one to three pearl onions. Either Gin or Vodka may be used.

GILROY COCKTAIL

Juice of ¼ lemon
½ oz. Dry Vermouth
¾ oz. Wild Cherry Flavored Brandy
¾ oz. Dry Gin
1 dash orange bitters
Shake well with cracked ice and strain into 3 oz. cocktail glass.

GIMLET

Juice of 1 lime
1 teaspoon powdered sugar
1½ oz. Dry Gin or Vodka
Shake well with cracked ice and strain into 4 oz. cocktail glass; fill balance with carbonated water and stir.

GIN AND BITTERS

Put ½ teaspoon bitters into 3 oz. cocktail glass and revolve glass until it is entirely coated with the bitters. Then fill with Dry Gin. *No ice used in this drink.*

GIN AND IT

2 oz. Dry Gin
1 oz. Sweet Vermouth
Stir. No ice is used in this drink. Serve in 3 oz. cocktail glass.

GIN AND TONIC

2 oz. Dry Gin
Cube of ice
Fill glass with quinine water and stir. Use 12 oz. Tom Collins glass.

the
juniper
drink

By HUNTER BARNHALL

IT IS a hot summer evening, and you have just finished a day
of toil in your office or your home. You slip out of your
shoes, unloosen your tie and if you've got a swimming pool,
you head for it.

If you head for a drink, the one you'll choose will probably
be Gin. Gin, an ancient drink, is certainly the most favored of
all during the warm months—even in such lands as Scotland,
where whisky is almost a religion. Gin goes well—almost bril-
liantly—with any kind of fruit juice, and its marriage to orange
or lemon juice, is, of course, celebrated. Gin is refreshing and
light, whereas whiskey or Brandy tend to be somewhat heavy
for hot weather drinking. It is hard to think of anything more
delightful on a summer evening than a Tom Collins, whose
recipe (Gin, lemon juice and soda) is just about as simple
as a simple glass of water. In fact, Gin and the tinkling of ice
in a glass—a melody harmonious to almost any ear—are almost synonymous.

Most people seem to think that Gin is of modern origin.
This is an interesting notion, except that it is wrong. Gin is
really historic and may well be one of the oldest of man's

distilled potables. The history of all man's food and drink is misty and that of Gin is no exception.

People started drinking Gin in England some time in the 17th century. The distilling processes of those days were so primitive that the drink was about as palatable as a case of double-pneumonia. Enterprising distillers then took to flavoring their newfangled concoction with various herbs—almost anything they could lay their hands on to make the Gin drinkable.

They took to such herbs as caraway, ginger, an antique herb known as Grains of Paradise, coriander, cloves and, in fact, almost anything they could rifle out of their wives' kitchen cabinets. However, one François DuBois de la Boe, a professor at the University of Lyden, chanced upon the juniper berry which grew on squat bushes in the marshes around his homeland, and which, until then, was a fairly obscure fruit. He infused the juniper berry with the distillation and called his drink "Geneva." The drink with the juniper flavor found its way into England where the British, traditionally indifferent, as we all know to large amounts of talk, shortened it to "Gin." The English, who can be said to have fathered Gin, fiddled about with the new drink, adding their own aromatic spices to it, and modern Gin was born. It contains today a complex series of herbs, including juniper, angelica, caraway and cinnamon.

As it is with all things, economics played an important part in the growing popularity of Gin. In the 18th century in England, George III, in a frantic anti-French gesture, drastically increased the duties on French Brandies and whiskies so that Gin became a thrifty drink, and it remains so to this day, although in recent years its comparatively modest price has not prevented it from becoming an extremely fashionable drink.

In the year 1830, an Englishman, unnamed and unsung, first put bitters in his Gin, and at *this* resplendent moment in history, the cocktail was born. People have been putting everything into Gin ever since. Gin is the only drink known to mankind with which an olive is traditionally served, and some 20 years ago, the citrus industry in the United States began an active lobby to squeeze a lemon rind into a Martini. This caught on and now bartenders and housewives find themselves staring at piles of peeled, but generally unusable, lemons. No drink other than Gin lends itself to so many different cocktails and there are now about 300 different Gin cocktails. Bartenders—and possibly even you—are busily creating new ones all the time.

Lots of Gin drinks bear the name of their inventors. Take,

for instance, the Tom Collins. Obviously, there must have been a Tom Collins, but who he was or where he lived, nobody knows. All early cocktail recipe books list the Tom Collins as a whiskey drink and for years the drink was known as a Tom Collins Whiskey. It appears—but this can't be authenticated —that on one fine hot day, probably, some wizard decided to put Gin instead of whiskey with his lemon juice; thus the modern version of the Tom Collins was created. We know that the Pink Lady, a popular drink of the frou-frou early part of the century, was named for Hazel Dawn, who starred in a play called "The Pink Lady" in 1912. The Chocolate Soldier, the Merry Widow and Za Za, were all named for early 20th century theatrical productions. The Clover Club was introduced in 1923 at the Clover Club, a fancy social group which met at the Bellevue-Stratford in Philadelphia. The Gin Rickey was invented and named for Colonel Joe Rickey, a Washington politician, along about the same time. These drinks are now more or less out of vogue, but occasionally bartenders hear a request for them and any conscientious bartender keeps them in his repertoire.

What did in most of these Gin drinks was a little pirate called the Martini. Although hardly anybody knows it, the Martini is not a modern drink, though its rise in popularity is of comparatively recent date. The Martini—iced Gin with Vermouth—has been known since at least 1845. It was originally made with Italian Vermouth, which caused the British, with their above noted fondness for brevity, to change it to "Gin and It," the "It" being an abbreviation for Italian. The Martini people, who made that Vermouth, realized that they had involuntarily latched on to a good thing, and propagandized so successfully that the cocktail came to be known as the Martini, although as of today, by no means all of the Vermouth in a Martini is Martini Vermouth. For those who have any liking for traditionalism, the British still stubbornly call the Martini "Gin and It." But the British "Gin and It" bears about as much resemblance to the Martini we know as Sophia Loren bears to Lassie.

Everybody knows that the Martini is lethal. But—know what? Nobody knows why. Yale University, which has been conducting a survey on alcohol for many years, put its double domes to work on the subject of, "Why the Martini is more intoxicating than any other drink," and though their scientific study was lengthy, it was inconclusive. There is no particular reason—from a scientific standpoint—why 3 ounces of Martini should be more crippling than 3 ounces of any other drink, but it would seem that this is the case. Some experts on the subject believe that the combination of Gin and Vermouth has a firing-squad effect on a drinker and this may well be true, since the same combination of whiskey and Vermouth—a Manhattan—is not nearly so notorious as the Martini. And to add to the mystery, it must be remembered that a Martini is diluted with water from the melting ice with which it is cooled.

The truth, which probably accounts for the reason that most people slump off the bar stool after demolishing Martinis, is that bibbers drink them before meals when their stomachs are empty and their systems are thus more susceptible to the effects of alcohol. However, people drink other drinks before dinner and seem to make it into the dining room, whereas the Martini drinker—a victim of every cartoonist in the country—has often been known to go to bed without a bite. It seems to be true, in addition, that drinking the same amount of Gin without the Vermouth is not nearly so numbing. In any case, paralyzing as it may be, the Martini is by far the *most* popular of cocktails around the world, and its popularity in this country in the past 25 years has been nothing short of phenomenal.

Gin is hospitable to various flavoring agents. Distillers put mint in to get mint Gin; rock candy to get a pre-sweetened Gin; and various fruit concentrates as well. The British, who took on Gin when it was a baby, currently make it into something called Pimm's Cup, and in the Pimm's Cup mixture they make a drink into which—hold your hats—they weave a cucumber rind. This drink, which has the effect of an arrow in your heart, is fed to young ladies at cricket matches on summer Sundays, and the mixture so disguises the flavor, but of course not the potency of the Gin, that flower-like English beauties have been known to topple off their chairs while the cricket match is going on. When picked up by the cricketers in their white sweaters, the young flower-like beauties often say, "What hit me?"

In the past 20 years, the sale of Vodka in this country, as everyone knows, has made spectacular gains, and when the Gin manufacturers first noticed this development they did so with considerable alarm, since Vodka can be and often is used as a substitute in drinks which traditionally use Gin. For some reason which the liquor industry doesn't fully seem to understand, the increased sale of Vodka has not only *not* decelerated Gin sales, but has actually increased it.

It may be that the growing vogue for Gin and tonic, a drink almost unknown in this country until 25 years ago, accounts for the steadily increasing Gin sales, because there is hardly a better summer drink than Gin and tonic. No other drink seems to be as broad in social appeal as Gin. It is both the working man's drink and the drink of the frothy socialite in the land's fancy supper clubs. It is consumed on both coasts with avidity, but is also popular amongst the residents of the Middle West.

A lot of jokes have been made about the increased dryness of Martinis. It started with the 3 to 1 Martini, then the 5 to 1 Martini, and now some hosts insist on a 10 to 1. One celebrated host used to make his Martinis as dry as possible by the simple expediency of bypassing the iced Gin repeatedly with an open Vermouth bottle in his hand. Some of his guests complained that too much Vermouth somehow happened to get into some of his drinks. In order to appease them, he now passes rapidly past the Gin, but he keeps the cork in the Vermouth bottle.

GIN BUCK

> 1 cube of ice
> Juice of ½ lemon
> 1½ oz. Dry Gin
> *Fill 8 oz. highball glass with ginger ale and stir.*

GIN COBBLER

> *Dissolve* 1 teaspoon powdered sugar *in* 2 oz. carbonated water, *then fill 10 oz. goblet with shaved ice, and add*
> 2 oz. Dry Gin
> *Stir well and decorate with fruits in season. Serve with straws.*

GIN COCKTAIL

> 2 oz. Dry Gin
> 2 dashes bitters
> *Stir well with cracked ice and strain into 3 oz. cocktail glass. Serve with a twist of lemon peel.*

GIN COOLER

> *Into 12 oz. Tom Collins glass put:*
> ½ teaspoon powdered sugar
> 2 oz. carbonated water, and stir
> *Fill glass with cracked ice and add*
> 2 oz. Dry Gin
> *Fill with carbonated water or ginger ale and stir again. Insert spiral of orange or lemon peel (or both) and dangle end over rim of glass.*

119

GIN DAISY

Juice of ½ lemon
½ teaspoon powdered sugar
1 teaspoon raspberry syrup or Grenadine
2 oz. Dry Gin
Shake well with cracked ice and strain into stein or 8 oz. metal cup. Add cube of ice and decorate with fruit.

GIN FIX

Juice of ½ lemon
1 teaspoon powdered sugar
1 teaspoon water
Stir and fill glass with shaved ice. Add
2½ oz. Dry Gin
Use 8 oz. highball glass. Stir well. Add slice of lemon. Serve with straws.

GIN FIZZ

Juice of ½ lemon
1 teaspoon powdered sugar
2 oz. Dry Gin
Shake well with cracked ice and strain into 7 oz. highball glass. Fill with carbonated water and stir.

GIN HIGHBALL

1 cube of ice
2 oz. Dry Gin
Fill 8 oz. highball glass with ginger ale or carbonated water. Add twist of lemon peel, if desired, and stir.

GIN MILK PUNCH

1 teaspoon powdered sugar
2 oz. Dry Gin
½ pt. milk
Shake well with cracked ice, strain into 12 oz. Tom Collins glass and grate nutmeg on top.

GIN RICKEY

1 cube of ice
Juice of ½ lime
1½ oz. Dry Gin
Fill 8 oz. highball glass with carbonated water and stir. Leave lime in glass.

GIN SANGAREE

Dissolve ½ teaspoon powdered sugar in 1 teaspoon of water. Add:
2 oz. Dry Gin
2 cubes of ice
Serve in 8 oz. highball glass. Fill balance with soda water. Stir, leaving enough room on which to float a tablespoon of Port Wine. *Sprinkle lightly with nutmeg.*

GIN SLING

Dissolve 1 teaspoon powdered sugar in 1 teaspoon water and juice of ½ lemon.
2 oz. Dry Gin
Serve in old fashioned cocktail glass and stir. Twist of orange peel and drop in glass.

GIN SMASH

Muddle 1 lump of sugar with:
1 oz. carbonated water
4 sprigs of green mint
Add 2 oz. Dry Gin and a cube of ice. Stir and decorate with a slice of orange and a cherry. Twist of lemon peel on top. Use old fashioned cocktail glass.

GIN SOUR

Juice of ½ lemon
½ teaspoon powdered sugar
2 oz. Dry Gin
Shake well with cracked ice and strain into 6 oz. sour glass. Fill with carbonated water and stir. Decorate with a half-slice of lemon and a cherry.

GIN SQUIRT

1½ oz. Dry Gin
1 tablespoon powdered sugar
1 teaspoon raspberry syrup or Grenadine
Stir well with cracked ice and strain into 8 oz. highball glass; fill with carbonated water and stir. Decorate with cubes of pineapple and strawberries.

GIN SWIZZLE

Juice of 1 lime
1 teaspoon powdered sugar
2 oz. carbonated water
Fill 12 oz. Tom Collins glass with shaved ice and stir
thoroughly with swizzle stick. Then add
2 dashes bitters
2 oz. Dry Gin
Fill with carbonated water and serve with swizzle stick
in glass, allowing drinker to do final stirring.

GIN TODDY

½ teaspoon powdered sugar
2 teaspoons water *and stir.*
2 oz. Dry Gin
1 lump of ice
Stir well in old fashioned glass and twist lemon peel
on top.

GIN TODDY (Hot)

Put lump of sugar into hot whiskey glass and fill two-
thirds with boiling water. Add 2 oz. Dry Gin. Stir and
decorate with slice of lemon. Grate nutmeg on top.

GLOOM CHASER

Juice of ¼ lemon
⅓ jigger Grenadine
⅓ jigger Grand Marnier
⅓ jigger Curaçao
Ice
Shake well. Strain into cocktail glass.

GLOOM LIFTER

1 part sugar syrup
2 parts lemon juice
6 parts Irish whiskey
1 egg white to each 2 drinks
Shake with cracked ice.

GLÜG (a skiiers' drink)

1 qt. Claret
2 oranges, sliced with peel
2 lemons, sliced with peel
8 sticks cinnamon
12 cloves

Place ingredients in the wine while it is cold. Then heat wine to a point just below boiling, or steaming, and serve in wine mug.

GOLDEN FIZZ

Juice of ½ lemon
1 teaspoon powdered sugar
2 oz. Dry Gin
Yolk of 1 egg

Shake well with cracked ice and strain into 8 oz. high-ball glass. Fill with carbonated water and stir.

GOLDEN GATE COCKTAIL

1½ oz. Dry Gin
1 scoop orange sherbert

Shake well and strain into 4 oz. cocktail glass.

GOLDEN SLIPPER COCKTAIL

¾ oz. Yellow Chartreuse
2 oz. Apricot Flavored Brandy

Stir well with cracked ice and strain into 4 oz. cocktail glass. Float yolk of egg on top.

GOLF COCKTAIL

1½ oz. Dry Gin
¾ oz. Dry Vermouth
2 dashes bitters

Stir well with cracked ice and strain into 3 oz. cocktail glass.

GOURMET COCKTAIL

3 tablespoons Gin
1 tablespoon Dry Vermouth
⅛ teaspoon Campari bitters
*Stir well with ice. Serve in a chilled 4 oz. cocktail glass
with a sliver of grapefruit peel.*

GRAND PASSION

1 part Passion-Fruit Nectar
2 part Gin
1 dash bitters to each drink

GRAND ROYAL FIZZ

Juice of ¼ orange
Juice of ½ lemon
1 teaspoon powdered sugar
2 oz. Dry Gin
½ teaspoon Maraschino Liqueur
2 teaspoons sweet cream
*Shake well with cracked ice and strain into 8 oz. high-
ball glass. Fill with carbonated water and stir.*

GRAND SLAM

Juice of ½ lemon
1 teaspoon sugar
1 jigger Carioca Rum
½ jigger Brandy
½ jigger Curaçao
1 dash Kirschwasser
Ice
*Shake well. Strain into saucer champagne glass. Deco-
rate with thin slice of lemon.*

GRAPEFRUIT COCKTAIL

1 oz. grapefruit juice
1 oz. Dry Gin
1 teaspoon Maraschino Liqueur
*Shake well with cracked ice and strain into 3 oz. cock-
tail glass. Serve with a cherry.*

GRASSHOPPER COCKTAIL

¾ oz. Crème de Menthe (Green)
¾ oz. Crème de Cacao (White)
¾ oz. light sweet cream
Shake well with cracked ice and strain into 3 oz. cocktail glass.

GREEN DRAGON COCKTAIL

Juice of ¼ lemon
½ oz. Kümmel
½ oz. Crème de menthe (Green)
1½ oz. Dry Gin
4 dashes orange bitters
Shake well with cracked ice and strain into 4 oz. cocktail glass.

Fellow we know swears this really happened. He has a well-earned reputation for being a wolf. So one night he takes this girl out for a drive and, suddenly, the car stops. "I guess we're out of gas," he leers. With this announcement, the girl carefully opens her purse and pulls out a bottle.

"Wow!" says our friend. "You've got a whole fifth. What kind is it?"

She purrs, "Esso Regular."

GREEN EYE OPENER

Prepare 8 oz. glass of Bromo Seltzer or Alka Seltzer, include a couple of ice cubes. Add two teaspoonsful of white or green Crème de Menthe.

GREEN FIZZ

1 teaspoon powdered sugar
White of 1 egg
Juice of ½ lemon
2 oz. Dry Gin
1 teaspoon Crème de Menthe (Green)
Shake well with cracked ice and strain into 8 oz. highball glass. Fill with carbonated water and stir.

GREEN SWIZZLE

Make same as GIN SWIZZLE, and add 1 tablespoon Green Crème de Menthe. If desired, Rum, Brandy or Whiskey may be substituted for the Gin.

GREEN TREE

Juice of ½ lemon
7 parts light Rum
1 part Crème de Menthe (Green)
Ice
Shake well, and serve in cocktail glass.

GRENADINE RICKEY

1 cube of ice
Juice of ½ lime
1½ oz. Grenadine
Fill 8 oz. highball glass with cabonated water and stir.
Leave lime in glass.

GYPSY COCKTAIL

1¼ oz. Sweet Vermouth
1¼ oz. Dry Gin
Stir well with cracked ice and strain into 3 oz. cock-
tail glass. Serve with a cherry.

HARLEM COCKTAIL

¾ oz. pineapple juice
1½ Dry Gin
½ teaspoon Maraschino Liqueur
2 cubes of pineapple
Shake well with cracked ice and strain into 3 oz. cock-
tail glass.

HARVARD COCKTAIL

1½ oz. Brandy
¾ oz. Sweet Vermouth
1 dash bitters
1 teaspoon Grenadine
2 teaspoons lemon juice
Shake well with cracked ice and strain into 3 oz. cock-
tail glass.

HARVARD COOLER

½ teaspoon powdered sugar
2 oz. carbonated water
Stir above ingredients in 12 oz. Tom Collins glass and then fill with cracked ice and add
2 oz. Apple Brandy
Fill with carbonated water or ginger ale and stir again. Insert spiral of orange or lemon peel (or both) and dangle end over rim of glass.

HASTY COCKTAIL

¾ oz. Dry Vermouth
1½ oz. Dry Gin
¼ teaspoon Pernod (Absinthe substitute)
1 teaspoon Grenadine
Stir well with cracked ice and strain into 3 oz. cocktail glass.

HAVANA COCKTAIL

1¼ oz. pineapple juice
½ teaspoon lemon juice
¾ oz. Rum
Shake well with cracked ice and strain into 3 oz. cocktail glass.

HAVANA DAIQUIRI

½ teaspoon superfine sugar
2¼ tablespoons White Rum
1 tablespoon Banana Cordial
Shake well with ice and serve in a parfait glass.

HAWAIIAN COCKTAIL

2 oz. Dry Gin
½ oz. pineapple juice
½ oz. Curaçao
Shake well with cracked ice and strain into 4 oz. cocktail glass.

HAWAIIAN COLLINS

1½ oz. pineapple juice
1½ oz. White Rum
Shake well, garnish with a slice of orange, one cherry and serve in a tall glass with ice.

HAWAIIAN SOUR

1 part sugar syrup
1 part lemon juice
2 parts pineapple juice
6 parts Bourbon
Shake well with cracked ice. Add slice of pineapple.
Serve in brandy pony or cognac glass.

HICKS' HANGOVER RECIPE

Juice of ½ lemon or 1 orange
⅛ teaspoon brown sugar
Enough ice water to make an 8 oz. total. Drink it fast.

HI-DE-HO SPECIAL

2 oz. Orange Flavored Gin
Juice of ½ lemon
1 teaspoon powdered sugar
Shake well with cracked ice and strain into 8 oz. high-
ball glass. Fill with seltzer water and stir. Decorate
with slice of lemon.

HIGH HAT

1 part Kijafa
2 parts lemon juice
4 parts Bourbon
Mix ingredients with shaved ice, strain and serve.

HIGH LIFE

1 part Cherry Heering
2 parts lemon juice
4 parts Rye or Scotch
Shake with cracked or crushed ice.

HIGHBALL

1 jigger Spirits
Cracked ice
Carbonated water
Pour liquor over ice in highball glass. Add carbonated
water.

HIGHLAND COOLER

½ teaspoon powdered sugar
2 oz. carbonated water
*Stir above ingredients into a 12 oz. Tom Collins glass
with cracked ice and add:*
2 oz. Scotch
*Fill with carbonated water or ginger ale and stir again.
Insert spiral of orange or lemon peel (or both) and
dangle end over rim of glass.*

HIGHLAND FLING COCKTAIL

¾ oz. Sweet Vermouth
1½ oz. Scotch
2 dashes orange bitters
*Stir well with cracked ice and strain into 3 oz. cock-
tail glass. Serve with an olive.*

HOFFMAN HOUSE COCKTAIL

¾ oz. Dry Vermouth
1½ oz. Dry Gin
2 dashes orange bitters
*Stir well with cracked ice and strain into 3 oz. cock-
tail glass. Serve with an olive.*

HOLE-IN-ONE COCKTAIL

1½ oz. Scotch
¾ oz. Dry Vermouth
¼ teaspoon lemon juice
1 dash orange bitters
*Shake well with cracked ice and strain into 3 oz. cock-
tail glass.*

HOLLYWOOD COOLER

2 oz. frozen orange juice
5 oz. California Sauterne
Ice cubes or shaved ice
Sweeten as desired
*Stir well into a 12 oz. Tom Collins glass. Garnish with
mint and half slice of orange.*

HOMESTEAD COCKTAIL

1½ oz. Dry Gin
¾ oz. Sweet Vermouth
Shake well with cracked ice and strain into 3 oz. cocktail glass and serve with slice of orange.

HONEST JOHN

2 jiggers Bonded Bourbon
Dash ginger ale
2 lumps ice
Twist of lemon peel
Serve in old fashioned glass. Fill with carbonated water and top with twist of lemon peel.

HONEYMOON COCKTAIL

¾ oz. Benedictine
¾ oz. Apple Brandy
Juice of ½ lemon
1 teaspoon Curaçao
Shake well with cracked ice and strain into 3 oz. cocktail glass.

HONOLULU COCKTAIL NO. 1

1 dash bitters
¼ teaspoon orange juice
¼ teaspoon pineapple juice
¼ teaspoon lemon juice
½ teaspoon powdered sugar
1½ oz. Dry Gin
Shake well with cracked ice and strain into 3 oz. cocktail glass.

HONOLULU COCKTAIL NO. 2

¾ oz. Dry Gin
¾ oz. Maraschino Liqueur
¾ oz. Benedictine
Stir well with cracked ice and strain into 3 oz. cocktail glass.

HOOT MON COCKTAIL

¾ oz. Sweet Vermouth
1½ oz. Scotch
1 teaspoon Benedictine
Stir well with cracked ice and strain into 3 oz. cocktail glass. Twist of lemon peel and drop in glass.

HOP TOAD COCKTAIL

Juice of ½ lime
¾ oz. Apricot Flavored Brandy
¾ oz. Rum
Stir well with cracked ice and strain into 3 oz. cocktail glass.

HORSE'S NECK (with and without a kick)

Peel rind of whole lemon in spiral fashion and put in 12 oz. Tom Collins glass with one end hanging over rim. Fill glass with ice cubes.
Add 2 oz. Whiskey (tee-totalers leave this out) Fill with ginger ale and stir.

HOT APPLE TODDY

12 Winesap or Pippin apples
12 lumps of sugar
2 bottles Jamaica Rum (Light)
1 bottle Cognac
2 qt. boiling water
Place apples in oven with lump of sugar on each apple. Do not core them. When baked, place apples in an earthenware crock and add Rum (a light variety), Cognac, and boiling water. Keep crock close to an open fire, pouring the contents of the jug back and forth from time to time. Take care not to bruise or break apples. Do not boil.

HOT BRANDY FLIP

1 egg
1 teaspoon powdered sugar
1½ oz. Brandy
Beat egg, sugar and brandy and pour into Tom & Jerry Mug and fill with hot milk. Grate nutmeg on top.

HOT BRICK TODDY

1 teaspoon butter
1 teaspoon powdered sugar
3 pinches cinnamon
1 oz. hot water
Dissolve thoroughly in hot whiskey glass then add 1½ oz. Whiskey. Fill with boiling water and stir.

HOT BUTTERED RUM

Put lump of sugar into hot whiskey glass and fill two-thirds with boiling water. Add square of butter and 2 oz. Rum. Stir and grate nutmeg on top.

HOT BUTTERED WINE

For each serving, heat ½ cup Muscatel Wine. Add ¼ cup water just to simmering; do not boil. Preheat mug or cup with boiling water. Pour heated wine mixture into mug and add 1 teaspoon butter and 2 teaspoons maple syrup. Stir well and sprinkle nutmeg on top. Serve at once.

HOT SPRINGS COCKTAIL

1½ oz. Dry White Wine
½ oz. pineapple juice
½ teaspoon Maraschino Liqueur
1 dash orange bitters
Stir well with cracked ice and strain into 3 oz. cocktail glass.

HOT TODDY

1 jigger Spirits
1 lump sugar
3 teaspoons hot water
Put sugar in glass and dissolve in water. Add liquor, lump of ice, and dash of nutmeg. Serve in old fashioned glass. (Among the popular Toddies are Applejack, Bourbon, Brandy, Gin, Rum and Rye.)

H. P. W. COCKTAIL

¼ oz. Dry Vermouth
¼ oz. Sweet Vermouth
1½ oz. Gin
Stir well with cracked ice and strain into 3 oz. cocktail glass. Twist of orange peel and drop in glass.

HULA-HULA COCKTAIL

¾ oz. orange juice
1½ oz. Dry Gin
¼ teaspoon powdered sugar
Stir well with cracked ice and strain into 3 oz. cocktail glass.

HUNTSMAN COCKTAIL

1½ oz. Vodka
½ oz. Jamaica Rum
Juice of ½ lime
Powdered sugar to taste
*Shake well with cracked ice and strain into 3 oz. cock-
tail glass.*

ICE CREAM FLIP

1 egg
1 oz. Maraschino Liqueur
1 oz. Curaçao
1 small scoop vanilla ice cream
*Shake well with cracked ice and strain into 5 oz. flip
glass. Grate a little nutmeg on top.*

John Barleycorn

By RICHARD SHARPE

CLEAR back in the days of the Civil War, to be a brewer, to Make Your Money Through Drink, was considered not quite nice. True it was that some of the grandest of dowagers swept up to the family entrances of cafes and restaurants, and had a cup of "tea" brought to them which was really Bourbon or Gin. True it was that most closets had a bottle in them (like a family skeleton), always referred to as "for medicinal purposes." True it was that all our Founding Fathers were good two-fisted drinking men. But by the middle of the Nineteenth Century, there was a prodigious amount of Uplift going on in the land.

Harriet Beecher Stowe was fighting slavery. Another Beecher, the great preacher Henry Ward Beecher, was attacking all the sins of the world—among them a neighborly nip with a friend—to packed houses year in and year out. Mrs. Stowe's husband, Dr. Calvin Stowe, was touring America and Europe, agitating for equal education for women, trying to found colleges for women.

Mrs. Elizabeth Cady Stanton, Susan B. Anthony, Lucretia Mott, Martha Wright, Mrs. Mary Ann McClintock, and even Mrs. Amelia Bloomer, whose Turkish Trousers got her name immortalized in the dictionary forevermore, were all campaigning furiously for Woman Suffrage and for Equal Rights for Women.

All noble causes, all so obviously right and righteous that, nowadays, it seems incredible that there was ever such a stench raised over any of them. Maybe it was because all these worthy crusades came in a bunch and all seemed to have an interchangeable cast of characters. Anyone who was for freeing the slaves seemed somehow, automatically, also to be in favor of equal rights for women, the women's vote, education for women, vegetarianism, the abolition of capital punishment, and even prohibition. For a time, since they all were prodigious speakers, and would all mount a rostrum and denounce, wave a banner, sign a petition, lead a parade at the drop of a hat (or even at the suggestion that a hat might be dropped), somehow it seemed as if these people swarming on all sides like so many bees, were Agin' Everything.

People, perhaps foolishly, got scared of them and struck back. They were sued, stoned, rioted against, jailed, run out of towns, ridiculed and reviled. It only seemed to make them stronger and more vociferous. They were like a sort of blight of propriety descending on the land, bunching Right Causes and Wrong Causes into one great single bludgeon of All Causes, to browbeat the public. It looked for a while as if the Puritans themselves had risen from their graves to scourge the land. And at that, it is true that the majority of the crusaders did seem to stem from old Puritan families.

However, it is also possible that their incessant speaking and their interminable agitation may have been caused by an inner nervousness, by their own embarrassment at a small item, generally overlooked. This was the identity of the man who was their greatest patron, their most generous contributor, who hired them halls, who subsidized their lecture tours and their trips abroad, who even, in moment of crisis, bailed some of the more rabid of them out of jails. For this gentleman operated with Tainted Money. He was a brewer and a distiller. But there was worse.

As the man who introduced the successful growing of barley into America, thus producing better malts for stronger beers and ales, better bases for far more potent spirits yet, he was known on two continents as Mr. Barleycorn.

He was quite a character. Descended from a French Huguenot refugee in England named Vasseur, with liberal doses of Irish, German, Scotch, English, a little Dutch and maybe even a dash of Spanish blood flowing in his veins, he was a forerunner of our modern product of the American melting pot of our modern American Go-Getter, of our Self-Made Man. As such, he was sneered at and cold-shouldered from Poughkeepsie to Paris, from Oberlin to Otranto, from Brooklyn to London to Rome, and it fazed him not one bit.

He murdered the King's English. He wrote long and overly florid letters in which he invariably made a fool of himself through misused words. He put on airs. He fancied himself a philosopher. He gave advice to people used to being considered the Best Minds of the Day. But he did even worse than that. His letters, stripped of their flourishes, made wonderful sense. His airs were justified by the plain horse sense he constantly displayed. And his advice was almost invariably right. People don't like to be corrected by men whom they consider their inferiors, but, when the correction is inspired, when it is luminously and obviously right, it is apt to rouse that famed old Urge to Kill.

Hence, our Mr. Barleycorn, popular as he might be with the tipplers of his brews, was not popular with the pundits of his age. They spurned his overtures of friendship, but, when they were accompanied by cash, they usually managed to find some reason for accepting. Then, having been bought and paid for, they were stuck with him. One of the great popular pastimes of the day, among the Better People, was making excuses for being acquainted with Mr. Matthew Vassar. (His family had Anglicized their name. Or, more likely, being somewhat illiterate for several generations before Matthew came along, they had forgotten how to spell it.)

Matthew came to the young United States at the age of 4, in 1796, with his father and his uncle (both brewers), and their families. They had been prosperous brewery-owners back in East Tuddingham, in the County of Norfolk in England, but they had got sick and tired of never being spoken to by the Gentry, since they were not only in Trade; they were in the liquor trade. They thought things would be better in that brave new world across the sea.

They chose to settle, of all places, in Dutchess County up along the Hudson in New York, where the Dutch aristocrats had been entrenched for generation after generation, and were far more stuffy and haughty than the neighbors back in East Tuddingham.

For the first few years, they were too busy establishing their brewery, trying to get decent barley to thrive in this country, and growing rich, to care much what the neighbors thought. But then Uncle Tom and little Matt went back to England, toured the Isle and came back with a better barleycorn which flourished in the American climate. Soon the family was famous for its powerful product, roundly denounced in the pulpits, and Uncle Tom was known as Old Tom Barleycorn, the Whiskey King.

In the Little Red Schoolhouse, the young lad Matt was shunned. The others were forbidden to play with him, or even address him. He was considered a Limb of Satan for sure, and he didn't like it. At the ripe old age of 13, he ran away from home, tended store, worked a farm, and, by the time he was 16, through growing and raising the newly imported barley, was well-to-do in his own right, and didn't give a hoot what the neighbors thought. He came back home and joined his family, adding his farms to theirs.

When he was a mere 19, the family brewery burned (and some suspected arson on the part of an ardent prohibitionist inspired with the urge to put an end to the Barleycorns and all their works). The older Vassars were discouraged, and decided to drop the whole thing and concentrate on growing barley for other brewers. But not Matt.

He mortgaged his own farms, and, on the strength of his own face and ability, borrowed the money necessary to put up a bigger and better brewery, this time in Poughkeepsie. One of the first men in America to understand the values of publicity, he gloried in the nickname of Mr. Barleycorn and quoted it everywhere; his Beers and Ale sold like hotcakes, he grew rich by leaps and bounds, and everyone was happy. For a while.

Happily married at 21 to a charming girl who loved him for his virtues and overlooked his lacks, he adored children. His brothers and sisters all had lots of them, but he had none. It was the sorrow of his life that he and his Dear Catherine were childless, and he began to lavish his love and affection, and his wealth, on his own nephews and nieces.

One of them, the apple of his eye, was as much a pioneer as uncle Matt, although a woman. Sent to Boston to a Finishing School, Miss Lydia Booth found it so deadly dull, offering no challenge to her mind, that she persuaded her aunt and uncle to let her switch to the fantastic Young Ladies' Academy conducted by the famed Miss Catherine Beecher at Hartford, Connecticut.

We have to thank Miss Beecher (sister, aunt, niece, daughter or cousin to all those famous Beecher Intellectuals of the era) for the invention of Calisthenics, of Interpretive Dancing, of Coeducation, and a number of things considered, in her day, quite shocking and totally unseemly in a spinster of a high-born line. We also have to thank her for the subsequent career of Miss Lydia Booth and, through her, of Uncle Matt.

On graduation, backed by her uncle's money, Lydia founded her own finishing school for young ladies called the Cottage Hill Seminary, outside Pittsburgh. She corresponded with the Beechers, the Stowes, the Motts, Cadys, Anthonys, with painter-inventor S. F. B. Morse (of portraits and telegraphs), with famed physicians and philosophers. From all of these she got statements of their opinion that "abstruse branches of learning are not injurious to women's health, nor likely to detract from their later proper roles as wives and mothers."

Uncle Matt got into the act, and he too began to write to all the bigwigs. They didn't answer, till the checks began to appear along with the correspondence. Then they did. Presently, a real uproar was raised, with half the wiseacres of New England up to their ears in Lydia's school, and editorials in the papers denouncing women's education as being akin to nudism, debauchery or mortal sin. Matthew loved it. He backed liberal magazines, subsidized high-minded newspapers, paid the bills for halls and lecture tours. And he also began to have a few ideas of his own on education, both for men and women, and this was resented.

Pay, but don't offer any advice, was the reaction. He continued to offer anyway, and also pay. In the midst of it, poor Lydia died. First Matthew, despondent, sold the school to a brilliant if brittle young educator named Milo P. Jewett. Then he began to miss the excitement and the fun, and he wanted back in. Mr. Jewett snubbed him, until one of his cronies pointed out that Uncle Barleycorn had often stated that he intended to leave all his money to some great foundation, and possibly even to his niece's school. To make it a Women's College, a thing unheard of in that age.

Jewett changed his tune. He became like a nephew to Vassar, and then like a son. He laughed at the old man to his face, he sneered at him to all his famous friends. But he was well aware that there was a cool million dollars in the deal, and this in a day of no taxes when 1 million would be the equivalent of 50 today. So he took "that uncouth old distillery man's advice." Then he published the ideas as his own, and was universally applauded for them by the best minds of the time. Matt paid a committee of doctors and scientists to work for five years, testing to prove conclusively that a woman, using her brain, did not destroy her capacity for motherhood. They did, and it was a stunner in those days; women with brains kept them dark. It must have been a very peculiar era altogether!

Abraham Lincoln approved the prospectus that Matt "Barleycorn" Vassar got up for his Women's College, and became its sponsor. Jewett took the bows, but it was Matt's ideas which brought in the great names of America as his Board of Directors. And it was his use of ballyhoo, his unerring eye for a good news item, which made the four-year-long building of the college (during the Civil War from 1861 to 1865) a front-page item for all the major newspapers of the civilized world. Queen

Victoria, though shocked, sent best wishes. Emperor Dom Pedro II of Brazil sent his Ambassador to investigate the project for Brazil. The Empress Eugenie thought that France should have a women's college too. And the Beer and Ale continued to sell, and old Mr. Barleycorn's ideas continued to jell, and the opening of the college was an international event. Cottage Hill College was a world sensation.

With a college actually in his hands, young Jewett threw discretion to the winds. He wrote to S. F. B. Morse, and to Professor Stowe, "The man is not only illiterate, he is childish . . . The man is mad to immortalize his name. . . You have no idea of the horrors I have been through in this association."

Shocked at the ingratitude of the young snip, they both promptly shipped his letters straight back to Mr. Vassar. It threw the wonderful, naturally brilliant old man into a complete funk. He was in the act of writing out his resignation to the Board of Directors, when he had a heart attack.

His family asked him to change his will. He didn't. Because the fine men who had been associated with him at last realized his qualities. They forced Jewett to resign as head of the College. They changed the name at once to Vassar College. On his deathbed, old Matthew Barleycorn persuaded his two brewer-nephews that they too should leave their fortunes to his college, and supervised their wills. And then he died, and left his money to the famous Vassar College.

Through 2 generations, the Vassars poured $2 millions into Mr. Barleycorn's fantastic dream. The money from Beer, from Ale and from whiskey worked for women's rights, for women's votes, for all the better causes which drew their skirts aside from their associating with a—pardon the word, shall we?—brewer. From Mr. Barleycorn.

How the name John became attached to Mr. Barleycorn, our closest research fails to show. Suffice to say, the good this one did lived after him, and continues ever more successful to this day.

IDEAL COCKTAIL

    1 oz. Dry Vermouth
    1 oz. Gin
    ¼ teaspoon Maraschino Liqueur
    ½ teaspoon grapefruit or lemon juice
Shake well with cracked ice and strain into 3 oz. cocktail glass. Serve with a cherry.

IMPERIAL COCKTAIL

1¼ oz. Dry Vermouth
1¼ oz. Gin
¼ teaspoon Maraschino Liqueur
1 dash bitters
Stir well with cracked ice and strain into 3 oz. cocktail glass. Serve with a cherry.

IMPERIAL FIZZ

Juice of ½ lemon
½ oz. Rum
1½ oz. Whiskey
1 teaspoon powdered sugar
Shake well with cracked ice and strain into 7 oz. highball glass. Fill with carbonated water and stir.

INCOME TAX COCKTAIL

¼ oz. Dry Vermouth
¼ oz. Sweet Vermouth
1 oz. Dry Gin
1 dash bitters
Juice of ¼ orange
Shake well with cracked ice and strain into 3 oz. cocktail glass.

IRISH COFFEE

Into a pre-warmed 8 oz. stemmed glass (or coffee cup), pour 1½ oz. Irish Whiskey. Add 1 or 2 teaspoons sugar and fill to within ½ inch of top with strong, very hot black coffee. Stir to dissolve sugar. Float to brim with chilled whipped cream. Do not stir. Drink through floating cream.

IRISH RICKEY

1 cube of ice
Juice of ½ lime
1½ oz. Irish Whiskey
Fill 8 oz. highball glass with carbonated water and stir. Leave lime in glass.

IRISH SHILLELAGH

Juice ½ lemon
1 teaspoon powdered sugar
1½ oz. Irish Whiskey
½ oz. Sloe Gin
½ oz. Rum
2 peach slices
Shake well with cracked ice and strain into 5 oz. punch glass. Decorate with fresh raspberries, strawberries, a cherry and two peach slices.

IRISH WHISKEY COCKTAIL

½ oz. Curaçao
½ teaspoon Pernod (Absinthe substitute)
¼ teaspoon Maraschino Liqueur
1 dash bitters
2 oz. Irish Whiskey
Stir well with cracked ice and strain into 3 oz. cocktail glass. Serve with an olive.

IRISH WHISKEY HIGHBALL

1 cube of ice
2 oz. Irish Whiskey
Fill 8 oz. highball glass with ginger ale or carbonated water. Add twist of lemon peel, if desired, and stir.

ISLE OF PINES

1 part sugar syrup
2 parts grapefruit juice
6 parts Rum
Shake with cracked ice.

JACK-IN-THE-BOX COCKTAIL

1 oz. Apple Brandy
1 oz. pineapple juice
Dash of bitters
Shake well with cracked ice and strain into 3 oz. cocktail glass.

JACK ROSE COCKTAIL

1 oz. Apple Brandy
Juice of ½ lime
1 teaspoon Grenadine
Shake well with cracked ice and strain into 3 oz. cocktail glass.

JAILAI

1 part Kahlua
2 parts Bourbon
Cinnamon stick
Shake Kahlua and Bourbon with ice and strain into brandy or small wine glass.

JAMAICA GLOW COCKTAIL

1 oz. Dry Gin
½ oz. Claret
½ oz. orange juice
1 teaspoon Jamaica Rum
Shake well with cracked ice and strain into 3 oz. cocktail glass.

JAMAICA GRANITO

Small scoop of either lemon or orange sherbet
1½ oz. Brandy
1 oz. Curaçao
Use 12 oz. Tom Collins glass and fill balance with carbonated water and stir. Grate nutmeg on top.

JAMAICA RUM COBBLER

3 oz. Jamaica Rum
1 teaspoon sugar
Fill wine goblet ¼ full with cracked ice. Add sugar and Rum. Fill glass with water, stir well. Decorate with half a slice of orange, maraschino cherry and pineapple stick.

JAMAICA RUM COLLINS

Juice of ½ lemon
½ barspoon powdered sugar
1 jigger Jamaica Rum
Shake well and strain into Collins glass. Add lump ice and fill glass with carbonated water.

JAMAICA RUM SOUR

Juice of ½ lemon
½ barspoon powdered sugar
1 jigger Jamaica Rum
Shake well with cracked ice and strain into Delmonico glass. Add dash carbonated water, half a slice of orange, and maraschino cherry.

JAPANESE FIZZ

Juice of ½ lemon
1 teaspoon powdered sugar
1½ oz. Whiskey
½ oz. Port Wine
White of 1 egg
Shake well with cracked ice and strain into 8 oz. highball glass. Fill with carbonated water and stir. Serve with slice of pineapple.

JERSEY LIGHTNING COCKTAIL

1½ oz. Apple Brandy
½ oz. Sweet Vermouth
Juice of 1 lime
Shake well with cracked ice and strain into 3 oz. cocktail glass.

JEWEL COCKTAIL

¾ oz. Green Chartreuse
¾ oz. Sweet Vermouth
¾ oz. Dry Gin
1 dash orange bitters
Stir well with cracked ice and strain into 3 oz. cocktail glass. Serve with a cherry.

JEYPLAK COCKTAIL

1½ oz. Dry Gin
¾ oz. Sweet Vermouth
¼ teaspoon Pernod (Absinthe substitute)
Stir well with cracked ice and strain into 3 oz. cocktail glass. Serve with a cherry.

Danny, the gregarious proprietor of the French Bootery in Las Vegas, told us the one about the young couple who had been lifting a few too many at the town's bars and were both getting somewhat maudlin. "You want to know something?" said the girl, with tears rolling down her cheeks. "I don't know who in the world I am. I was left on the doorstep!"

"S-a-y!" exclaimed her date. "Maybe you're a milk bottle!"

JOCKEY CLUB COCKTAIL

1 dash bitters
¼ teaspoon Crème de Cacao
Juice of ¼ lemon
1½ oz. Dry Gin
Shake well with cracked ice and strain into 3 oz. cocktail glass.

JOHN COLLINS

Juice of ½ lemon
1 teaspoon powdered sugar
2 oz. Holland Gin
Shake well with cracked ice and strain into 12 oz. Tom Collins glass. Add several cubes of ice, fill with carbonated water and stir. Decorate with slice of orange, lemon and a cherry. Serve with straws.

JOHNNIE COCKTAIL

¾ oz. Curaçao
1½ oz. Sloe Gin
1 teaspoon Anisette
Stir well with cracked ice and strain into 3 oz. cocktail glass.

JOURNALIST COCKTAIL

¼ oz. Dry Vermouth
¼ oz. Sweet Vermouth
1½ oz. Dry Gin
½ teaspoon lemon juice
½ teaspoon Curaçao
1 dash bitters
Shake well with cracked ice and strain into 3 oz. cocktail glass.

JUDGE JR. COCKTAIL

¾ oz. Dry Gin
¾ oz. Rum
Juice of ¼ lemon
½ teaspoon powdered sugar
¼ teaspoon Grenadine
*Shake well with cracked ice and strain into 3 oz.
cocktail glass.*

JUDGETTE COCKTAIL

¾ oz. Peach Flavored Brandy
¾ oz. Dry Gin
¾ oz. Dry Vermouth
Juice of ¼ lime
*Shake well with cracked ice and strain into 3 oz.
cocktail glass. Serve with a cherry.*

KAHLUALEXANDER

1 part sweet cream
1 part Kahlua
3 to 4 parts Gin (or Cognac)
Shake with cracked or crushed ice.

KATZ' MEOW

1½ oz. Vodka
¾ oz. Dry Vermouth
*Stir well with cracked ice and strain into 3 oz. cock-
tail glass. Serve with twist of lemon peel.*

KENTUCKY COCKTAIL

1½ oz. pineapple juice
¾ oz. Kentucky Bourbon
*Shake well with cracked ice and strain into 3 oz.
cocktail glass. Serve with twist of lemon peel.*

KENTUCKY COLONEL COCKTAIL

½ oz. Benedictine
1½ oz. Kentucky Bourbon
Twist of lemon peel
*Stir well with cracked ice and strain into a 3 oz.
cocktail glass.*

KENTUCKY HORSE'S NECK

1 jigger Bourbon
Rind of lemon
Ginger ale
Pour ingredients over ice cubes in glass and serve.

KING COLE COCKTAIL

1 slice of orange
1 slice of pineapple
½ teaspoon powdered sugar
Muddle well in old fashioned cocktail glass and add
2 oz. Whiskey
1 cube of ice
Stir well.

KISS-IN-THE-DARK COCKTAIL

¾ oz. Dry Gin
¾ oz. Wild Cherry Flavored Brandy
¾ oz. Dry Vermouth
Stir well with cracked ice and strain into 3 oz. cocktail glass.

KLONDIKE COOLER

½ teaspoon powdered sugar
2 oz. carbonated water
Stir and fill glass with cracked ice and add:
2 oz. Whiskey
Fill 12 oz. Collins glass with carbonated water or ginger ale and stir again. Insert spiral of orange or lemon peel (or both) and dangle end over rim of glass.

KNICKERBOCKER COCKTAIL

¼ teaspoon Sweet Vermouth
¾ oz. Dry Vermouth
1½ oz. Dry Gin
Stir well with cracked ice, strain into 3 oz. glass. Add twist of lemon peel and drop in glass.

KOPMAN CAPRICE

1 oz. Blackberry Brandy
1½ oz. Dry Gin
Juice of ½ lemon
Lemon slice
Blackberries (fresh are preferable)
Pour Brandy, Gin and lemon juice in 12 oz. Collins glass. Fill with shaved ice and 2-3 oz. carbonated water. Mix. Garnish with 2 or 3 blackberries and lemon slice.

LADIES' COCKTAIL

1¾ oz. Whiskey
½ teaspoon Pernod
½ teaspoon Anisette
2 dashes bitters
Stir well with cracked ice and strain into 3 oz. cocktail glass. Serve with a piece of pineapple on top.

LADY ALEXANDER

1 part Crème de Cacao
1 part Sloe Gin
White of 1 egg
1 dash bitters
Shake with cracked ice.

LADY LOVE FIZZ

1 teaspoon powdered sugar
Juice of ½ lemon
White of 1 egg
2 oz. Dry Gin
2 teaspoons sweet cream
Shake well with cracked ice and strain into 8 oz. highball glass. Fill with carbonated water and stir.

LEATHERNECK

Juice of ½ lime
3 parts Rye
1 part Curaçao
Ice
Shake well. Strain into cocktail glass.

LEAVE IT TO ME COCKTAIL NO. 1

½ oz. Apricot Flavored Brandy
½ oz. Dry Vermouth
1 oz. Gin
¼ teaspoon lemon juice
¼ teaspoon Grenadine
Shake well with cracked ice and strain into 3 oz. cocktail glass.

LEAVE IT TO ME COCKTAIL NO. 2

1 teaspoon raspberry syrup
1 teaspoon lemon juice
¼ teaspoon Maraschino Liqueur
1½ oz. Dry Gin
Stir well with cracked ice and strain into 3 oz. cocktail glass.

LEMON SQUASH (Non-alcoholic)

1 lemon, peeled and quartered
2 teaspoons powdered sugar
Muddle well in 12 oz. Tom Collins glass until juice is well extracted. Then fill glass with cracked ice. Add carbonated water and stir. Decorate with fruits.

LEMONADE (Non-alcoholic, Carbonated)

2 teaspoons powdered sugar
Juice of 1 lemon
Stir. Then fill 12 oz. Tom Collins glass with shaved ice. Add enough carbonated water to fill glass and stir. Decorate with slice of orange, lemon and a cherry. Serve with straws.

LEMONADE (Claret)

2 teaspoons powdered sugar
Juice of 1 lemon
Stir. Then fill 12 oz. Tom Collins glass with shaved ice. Add enough water to fill glass, leaving room to float 2 oz. Claret. Decorate with slice of orange, lemon and a cherry. Serve with straws.

LEMONADE (Egg)

Juice of 1 lemon
2 teaspoons powdered sugar
1 whole egg
Shake well and strain into 12 oz. Tom Collins glass filled with shaved ice. Add enough water to fill glass. Serve with straws.

LEMONADE (Fruit)

Juice of 1 lemon
2 teaspoons powdered sugar
1 oz. raspberry syrup
Stir. Then fill 12 oz. Tom Collins glass with shaved ice. Add enough water to fill glass and stir. Decorate with a slice of orange, lemon and a cherry. Serve with straws.

LEMONADE (Golden)

Juice of 1 lemon
2 teaspoons powdered sugar
Yolk of 1 egg
6 oz. water
Shake well with cracked ice and strain into 12 oz. Tom Collins glass. Decorate with a slice of orange, lemon and a cherry.

LEMONADE (Modern)

2 teaspoons powdered sugar
1½ oz. Sherry
1 oz. Sloe Gin
Cut lemon in quarters and muddle well with sugar. Add Sherry and Sloe Gin. Shake well with cracked ice and strain into 12 oz. Tom Collins glass. Fill glass with carbonated water.

LEMONADE (Plain)

2 teaspoons powdered sugar (or 1 tablespoon sugar syrup)
Juice of 1 lemon
Stir. Then fill 12 oz. Tom Collins glass with shaved ice. Add enough water (plain or charged) to fill glass and stir well. Decorated with slice of orange, lemon and a cherry.

LEVIATHAN 477

1 part sugar syrup
2 parts lemon juice
2 parts orange juice
4 parts Scotch
Shake.

LIMEADE

Juice of 3 limes
3 teaspoons powdered sugar
Fill 12 oz. Tom Collins glass with lime juice, sugar and shaved ice. Add enough water to fill glass. Stir well and drop lime in glass. Add a cherry. Serve with straws.

LITTLE COLONEL

1 part lime juice
2 parts Bourbon
4 parts Southern Comfort
Shake with cracked or crushed ice.

LONDON COCKTAIL

2 oz. Dry Gin
2 dashes orange bitters
½ teaspoon simple syrup
½ teaspoon Maraschino Liqueur
Stir well with cracked ice and strain into 3 oz. cocktail glass. Add twist of lemon peel to glass.

LONDON SPECIAL COCKTAIL

Put rind of ½ orange into 6 oz. champagne glass. Add
1 lump of sugar
2 dashes bitters
Fill with Champagne, well chilled, and stir gently.

LONE TREE COCKTAIL

¾ oz. Sweet Vermouth
1½ oz. Dry Gin
Stir well with cracked ice and strain into 3 oz. cocktail glass.

LONE TREE COOLER

½ teaspoon powdered sugar
2 oz. carbonated water
Stir and fill 12 oz. Tom Collins glass with cracked ice and add
2 oz. Dry Gin
½ oz. Dry Vermouth
Fill with carbonated water or ginger ale and stir again. Insert spiral of orange or lemon peel (or both) and dangle end over rim of glass.

words
on drink

THE literary brains of the young century gathered at Schlogl's which was, to the scribes of Chicago's Newspaper Row, what the Maitre Tavern on Fleet Street was to the London writers of Samuel Johnson's day. Around the walnut tables, under the ornate tin ceiling and surrounded by the large oil paintings which depicted monks drinking wine in old cellars, would sit George Ade, Harry Hansen, Carl Sandburg, Ben Hecht, and others. The customers would raise their drinks at regular intervals and toast one another with verse:

> *"Then stand to your glasses steady*
> *We drink to our comrades' eyes.*
> *A cup to the dead already*
> *Hurrah for the next who dies."*

From ON THE HOUSE by Matty and Don Simmons.
Published by Coward-McCann, 1955.

All the great villainies of history have been perpetrated by sober men, and chiefly by tee-totalers. But all the charming and beautiful things, from the Song of Songs to terrapin à la Maryland, and from the nine Beethoven symphonies to the Martini cocktail, have been given to humanity by men who, when the hour came, turned from well water to something with color to it, and more in it than mere oxygen and hydrogen.

—H. L. Mencken
PREJUDICES: fourth series

153

LOVE COCKTAIL

2 oz. Sloe Gin
White of 1 egg
1 half teaspoon lemon juice
½ teaspoon raspberry juice
*Shake well with cracked ice and strain into 4 oz.
cocktail glass.*

LOVER'S DELIGHT

1 part Cointreau
1 part Forbidden Fruit Liqueur
2 parts Cognac
Shake.
Optional—add 2 parts lemon juice and increase proportion of Cognac to 8 parts.

LOVING CUP

4 teaspoons powdered sugar
6 oz. carbonated water
1 oz. Triple Sec
2 oz. Brandy
*Fill large glass pitcher with cubes of ice. Add 1 pint
Claret. Stir well and decorate with as many fruits
as available and also rind of cucumber inserted on
each side of pitcher. Top with small bunch of mint
sprigs. Serve in 5 oz. claret glasses.*

LUXURY COCKTAIL

3 oz. Brandy
2 dashes orange bitters
3 oz. well chilled Champagne
Stir very gently. Use 6 oz. saucer champagne glass.

MAD HATTER

Juice of ¼ lemon
Juice of ¼ lime
1 teaspoon powdered sugar
1 jigger Whiskey
Ice
Shake. Strain into cocktail glass. Add dash of Pernod.

MADEIRA EGGNOG

1 egg
1½ oz. Madeira
1 tablespoon powdered sugar
1 glass milk
Break egg into shaker. Add ice and ingredients. Shake well and strain into tall highball glass. Grate a little nutmeg on top.

MAIDEN'S BLUSH COCKTAIL NO. 1

¼ teaspoon lemon juice
1 teaspoon Curaçao
1 teaspoon Grenadine
1½ oz. Dry Gin
Shake well with cracked ice and strain into 3 oz. cocktail glass.

MAIDEN'S BLUSH COCKTAIL NO. 2

¾ oz. Pernod
1½ oz. Dry Gin
1 teaspoon Grenadine
Stir well with cracked ice and strain into 3 oz. cocktail glass.

MAIDEN'S PRAYER COCKTAIL

¼ teaspoon orange juice
¼ teaspoon lemon juice
¼ teaspoon Triple Sec
2 oz. Dry Gin
Shake well with cracked ice and strain into 3 oz. cocktail glass.

MAINBRACE COCKTAIL

¾ oz. Dry Gin
¾ oz. Triple Sec
¾ oz. grape juice
Shake well with cracked ice and strain into 3 oz. cocktail glass.

MAJOR BAILEY

¼ oz. lime juice
¼ oz. lemon juice
½ teaspoon powdered sugar
12 mint leaves
Muddle well and pour into 12 oz. Tom Collins glass filled with shaved ice, and add: 2 oz. Dry Gin. Stir gently, until glass is frosted. Decorate with sprig of mint and serve with straws.

MAMIE GILROY

Juice of ½ lime
2 cubes of ice
2 oz. Scotch
1 dash bitters
Fill 12 oz. Tom Collins glass with carbonated water and stir gently.

MAMIE TAYLOR

Juice of ½ lime
2 cubes of ice
2 oz. Scotch
Fill 12 oz. Tom Collins glass with ginger ale and stir gently.

MANHATTAN COCKTAIL

1 dash bitters
¾ oz. Sweet Vermouth
1½ oz. Whiskey
Stir well with cracked ice and strain into 3 oz. cocktail glass. Serve with a cherry.

MANHATTAN COCKTAIL (Dry)

1 dash bitters
¾ oz. Dry Vermouth
1½ oz. Whiskey
Stir well with cracked ice and strain into 3 oz. cocktail glass. Serve with a twist of lemon peel or a cherry.

MANHATTAN PERFECT

4 parts Bourbon
1 part Vermouth (equal amounts of Sweet and Dry)
Stir and serve with lemon rind or cherry.

MANHATTAN SWEET

1 part Sweet Vermouth
4 parts Bourbon
1 dash bitters
Add twist of lemon if desired. Mix and serve in cocktail glass.

MARGARITA COCKTAIL

1½ oz. Tequila
½ oz. Triple Sec
Juice of ½ lemon or lime
Stir with crushed ice. Rub rim of 3 oz. cocktail glass with rind of lemon or lime, dip rim in salt, pour and serve.

MARTINI

Martini Mixing: Chill 3-oz. cocktail glasses to the point of frost. Fill Martini pitcher with cracked ice. Ice should be dry and hard frozen. Pour Gin in first, then the Dry Vermouth. Stir (don't shake) until drink is very cold. Strain into frosty, stemmed cocktail glasses. (Vodka may be substituted for Gin in any of the following recipes.) Martinis "on the rocks" call for pre-chilled old fashioned glasses filled with cubes of ice, served with olive or lemon peel.

GIBSON

A dry or Extra Dry Martini with a twist of lemon peel and one to three pearl onions.

MARTINI (Traditional 3 to 1)

1½ oz. Gin
½ oz. Dry Vermouth
Drop in an olive.

MARTINI (Medium)

1½ oz. Gin
½ oz. Dry Vermouth
½ oz. Sweet Vermouth
Drop in an olive.

MARTINI (5 to 1)

1⅔ oz. Gin
⅓ oz. Dry Vermouth
Drop in an olive.

The Scene: The Chambers of the Senate Investigating Committee. Senator McClellan calls this brassy blonde "B-Girl" to the stand to testify. "Miss LaRue," sternly demands the Senator from Arkansas, "do you swear to tell the truth, to give us the whole story—the inside story—on 'B-Girl' operations in your city?" And she says, "I will if you buy me a drink!"

MARTINI, EXTRA DRY (7 to 1)

1¾ oz Gin
¼ oz. Dry Vermouth
Drop in an olive.

MARY GARDEN COCKTAIL

1½ oz. Dubonnet
¾ oz. Dry Vermouth
Stir well with cracked ice and strain into 3 oz. cocktail glass.

MARY PICKFORD COCKTAIL

1 oz. Rum
1 oz. pineapple juice
¼ teaspoon Grenadine
¼ teaspoon Maraschino Liqueur
Shake well with cracked ice and strain into 3 oz. cocktail glass.

MERRY-GO-ROUND

1 jigger Bourbon
2 dashes Curaçao
2 dashes Dubonnet
A twist of orange
Stir well, pour over ice cubes in glass.

MERRY WIDOW COCKTAIL NO. 1

1¼ oz. Gin
1¼ oz. Dry Vermouth
½ teaspoon Benedictine
½ teaspoon Pernod
1 dash orange bitters
Stir well with cracked ice and strain into 3 oz. cocktail glass. Add twist of lemon peel and drop in glass.

MERRY WIDOW COCKTAIL NO. 2

1¼ oz. Maraschino Liqueur
1¼ oz. Wild Cherry Flavored Brandy
Stir well with cracked ice and strain into 3 oz. cocktail glass. Serve with a cherry.

MERRY WIDOW FIZZ

Juice of ½ orange
Juice of ½ lemon
White of 1 egg
1 teaspoon powdered sugar
1½ oz. Sloe Gin
Shake well with cracked ice and strain into 8 oz. highball glass. Fill with carbonated water and stir.

MIAMI BEACH COCKTAIL

¾ oz. Scotch
¾ oz. Dry Vermouth
¾ oz. grapefruit juice
Stir well with cracked ice and strain into 3 oz. cocktail glass.

MIKE'S MUDDLER

1 oz. Bourbon
2 oz. Crème de Banana
½ oz. Triple Sec
1 oz. cream
Pour over crushed ice, blend well and strain into 4 oz. champagne glass.

MILK PUNCH

1 teaspoon powdered sugar
2 oz. Whiskey
½ pt. milk
Shake well with cracked ice and strain into 12 oz. Tom Collins glass. Grate nutmeg on top.

MIMOSA

Orange juice and champagne, half and half.

MINT COLLINS

Juice of ½ lemon
2 oz. Mint Flavored Gin
Shake well with cracked ice and strain into 12 oz.
Tom Collins glass. Add several cubes of ice, fill with
carbonated water and stir. Decorate with slice of
lemon, orange and a cherry. Serve with straws.

MINT HIGHBALL

1 cube of ice
2 oz. Crème de Menthe
Fill 8 oz. highball glass with ginger ale or carbonated
water. Add twist of lemon peel, if desired, and stir.

MINT JULEP

4 mint sprigs
1 teaspoon powdered sugar
2 teaspoons water
Fill 12 oz. Tom Collins glass or silver mug with above
ingredients plus shaved ice, and muddle. Add 2½ oz.
Bourbon, and stir until glass is frosted. Decorate with
slice of orange, lemon, pineapple and a cherry. In-
sert 5 or 6 sprigs of mint on top. Serve with straws.

MINT JULEP (Southern Style)

Fill silver mug or Tom Collins glass with finely shaved ice. Add 2½ oz. Kentucky Straight Bourbon Whiskey and stir until glass is heavily frosted. (Do not hold glass with hand while stirring.) Add 1 teaspoon powdered sugar and fill balance with water, and stir. Decorate with 5 or 6 sprigs of fresh mint so that the tops are about 2 inches above rim of mug or glass. Use short straws so that it is necessary to bury nose in mint. The mint is intended for odor rather than taste.

there's a town
called Cognac

By MYRA WALDO

THE town of Cognac, an apparently somnolent town in the
southwest of France, for all its appearances is about as somnolent as a Madison Avenue ad agency. Cognac is ancient;
Caesar probably rode through Cognac on a horse. But Cognac
is about as ancient these days as a jet plane. It is as full of lore
of the past as your teen-age son's history book. But it is also
as full of the present as the newspaper you read this morning.

In a sense, Cognac—and the drink which it produces—are
preposterous. Most communities based upon agricultural produce (and the grape is a product of agriculture as clearly as
wheat or cotton is) are predicated on fertile earth. One of the
secrets of the Cognac region is that its earth, by any standards,
is slightly more productive than a child's sandbox. You probably wouldn't try to grow a shock of corn in Cognac, nor
produce an edible bean, but what you can produce is a peculiar kind of grape which produces a peculiar kind of wine
which, in turn, produces a unique kind of drink called *Cognac*.
The word *Cognac* is regarded by the growers in Cognac as
other men regard their right eye. By French law and international agreements, no drink produced in any place other
than the 138,863 acres surrounding the town of Cognac can
be called *Cognac*. Brandy from Italy can be called grappa,
"slivowicz" is from Poland and "Brandy" is from any one
of a number of wine producing countries; but *Cognac* can
come only from the Cognac region.

162

The soil of the area around Cognac is chalky and harsh. It is a milieu in which one would think a plant could not flourish. But the grapes, from which *Cognac* is eventually made, disagree; they flourish. Oddly enough the wine which is pressed from these grapes is not very palatable, but nobody cares because the *Cognac* produced from the grapes is the most palatable brandy in the world.

Cognac is not a large town—it has 17,523 people. There's really no outstanding restaurant in town and no really well-known cathedral, which is comparatively rare for even a small town in France. Cognac has not produced a great cheese nor a great painter nor a great jazz musician. But in a sense, it shouldn't be expected to, since it makes *Cognac*. And oddly enough, at the beginning, *Cognac* probably produced itself.

It happened this way. About the year 1655, the vineyards of the Cognac region, blessed by a beautiful spring and summer sun, produced an exceedingly bountiful harvest.

Since the wine made from the grapes was thin and peevish and not very good for ordinary drinking, some of the vineyard owners—so the popular belief goes—decided to distill it, both to preserve it and to hoard it in the form of spirits for future sale. (They saved for a rainy day in those days, too.)

The good people of Cognac were to find, upon sampling their distillation, that they had on their hands a Brandy rich with flavor and bouquet. The town rejoiced over this, and it wasn't long after that that sailing ships were putting into the port of La Rochelle (near the town of Cognac) to fill their holds.

As the stock of *Cognac* grew, the vineyard owners had to store it in something and here we come to one of those unexplained happenstances of nature: the French stored their *Cognac* in casks made of oak from the neighboring Limousin forest. In a sense it was like the discovery of penicillin.

The raw, distilled, newly-made *Cognac* and the casks from Limousin were meant for each other. The marriage that took place between them produced a drink which the world hailed for its mellow taste, its delightful bouquet, its golden color. *Cognac* was the essence of the grape, the very soul of the wine.

It had none of the characteristics of whiskey, which, at this point, was being produced in Scotland, England and Ireland; it had none of the characteristics of Vodka which, at this point, was being made in localities we now call countries behind the Iron Curtain. Nor did it have the syrupy and sweet flavor of the drinks we now call Cordials—Blackberry Brandy, Apricot Brandy, Plum Brandy, and the rest. (The difference between Brandy and *Cognac* is very simple. All *Cognac* is Brandy, but not all Brandy is *Cognac*.)

163

The people of Cognac didn't know quite what to call their new drink, so they simply called it after the capital of their rather small area. The fame of *Cognac* spread very quickly. *Cognac* migrated to England where the culture of the grapes, except in greenhouses, is impossible because of the inclement climate of the British Isles. (Britain today is still the first country, outside of France, in the consumption of *Cognac;* the United States is a very close second. In England small bottles of *Cognac* are kept in medicine chests in case his Lordship comes down with a cold.)

In connection with the economics of Cognac, it is interesting to note that in the Cognac region, *Cognac* has, to a certain degree, taken on the function of currency. The French farmer, always suspicious of anything so transitory as a thousand-franc note, sees in *Cognac* a solidity that he can appreciate. He therefore typically buys a barrel of raw *Cognac* for about $300, ages it in his cellar for from 5 to 10 years and then sells it for $600 or maybe even more. Furthermore, barrels of *Cognac* or the empty casks themselves in the Cognac region often comprise part of a girl's dowry, and a particularly unattractive girl may be obliged to provide as much as 10 barrels before her suitor stops looking at Brigitte Bardot.

As this is being written, the last of the grapes have been picked and mists from the Atlantic Ocean are drifting over the little town of Cognac. The sun, which has poured mercilessly on the area all summer, is somewhat obscured. The fields, which echoed to the songs of the harvest pickers in October, are now barren and desolate. The vines, naked of grapes, are wet with the salt sea dew.

Times haven't changed in the *Cognac* country. The harvesting is still done by hand through the use of baskets and animal-drawn carts and the same technique used centuries ago is still used to make the *Cognac* that you will drink tonight. In the quiet autumn air, the smell of *Cognac*, the fermentation of the *Cognac* grape and the distillation of the *Cognac* itself hang over the little town like a blanket. Frenchmen think that during the fermentation and distilling time of *Cognac*, a man can get drunk simply by walking down the main street. But a friend of this writer, on hearing the legend, tried it and is now in position to dispute that: the best way to get drunk on *Cognac* in Cognac is to drink *Cognac*.

The vineyard owners, half of whom have their own highly secret formulae for making *Cognac* (largely by combining different years, that is, the different years they have access to) are busily sampling their product. It doesn't taste very good right now, but the man who ate the first oyster probably didn't like it, either. The *Cognac* the French farmers will be tasting now is colorless and peppery in flavor. Only time and the action of the good oak from Limousin can transform it into the *Cognac* which may grace your dinner table five years hence.

Cognac appears to achieve stature when it is about 5 years old, which is the age at which most *Cognacs* are sold. Some experts believe that it achieves greater subtleties from about the age of 5 to 15 years, at which point it would seem to remain static. At the age of 40 it suddenly appears to lose its verve, although in some cases this isn't always true.

Now, about those stars which often appear in the labels of *Cognac* bottles, here's the story that's most popular: 1811, the year of the Comet, was also a great year for the vineyard owners. As a means of dramatizing the quality of the grape, as well as the Comet, the *Cognac* makers put a star on their *Cognac*. The next year, although there was no Comet, was another superior year, so on went a second star. When, with luck, they had another successful year they identified it with three stars. This all seems to have stopped, though, at five stars.

Cognac drinkers also find letters on their bottles that indicate the quality of their brandy—letters such as V, O, VSOP, R, E, X, and C. Well, V stands for Very; S for Superior; O for Old, P for Pale, F for Fine (pronounced "feen"), R for Rare, E for Especially, X for Extra and C, simply for *Cognac*.

MINT ON ROCKS

Pour 2 oz. Crème de Menthe (Green) *on ice cubes in old fashioned cocktail glass.*

MISSOURI MULE

1 goblet or mug of cracked ice
2 oz. Southern Comfort
Juice of ¼ large lemon
Fill mug with ginger ale. Stir and serve.

MOGEL'S MILLIONS

White of 1 egg
¼ teaspoon Grenadine
½ oz. Curaçao
1½ oz. Whiskey
Shake well with cracked ice and strain into 4 oz. cocktail glass.

MONKEY GLAND

1 part Grenadine
2 parts orange juice
6 parts Gin
1 or 2 dashes Pernod to each drink
Shake well with crushed ice.

MONTE CARLO IMPERIAL HIGHBALL

2 oz. Dry Gin
½ oz. Crème de Menthe (White)
Juice of ¼ lemon
Shake well with cracked ice and strain into 8 oz. highball glass. Fill glass with Champagne and stir.

MONTMARTRE COCKTAIL

1¼ oz. Dry Gin
½ oz. Sweet Vermouth
½ oz. Triple Sec
Stir well with cracked ice and strain into 3 oz. cocktail glass. Serve with a cherry.

MORNING COCKTAIL

1 oz. Brandy
1 oz. Dry Vermouth
¼ teaspoon Curaçao
¼ teaspoon Maraschino Liqueur
¼ teaspoon Pernod
2 dashes orange bitters
Stir well with cracked ice and strain into 3 oz. cocktail glass. Serve with a cherry.

MORNING GLORY FIZZ

Juice ½ lemon or 1 lime
1 teaspoon powdered sugar
White of 1 egg
½ teaspoon Pernod
2 oz. Scotch
Shake well with cracked ice and strain into 8 oz. high-ball glass. Fill with carbonated water and stir.

MOSCOW MULE

1½ oz. Vodka
Juice of ½ lime
Add ice cubes and fill copper mug with ginger beer. Drop lime in mug to decorate.

MOULIN ROUGE COCKTAIL

1½ oz. Sloe Gin
¾ oz. Sweet Vermouth
1 dash bitters
Stir well with cracked ice and strain into 3 oz. cocktail glass.

NAPOLEON COCKTAIL

2 oz. Dry Gin
½ teaspoon Curaçao
½ teaspoon Dubonnet
Stir well with cracked ice and strain into 3 oz. cocktail glass.

NEVADA COCKTAIL

1½ oz. Rum
1 oz. grapefruit juice
Juice of 1 lime
1 dash bitters
3 teaspoons powdered sugar
Shake well with cracked ice and strain into 4 oz. cocktail glass.

NEW ORLEANS GIN FIZZ

Juice of ½ lemon
1 teaspoon powdered sugar
White of 1 egg
2 oz. Dry Gin
1 tablespoon sweet cream
½ teaspoon orange flower water
Shake well with cracked ice and strain into Tom Collins glass. Fill with carbonated water and stir.

NEW ORLEANS MINT JULEP

2 oz. bonded Kentucky Bourbon
1 lump sugar
4 mint sprigs
Fill tall glass with crushed ice and set aside. In old fashioned glass crush sugar with a stick. Add mint leaves and bruise lightly. Add whiskey and mix all together. Pour over crushed ice in tall glass. Stir until outside of glass is frosted. Decorate with large sprig of mint on top and sprinkle with powdered sugar.

NEW ORLEANS PUNCH

1 jigger Bourbon
Juice of ½ lime
Dash of Cherry Liqueur
Shake well, pour over ice cubes in tall glass. Fill with cold black tea.

NEW YORK COCKTAIL

Juice of 1 lime or ½ lemon
1 teaspoon powdered sugar
1½ oz. Whiskey
½ teaspoon Grenadine
Twist of orange peel
Shake well with cracked ice and strain into 3 oz. cocktail glass. Add twist of lemon peel and drop in glass.

NEW YORK SOUR

Juice of ½ lemon
1 teaspoon powdered sugar
2 oz. Whiskey
Shake well with cracked ice and strain into 6 oz. sour glass, leaving about ½ inch on which to float Claret. Decorate with a half-slice of lemon and a cherry.

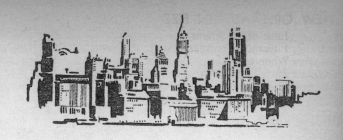

NIGHT CAP

2 oz. Rum
1 teaspoon powdered sugar
Add enough warm milk to fill a Tom & Jerry mug and stir. Grate a little nutmeg on top.

NINOTCHKA COCKTAIL

1½ oz. Vodka
½ oz. Crème de Cacao
½ oz. lemon juice
Shake well with cracked ice and strain into 3 oz. cocktail glass.

OLD CHARTER

2 parts Bourbon
1 part lemon juice
A dash of Grenadine
Stir well with ice and strain into glass.

OLD FASHIONED COCKTAIL

½ lump sugar
2 dashes bitters
Add enough water to cover sugar and muddle well in old fashioned glass.
1 cube of ice
2 oz. Whiskey
Stir well. Add twist of lemon rind and drop in glass. Decorate with slice of orange, lemon and a cherry. Serve with stirring rod.

OLYMPIC COCKTAIL

¾ oz. orange juice
¾ oz. Curaçao
¾ oz. Brandy
Shake well with cracked ice and strain into 3 oz. cocktail glass.

OMAR'S DELIGHT

*Omar Khayyam's
San Francisco*

1 jigger (100-proof) Southern Comfort
3 dashes Curaçao
Juice of ½ small lime
⅓ oz. lemon juice
½ level teaspoon sugar
Fine ice to chill
Shake, or mix in electric mixer. Strain, and serve in champagne glass.

OPAL COCKTAIL

1 oz. Dry Gin
½ oz. orange juice
½ oz. triple Sec
½ teaspoon orange flower water
¼ teaspoon powdered sugar
Shake well with cracked ice and strain into 3 oz. cocktail glass.

OPERA COCKTAIL

½ oz. Maraschino Liqueur
½ oz. Dubonnet
1½ oz. Dry Gin
Stir well with cracked ice and strain into 3 oz. cocktail glass.

ORANGE BLOOM COCKTAIL

½ oz. Sweet Vermouth
½ oz. Triple Sec
1½ oz. Dry Gin
Stir well with cracked ice and strain into 3 oz. cocktail glass. Serve with a cherry.

ORANGE BLOSSOM COCKTAIL

1 oz. Dry Gin
1 oz. orange juice
¼ teaspoon powdered sugar
Shake well with cracked ice and strain into 3 oz. cocktail glass.

ORANGE GIN COLLINS

Juice of ½ lemon
2 oz. Orange Flavored Gin
Shake well with cracked ice and strain into Tom Collins glass. Add several cubes of ice, fill with carbonated water and stir. Decorate with slice of lemon, orange and a cherry. Serve with straws.

ORANGE GIN FIZZ

Juice of ½ lemon
1 teaspoon powdered sugar
2 oz. Orange Flavored Gin
Shake well with cracked ice and strain into 7 oz. highball glass. Fill with carbonated water and stir.

ORANGE GIN HIGHBALL

1 cube of ice
2 oz. Orange Flavored Gin
Fill 8 oz. highball glass with ginger ale or carbonated water. Add twist of lemon peel, if desired, and stir.

ORANGE MILK FIZZ

Juice of ½ lemon
1 teaspoon powdered sugar
2 oz. Orange Flavored Gin
2 oz. milk
Shake well with cracked ice and strain into 8 oz. highball glass. Fill with carbonated water and stir.

ORANGE SMILE

1 egg
Juice of 1 large orange
1 tablespoon raspberry syrup or Grenadine
Shake well with cracked ice and strain into 8 oz. stem goblet.

ORANGEADE (Non-alcoholic)

Juice of 2 oranges
1 teaspoon powdered sugar
Add 2 cubes of ice and enough water to fill 12 oz. Tom Collins glass and stir well. Decorate with a slice of orange, lemon and 2 cherries. Serve with straws.

ORIENTAL COCKTAIL

½ oz. Whiskey
½ oz. Sweet Vermouth
½ oz. Curaçao
Juice of ½ lime
Shake well with cracked ice and strain into 3 oz. cocktail glass.

PADDY COCKTAIL

1¼ oz. Irish Whiskey
1¼ oz. Sweet Vermouth
1 dash bitters
Stir well with cracked ice and strain into 3 oz. cocktail glass.

PALISADES

1 part Gin
1 part Hard Cider
1 dash bitters
Shake.

PALM BEACH COCKTAIL

1½ oz. Dry Gin
¼ oz. Sweet Vermouth
¼ oz. grapefruit juice
Shake well with cracked ice and strain into 3 oz. cocktail glass.

PALMER COCKTAIL

2 oz. Whiskey
1 dash bittters
½ teaspoon lemon juice
Stir well with cracked ice and strain into 3 oz. cocktail glass.

PALMETTO COCKTAIL

    1¼ oz. Rum
    ¼ oz. Dry Vermouth
    2 dashes bitters
    Stir well with cracked ice and strain into 3 oz. cocktail glass.

PALS TROPICAL PUNCH

    Juice of ½ orange
    Sugar to taste
    Juice of ½ lemon or lime
    Few dashes Grenadine
    1½ oz. light Bacardi Rum
    Few dashes Orange Curaçao
    1½ oz. dark Bacardi Rum.
    Either shake well or mix in blender. Serve in tall Zombie glass topped with Port Wine and garnished with a stick of pineapple.

PANAMA COCKTAIL

    1 oz. Crème de Cacao
    1 oz. sweet cream
    1 oz. Brandy
    Shake well with cracked ice and strain into 4 oz. cocktail glass.

PARADISE COCKTAIL

    1 oz. Apricot Flavored Brandy
    ¾ oz. Dry Gin
    Juice of ¼ orange
    Shake well with cracked ice and strain into 3 oz. cocktail glass.

PARISIAN BLONDE COCKTAIL

    ¾ oz. sweet cream
    ¾ oz. Curaçao
    ¾ oz. Jamaica Rum
    Shake well with cracked ice and strain into 3 oz. cocktail glass.

PASSION DAIQUIRI COCKTAIL

1½ oz. Rum
Juice of 1 lime
1 teaspoon powdered sugar
½ oz. Passion Fruit Juice
Shake well with cracked ice and strain into 3 oz. cocktail glass.

PEACH BLOSSOM

1 teaspoon lemon juice
½ teaspoon powdered sugar
2 oz. Dry Gin
½ peach
Shake well with cracked ice and strain into 8 oz. highball glass. Fill with carbonated water and stir.

PEACH BLOW FIZZ

Juice of ½ lemon
White of 1 egg
2 teaspoons Grenadine
½ teaspoon powdered sugar
1 oz. sweet cream
2 oz. Dry Gin
Shake well with cracked ice and strain into 10 oz. highball gass. Fill with carbonated water and stir.

PEACH SANGAREE

2 oz. Peach Flavored Brandy
2 cubes of ice
Serve in 8 oz. highball glass. Fill balance with soda water. Stir, leaving enough room on which to float a tablespoon of Port Wine. Sprinkle lightly with nutmeg.

PEKING EXPRESS

Peking Restaurant
New York

½ oz. Cointreau
1 oz. Gin
White of 1 egg
Juice of ½ lime
1 drop Crème de Menthe
Shake well with cracked ice and strain into cocktail glass.

PERFECT COCKTAIL

¼ oz. Dry Vermouth
¼ oz. Sweet Vermouth
1½ oz. Dry Gin
1 dash bitters
Stir well with cracked ice and strain into 3 oz. cocktail glass.

PETER PAN COCKTAIL

2 dashes bitters
¾ oz. orange juice
¾ oz. Dry Vermouth
¾ oz. Dry Gin
Shake well with cracked ice and strain into 3 oz. cocktail glass.

PHOEBE SNOW COCKTAIL

1¼ oz. Dubonnet
1¼ oz. Brandy
¼ oz. Pernod
Stir well with cracked ice and strain into 3 oz. cocktail glass.

PICCADILLY COCKTAIL

¾ oz. Dry Vermouth
1½ oz. Dry Gin
¼ teaspoon Pernod
¼ teaspoon Grenadine
Stir well with cracked ice and strain into 3 oz. cocktail glass.

PIKE'S PEAK COOLER

Juice of ½ lemon
1 teaspoon powdered sugar
1 egg
Shake well with cracked ice and strain into 12 oz. Tom Collins glass and fill with Hard Cider and stir. Insert spiral of orange or lemon peel (or both) and dangle end over rim of glass.

PINEAPPLE BLOSSOM

1 part sugar syrup
1 part lemon juice
2 parts pineapple juice
4 parts Whiskey
Use fresh pineapple. Shake with cracked ice.

PINEAPPLE COCKTAIL

¾ oz. pineapple juice
1½ oz. Rum
½ teaspoon lemon juice
Shake well with cracked ice and strain into 3 oz. cocktail glass.

PINEAPPLE COOLER

½ teaspoon powdered sugar
2 oz. carbonated water
Stir into 12 oz. Tom Collins glass and fill with cracked ice Add 2 oz. Dry White Wine. Fill with carbonated water and stir again. Add crushed pineapple.

PINEAPPLE DREAM COCKTAIL

½ oz. pineapple juice
Juice of ½ lime
1 oz. Rum
Shake well with cracked ice and strain into 3 oz. cocktail glass.

PINEAPPLE FIZZ

1 oz. pineapple juice
½ teaspoon powdered sugar
2 oz. Rum
Shake well with cracked ice and strain into 7 oz. highball glass. Fill with carbonated water and stir.

PING-PONG COCKTAIL

Juice of ¼ lemon
White of 1 egg
1 oz. Sloe Gin
1 oz. Crème de Yvette
Shake well with cracked ice and strain into 4 oz. cocktail glass.

PINK LADY COCKTAIL

White of 1 egg
1 teaspoon Grenadine
1 teaspoon sweet cream
1½ oz. Dry Gin
Shake well with cracked ice and strain into 4 oz. cocktail glass.

PINK ROSE FIZZ

Juice of ½ lemon
1 teaspoon powdered sugar
White of 1 egg
½ teaspoon Grenadine
2 teaspoons sweet cream
2 oz. Dry Gin
Shake well with cracked ice and strain into 8 oz. highball glass. Fill with carbonated water and stir.

PINK WHISKERS COCKTAIL

¾ oz. Apricot Flavored Brandy
¾ oz. Dry Vermouth
1 oz. orange juice
1 teaspoon Grenadine
¼ teaspoon Crème de Menthe (White)
Shake well with cracked ice and strain into 4 oz. cocktail glass and top with a little Port Wine.

PISCO SOUR

1 jigger Pisco Brandy
Juice of ½ lemon
1 teaspoon sugar
1 egg white
Ice
Shake well. Strain into Delmonico glass.

PLANTATION PUNCH

2 oz. Planter's Punch Rum
1 oz. Puerto Rican Dark Rum
½ oz. Barbados Rum
2 oz. ginger beer
2 oz. frozen pineapple juice
Juice of 1 fresh lime
2 dashes bitters
2 dashes Pernod
Decorate with slice of lemon, orange, pineapple and cherry. Serve with straws in 12 oz. Collins glasses.

PLANTER'S PUNCH NO. 1

Juice of ¼ lemon
½ teaspoon powdered sugar
1½ oz. Jamaica Rum
Shake well with cracked ice and strain into 3 oz. cocktail glass.

PLANTER'S PUNCH NO. 2

Juice of 2 limes
2 teaspoons powdered sugar
2 oz. carbonated water
Fill 12 oz. Tom Collins glass with shaved ice and stir until glass is frosted. Add 2 dashes bitters, 2½ oz. Rum. Stir and decorate with slice of lemon, orange, pineapple and a cherry. Serve with straws.

PLANTER'S PUNCH NO. 3

Juice of 1 lime
Juice of ½ lemon
Juice of ½ orange
1 teaspoon pineapple juice
2 oz. Rum
Pour above into 16 oz. glass, well filled with shaved ice. Stir until glass is frosted. Then add 1 oz. Jamaica Rum, and top with ¼ teaspoon Curaçao. Decorate with slice of orange, lemon, pineapple and a cherry, also sprig of mint dipped in powdered sugar. Serve with straws.

POLONAISE COCKTAIL

2 parts Vodka
1 part Cherry Brandy
1 dash fresh lemon juice
Dash of sugar
Shake well with cracked ice and strain into cocktail glass.

POLYNESIAN COCKTAIL

1½ oz. Vodka
¾ oz. Wild Cherry Flavored Brandy
Juice of 1 lime
Shake well with cracked ice and strain into 4 oz. cocktail glass. Frost rim by rubbing with lime and dipping in powdered sugar.

179

PONCE DE LEON

½ oz. grapefruit juice
½ oz. Cointreau
½ oz. Rum
½ oz. Cognac
Shake with cracked ice and strain into a saucer champagne glass. Fill the glass with Champagne.

POOP DECK COCKTAIL

1¼ oz. Blackberry Flavored Brandy
½ oz. Port Wine
½ oz. Brandy
Stir well with cracked ice and strain into 3 oz. cocktail glass.

POPPY COCKTAIL

¾ oz. Crème de Cacao
1½ oz. Dry Gin
Shake well with cracked ice and strain into 3 oz. cocktail glass.

PORT AND STARBOARD

½ oz. Grenadine
½ oz. Crème de Menthe (Green)
Pour carefully into Pousse Café glass, so that Menthe floats on Grenadine.

PORT MILK PUNCH

1 teaspoon powdered sugar
3 oz. Port Wine
½ pt. milk
Shake well with cracked ice, strain into 12 oz. Tom Collins glass and grate nutmeg on top.

PORT WINE COBBLER

Dissolve 1 teaspoon powdered sugar in 2 oz. carbonated water; then fill 10 oz. goblet with shaved ice and add 3 oz. Port Wine. Stir well and decorate with fruits in season. Serve with straws.

PORT WINE COCKTAIL

2¼ oz. Port Wine
½ teaspoon Brandy
Stir slightly with cracked ice and strain into 3 oz. cocktail glass.

PORT WINE EGGNOG

1 egg
1 teaspoon powdered sugar
3 oz. Port Wine
Fill glass with milk. Shake well with cracked ice and strain into 12 oz. Tom Collins glass. Grate nutmeg on top.

PORT WINE FLIP

1 egg
1 teaspoon powdered sugar
1½ oz. Port Wine
2 teaspoons sweet cream (if desired)
Shake well with cracked ice and strain into 5 oz. flip glass. Grate a little nutmeg on top.

PORT WINE NEGUS

½ lump sugar
2 oz. Port Wine
Fill hot whiskey glass with hot water and stir. Grate nutmeg on top.

PORT WINE SANGAREE

Dissolve ½ teaspoon powdered sugar in 1 teaspoon of water.
2 oz. Port Wine
2 cubes of ice
Serve in 8 oz. highball glass. Fill balance with soda water. Stir, leaving enough room on which to float a tablespoon of Brandy. Sprinkle lightly with nutmeg.

POUSSE CAFÉ

1 part Curaçao
1 part Chartreuse
1 part Brandy
Place ingredients in parfait glass in order indicated, being careful to float one on top of the other.

POUSSE L'AMOUR

⅓ oz. Maraschino Liqueur
Yolk of 1 egg
⅓ oz. Benedictine
⅓ oz. Brandy
Pour carefully, in order given, into 2 oz. sherry glass, so that each ingredient floats on preceding one.

PRAIRIE OYSTER COCKTAIL (a "picker-upper")

1 oz. Cognac
1 whole egg
1 teaspoon Worcestershire sauce
1 teaspoon tomato catsup
½ teaspoon vinegar
Pinch of pepper
1 drop of Tabasco sauce
Use 5 oz. Delmonico glass. Swallow without breaking yolk.

PREAKNESS COCKTAIL

¾ oz. Sweet Vermouth
1½ oz. Whiskey
1 dash bitters
½ teaspoon Benedictine
Stir well with cracked ice and strain into 3 oz. cocktail glass. Add twist of lemon peel and drop in glass.

PRINCETON COCKTAIL

1 oz. Dry Gin
1 oz. Dry Vermouth
Juice of ½ lime
Stir well with cracked ice and strain into 3 oz. cocktail glass.

PUERTO RICAN COCKTAIL

Juice of ½ lime
½ oz. pineapple juice
2 oz. Puerto Rican Rum
Shake with shaved ice and pour unstrained into a chilled champagne glass.

PUSSYFOOT (Non-alcoholic)

1 part lemon juice
3 parts orange juice
1 teaspoonful Grenadine to each drink
1 egg yolk to each 2 or 3 drinks
Shake thoroughly with cracked ice.

QUAKER'S COCKTAIL

¾ oz. Rum
¾ oz. Brandy
Juice of ¼ lemon
2 teaspoons raspberry syrup
Shake well with cracked ice and strain into 3 oz. cocktail glass.

QUARTER DECK COCKTAIL

⅓ oz. Sherry Wine
1½ oz. Rum
Juice of ½ lime
Stir well with cracked ice and strain into 3 oz. cocktail glass.

QUEEN CHARLOTTE

2 oz. Claret Wine
1 oz. raspberry syrup or Grenadine
Pour into 12 oz. Tom Collins glass. Add cube of ice: fill with lemon soda and stir.

QUEEN ELIZABETH COCKTAIL

1½ oz. Dry Gin
½ oz. Dry Vermouth
¼ oz. Benedictine
Stir well with cracked ice and strain into 3 oz. cocktail glass.

RACQUET CLUB COCKTAIL

1½ oz. Dry Gin
¾ oz. Dry Vermouth
1 dash orange bitters
Stir well with cracked ice and strain into 3 oz. cocktail glass.

RAMOS FIZZ

Juice of ½ lemon
White of 1 egg
1 teaspoon powdered sugar
2 oz. Dry Gin
1 tablespoon sweet cream
½ teaspoon orange flower water
*Shake well with cracked ice and strain into 12 oz.
Tom Collins glass. Fill with carbonated water and stir.*

RHINE WINE CUP

4 teaspoons powdered sugar
6 oz. carbonated water
½ oz. Triple Sec
½ oz. Curaçao
2 oz. Brandy
1 pint Rhine Wine
*Fill large glass pitcher with cubes of ice. Add all above
ingredients. Stir well and decorate with as many fruits
as available and also rind of cucumber inserted on
each side of pitcher. Top with small bunch of mint
sprigs. Serve in 5 oz. claret glasses.*

ROB ROY COCKTAIL

¾ oz. Sweet Vermouth
1½ oz. Scotch
1 dash orange bitters
*Stir well with cracked ice and strain into 3 oz. cock-
tail glass.*

ROBERT E. LEE COOLER

Juice of ½ lime
½ teaspoon powdered sugar
2 oz. carbonated water
*Fill 12 oz. Tom Collins glass with above ingredients
and add*
¼ teaspoon Pernod
2 oz. Dry Gin
*Fill with ginger ale and stir again. Insert spiral of
orange or lemon peel (or both) and dangle end over
rim of glass.*

ROCK AND RYE

1 jigger Rye
2 teaspoons Rock Candy Syrup
Serve in whiskey glass.

ROCKETTE

Juice of ½ lemon
1 teaspoon sugar
3 sprigs fresh mint
1½ ounces Vodka
Shake well. Strain and pour in cocktail glass.

it's the fizz
that gets you . . .

A MAN who should be immortalized in every bar, restaurant or any other liquor-selling establishment, was Baltimore druggist, Isaac L. Emerson. A gent who enjoyed the pleasant memories of relaxation over a cup of brew, Mr. Emerson was prone to severe hangovers. While in this state, unlike Alexander, he would retire to the peaceful boundaries of his drugstore and experiment with various chemical mixtures which might relieve his condition.

One night, while his patient wife sat watching him, he mixed a little of just about anything into a glass. It started to fizz and snarled like a steam pipe. He swallowed the mixture. In a little while his head started to clear.

"Mi-God!" he suddenly shrieked. "That was it, but I can't remember what I put in the glass." Mrs. Emerson stood up from her chair and smiled delicately. "I remember," she whispered.

The next morning, Emerson was at the office of the neighborhood bank president. Again, good fortune was with him. The bank head himself was suffering from a hangover. The drink again turned the trick and Emerson got the financing needed to put Bromo Seltzer in business.

The late W. C. Fields suffered daily hangovers, attributed—rumor has it—to a leaning toward Bourbon, Scotch or anything bottled, canned, boxed or even resembling an alcoholic beverage. One bartender once asked the bulbous-nosed Fields if he might fix him a "Bromo." "Good Lord, no!" was the reply, "I couldn't stand the noise."

ROMAN PUNCH

1 jigger Jamaica Rum
½ jigger Brandy
¼ jigger Curaçao
Juice of ½ lemon
2 teaspoons sugar
2 teaspoons raspberry syrup
Port Wine
Shake all ingredients except Port. Pour over shaved ice in highball glass. Decorate with fresh fruit and a Port Wine float on top.

ROSE COCKTAIL (English)

½ oz. Apricot Flavored Brandy
½ oz. Dry Vermouth
1 oz. Dry Gin
½ teaspoon lemon juice
1 teaspoon Grenadine
Shake well with cracked ice and strain into 3 oz. cocktail glass. Frost edge of glass by rubbing with lemon and dipping in powdered sugar.

ROSE COCKTAIL (French)

½ oz. Wild Cherry Flavored Brandy
½ oz. Dry Vermouth
1¼ oz. Dry Gin
Stir well with cracked ice and strain into 3 oz. cocktail glass.

ROYAL COCKTAIL

1 whole egg
Juice of ½ lemon
1 teaspoon powdered sugar
1½ oz. Dry Gin
Shake well with cracked ice and strain into 4 oz. cocktail glass.

ROYAL FIZZ

Juice of ½ lemon
1 teaspoon powdered sugar
2 oz. Dry Gin
1 whole egg
Shake well with cracked ice and strain into 8 oz.
highball glass. Fill with carbonated water and stir.

RUM COBBLER

1 teaspoon powdered sugar
2 oz. carbonated water
Dissolve above ingredients in a 10 oz. goblet. Fill
goblet with shaved ice, and add
2 oz. Rum
Stir well and decorate with fruits in season. Serve
with straws.

RUM COLLINS

Juice of 1 lime
1 teaspoon powdered sugar
2 oz. Rum
Shake well with cracked ice and strain into 12 oz.
Tom Collins glass. Add several cubes of ice, fill with
carbonated water and stir. Decorate with slice of
lemon and a cherry and drop lime in glass. Serve
with straws.

RUM COOLER

½ teaspoon powdered sugar
2 oz. carbonated water
Stir; fill glass with cracked ice and add
2 oz. Rum
Fill with carbonated water or ginger ale and stir
again. Insert spiral of orange or lemon peel (or both)
and dangle end over rim of glass. Use 12 oz. Collins
glass.

RUM DAISY

Juice of ½ lemon
½ teaspoon powdered sugar
1 teaspoon raspberry syrup or Grenadine
2 oz. Rum
Shake well with cracked ice and strain into stein or 8 oz. metal cup. Add cube of ice and decorate with fruit.

RUM EGGNOG

1 egg
1 teaspoon powdered sugar
2 oz. Rum
Fill glass with milk. Shake well with cracked ice and strain into 12 oz. Tom Collins glass. Grate nutmeg on top.

the real spirit of '76

By MICHAEL FAIN

THE sign in the window of a liquor shop in Moscow carries this legend: "Portoriko Rum Made in Hungary—80 rubles per bottle."

Though the sign clearly does not refer to the genuine article, it graphically indicates the extent of the current Rediscovery of Rum. In this country, Rum's new-found popularity spreads from Park Avenue to Hollywood and Vine, as they say, and is America's traditional holiday season liquor, though still strong at other times of the year.

Rum, sometimes called "the Real Spirit of '76," is no stranger in the U. S., however. It's been around since the days of the Virginia and Plymouth colonies. Despite this, many present-day Americans are not well acquainted with Rum, perhaps because there are so many different kinds—almost as many as there are islands in the Caribbean.

When Columbus landed in the New World, he didn't find the makings of grog waiting for him. In fact, it was Columbus himself who first introduced sugar cane. He had brought seedlings along from the Canary Islands. By the time Ponce de Leon left Puerto Rico in search of his Fountain of Youth, sugar plantations were flourishing on the island. Just who made the happy discovery that a spirited drink could be made by fermenting the juice of the sugar cane and distilling it remains obscure. But the fine art of distilling was certainly known to the early Conquistadores and Rum historians credit them with setting up the first stills, probably in Puerto Rico or Hispañola.

In Virginia and Massachusetts, the settlers, badly in need of a warm and heartening spirit, were soon introduced to *Rum-bullion*. Even in those days, we Americans had a penchant for shortening names and Rum-bullion quickly became plain Rum.

Rum was in on the Revolution from the very start. Generous swigs of this invigorating spirit helped inspire the patriots to toss the tea into Boston Harbor. According to Paul Revere's own account of his famous ride, at his very first stop he was served several stirrup cups of old Rum.

George Washington, who was known to enjoy an occasional grog, considered Rum rations a necessity for the Continental Army. In 1777 he protested to Congress that Rum was available "in too small quantities." His complaint was backed by John Hancock who urged that the troops be "fill'd up and regularly supplied" with it.

Much of the lore connected with the Christmas and New Year's holidays takes us back to our roots. Eggnogs, Punches, Hot Buttered Rum and Tom and Jerry have all been a part of the American scene since the days of the tricorn hat.

The Rum Sour, first among the Rum cocktails, actually had its origins much further back in history than other Rum drinks. It was a Yankee adaptation of a favorite of the Spaniards— *"rony limon"* which they sipped from conch shells on the shores of the blue Caribbean.

The fact that all Rum is made from molasses or sugar cane juice leads some to infer that it is sweet. Nothing could be further from the truth. In point of fact, all grain spirits (Whiskey, Gin, Vodka) are made from sugar, the grain being converted to a form of sugar by the cooking process. Some Rums do have a strong molasses-like flavor, notably Jamaican, Barbados, Virgin Island, Demerara and New England. But of all the liquors in the world, none can justly claim a drier and more subtle flavor than the light-bodied Rums of Puerto Rico, Cuba and Haiti.

What kind of Rum should one buy? Most people prefer the light-bodied—it outsells the heavy, strongly flavored Rums ten to one. The light will appeal to you, particularly if your tastes in liquor run to blended whiskey, Scotch, Gin and Vodka. If you're a heavy Bourbon fan, then perhaps the heavy Rums are for you. But remember, their uses are restricted to special drinks and for flavoring. A little goes a long way.

What's the difference between lights and heavies? Much is due to differences in fermentation, distillation and blending. Take, for instance, the Puerto Rican brands which are all produced under strict government supervision. The Puerto Ricans ferment molasses by adding cultured yeast, then distilling in modern column stills which permit running the Rum off at very high proof (over 180). This results in a pure spirit free of impurities that cause unpleasant after-effects and congeners (chemicals) that impart pungent flavor. After this, the raw Rum, colorless at this stage, is aged in white oak barrels for periods from one to ten years or more. They then are blended. When it reaches you, it is a mild 80 proof.

Light-bodied Rums mellow quite rapidly in the barrel. But long ago, the ancestors of present-day distillers learned that the smoothest-sipping liquor results when straight Rums of different ages are "joined in marriage." Therein lies one of the major trade secrets of the producers. Each has his own special blending formula which has been handed down from father to son and zealously guarded along with the recipe for mixing and fermenting molasses. (The reason for the subtle differences between the Rums of various distillers on the same island.)

Heavy Rum is made from molasses fermented naturally (wild yeast) and distilled in pot stills at relatively low proof—about 160 proof. It is well aged, blended and reduced down to about 90 proof, although some rum as high as 150 proof—a dangerously potent potion—is marketed.

What about color? Not a too important factor in Rum. Both the heavies and the light may range from colorless to a deep golden or mahogany. Puerto Rican brands are marketed in "white label" (colorless) and "gold label" (dark). The "white" is an all-purpose Rum excellent for Daiquiris, Rum on the Rocks or Rum Collins. Use "gold" for the Christmas Eggnog.

The best Rums—light and heavy—bear labels with the name of the specific island where they originated. Hence, all Puerto Rican brands have "Puerto Rican Rum" printed conspicuously on the label. Let the buyer beware of cheap, unknown Rums vaguely labeled as to origin. Remember, the word "West Indian" mean only that the Rum came from who-knows-where in the West Indies. If you're a neophyte when it comes to buying Rum, the best advice is to try out several name brands in small quantities and then stick to the ones that appeal to you the most.

Today, people are rediscovering a fact well-known to our forefathers—good Rum blends with most anything: fruit juices, mixers, tea, coffee, milk and a host of other liquors. You don't have to be a mixologist to whip up a delectable Rum concoction. The easiest and certainly the one which im-

parts the true flavor of this rich liquor is Rum on the Rocks—
a jigger of light-bodied Rum, twist of lemon peel, ice and a
splash of soda. After one of these you'll have more than
enough courage to sally forth and make your own Rum dis-
coveries.

RUM FIX

Juice of ½ lemon or 1 lime
1 teaspoon powdered sugar
1 teaspoon water and stir
Fill glass with shaved ice.
2½ oz. Rum
*Use 8 oz. highball glass. Stir well. Add slice of lemon.
Serve with straws.*

RUM HIGHBALL

1 cube of ice
2 oz. Rum
*Fill 8 oz. highball glass with ginger ale or carbonated
water. Add twist of lemon peel, if desired, and stir.*

RUM MILK PUNCH

1 teaspoon powdered sugar
2 oz. Rum
½ pt. milk
*Shake well with cracked ice, strain into 12 oz. Tom
Collins glass and grate nutmeg on top.*

RUM OLD FASHIONED

1½ oz. Rum
1 cube sugar
Dash bitters
*Muddle sugar and bitters in old fashioned glass with
a dash of carbonated water. Add cracked ice, Rum
and twist of lemon peel. Stir. Decorate with half slice
orange, stick of fresh pineapple and maraschino
cherry, if desired.*

RUM RICKEY

1 cube of ice
Juice of ½ lime
1½ oz. Rum
Fill 8 oz. highball glass with carbonated water and stir. Leave lime in glass.

RUM SOUR

Juice of ½ lemon
½ teaspoon powdered sugar
2 oz. Rum
Shake well with cracked ice and strain into 6 oz. sour glass. Fill with carbonated water and stir. Decorate with a half-slice of lemon and a cherry.

RUM SWIZZLE

Made same as GIN SWIZZLE, using 2 oz. Rum.

RUM TODDY

½ teaspoon powdered sugar
2 teaspoons water
Stir in old fashioned glass.
2 oz. Rum
1 lump of ice
Stir again and twist lemon peel on top.

RUM TODDY (Hot)

Put lump of sugar into hot whiskey glass and fill two-thirds with boiling water. Add 2 oz. Rum. Stir and decorate with slice of lemon. Grate nutmeg on top.

RUSSIAN BEAR COCKTAIL

1 oz. Vodka
½ oz. Crème de Cacao
½ oz. sweet cream
Stir well with cracked ice and strain into 3 oz. cocktail glass.

RUSSIAN COCKTAIL

¾ oz. Crème de Cacao
¾ oz. Dry Gin
¾ oz. Vodka
*Shake well with cracked ice and strain into 3 oz.
cocktail glass.*

RYE EGGNOG

1 jigger Rye
1 egg
1 teaspoon sugar
½ pint milk
*Put in shaker with ice and shake well. Strain into
12 oz. goblet. Top with grated nutmeg.*

RYE HIGHBALL

1 cube of ice
2 oz. Rye
*Fill 8 oz. highball glass with ginger ale or carbonated
water. Add twist of lemon peel if desired, and stir.*

RYE OLD FASHIONED

1½ oz. Rye
Cube sugar
Dash bitters
*Muddle sugar and bitters in old fashioned glass with
dash carbonated water. Add cracked ice, Rye and
twist lemon peel. Stir.*

RYE RICKEY

1 jigger Rye
Juice and rind of ½ lime
Fill with carbonated water. Serve over ice in tall glass.

RYE WHISKEY COCKTAIL

1 dash Rye
1 teaspoon simple syrup
2 oz. Rye
*Stir well with cracked ice and strain into 3 oz. cocktail
glass. Serve with a cherry.*

ST. PATRICK'S DAY COCKTAIL

    ¾ oz. Crème de Menthe (Green)
    ¾ oz. Green Chartreuse
    ¾ oz. Irish Whiskey
    1 dash bitters
Stir well with cracked ice and strain into 3 oz. cocktail glass.

SALOME

    ½ jigger Dubonnet
    ½ jigger Italian Vermouth
    2 dashes Pernod
    Ice
Stir. Strain into cocktail glass.

SALTY DOG

    2 oz. Dry Gin
    4 oz. grapefruit juice
Fill 12 oz. Tom Collins glass almost full with shaved ice or ice cubes, and add above ingredients. Add pinch of salt and stir well.

SAN FRANCISCO COCKTAIL

    ¾ oz. Sloe Gin
    ¾ oz. Sweet Vermouth
    ¾ oz. Dry Vermouth
    1 dash bitters
    1 dash orange bitters
Shake well with cracked ice and strain into 3 oz. cocktail glass. Serve with a cherry.

SANDS-MARTIN COCKTAIL

    1 teaspoon Green Chartreuse
    1¼ oz. Sweet Vermouth
    1¼ oz. Gin
Stir well with cracked ice and strain into 3 oz. cocktail glass.

SANGAREE

½ jigger Sloe Gin
½ jigger French Vermouth
Dash carbonated water
3 dashes bitters
A drink made of wine and sugar served in a small bar glass with ice, topped with grated nutmeg; or red wine and water. Also can be made with Whiskey and Gin, Rum or Brandy; or with Ale and Porter, or Stout.

SANTIAGO COCKTAIL

½ teaspoon powdered sugar
¼ teaspoon Grenadine
Juice of 1 lime
1½ oz. Rum
Shake well with cracked ice and strain into 3 oz. cocktail glass.

SAPPHIRE

½ jigger Dry Gin
½ jigger Blue Curaçao
2 teaspoons heavy cream
Shake well with cracked ice. Strain into cocktail glass.

SARATOGA COCKTAIL

2 oz. Brandy
2 dashes bitters
½ teaspoon pineapple syrup
½ teaspoon Maraschino Liqueur
Stir well with cracked ice and strain into 3 oz. cocktail glass.

SARATOGA COOLER

Fill 12 oz. Tom Collins glass with cracked ice. Fill with sarsaparilla. Insert spiral of lemon and dangle end over rim of glass.

SAUCY SUE COCKTAIL

½ teaspoon Apricot Flavored Brandy
½ teaspoon Pernod
2 oz. Apple Brandy
Stir well with cracked ice and strain into 3 oz. cocktail glass.

SAUTERNE COBBLER

3 oz. Sauterne
¼ teaspoon sugar
Fill wine goblet ¼ full with cracked ice. Add sugar, Sauterne, and fill goblet with water. Stir well. Decorate with half slice orange, pineapple, stick, and maraschino cherry.

SAUTERNE CUP

4 teaspoons powdered sugar
6 oz. carbonated water
½ oz. Triple Sec
½ oz. Curaçao
2 oz. Brandy
Fill large glass pitcher with cubes of ice. Add 1 pint of Sauterne. Stir well and decorate with as many fruits as available and also rind of cucumber inserted on each side of pitcher. Top with small bunch of mint sprigs. Serve in 5 oz. wine glasses.

SAVANNAH

1 part orange juice
3 parts Gin
1 teaspoonful Crème de Cacao to each drink
1 egg white to each 2 drinks
Shake.

199

SAZERAC COCKTAIL

Put ¼ teaspoon Pernod into an old fashioned cocktail glass and revolve glass until it is entirely coated with the liquid. Then add
½ lump of sugar
2 dashes bitters
Sufficient water to cover sugar, and muddle well.
2 cubes of ice
2 oz. Whiskey
Stir very well. Add twist of lemon peel. (Best results come from putting glass on ice for a few minutes before using.)

SCARLETT O'HARA

1 part cranberry juice
2 parts lime juice
8 parts Southern Comfort
Shake with crushed ice.

SCOTCH BISHOP COCKTAIL

1 oz. Scotch
½ oz. orange juice
½ oz. Dry Vermouth
½ teaspoon Triple Sec
¼ teaspoon powdered sugar
Twist of lemon peel
Shake well with cracked ice and strain into 3 oz. cocktail glass.

SCOTCH COOLER

2 oz. Scotch
3 dashes Crème de Menthe
Stir into 8 oz. highball glass with ice cubes. Fill with chilled carbonated water and stir.

SCOTCH MILK PUNCH

2 oz. Scotch
6 oz. milk
teaspoon powdered sugar
Shake thoroughly with cracked ice. Pour into 12 oz. Tom Collins glass. Sprinkle with nutmeg.

SCOTCH MIST

Fill old fashioned cocktail glass with shaved ice. Pour in Scotch. Add twist of lemon peel. Serve with short straws.

SCOTCH OLD FASHIONED

Make same as RYE OLD FASHIONED COCKTAIL, except substitute Scotch.

SCOTCH RICKEY

1 cube of ice
Juice of ½ lime
1½ oz. Scotch
Fill 8 oz. highball glass with carbonated water and stir. Leave lime in glass.

They tell the story of the hard-drinking, quick-tempered Texan named Luke who was always getting into trouble because of his low boiling point. Finally, he hit somebody too hard and was sentenced to ten years in prison for manslaughter.

He was put in a lonely cell with no one to talk to—no one to pass the day with. But one day an ant crawled into the cell.

At first, Luke merely studied the movements of the ant. Soon he discovered what scientists have long known—that the ant is a remarkable little fellow with great strength and intelligence.

And so, with a small matchstick, Luke started to train the ant. At the end of a year, he could do somersaults. At the end of five years, he would do a back flip at a signal. Before Luke's term expired, the ant could sit up, dance to a tune whistled by the prisoner and actually count by hitting one tiny foot against the ground as Luke counted.

Finally, the day came when Luke was released from prison. With the ant in a small box in his pocket, he set out into the world, confident that his little friend was his passport to riches.

His first stop was at a small bar. He ordered a drink and then put his little trained ant—the only one of its kind on earth—on the bar and called the bartender.

"Bartender," he began proudly, "see this ant?"

The bartender took a look. "Oh," he said, "I'm sorry, sir!" And smack—down came the huge palm of his hand.

SCOTCH SOUR

1½ oz. Scotch
Juice of ½ lime
½ teaspoon powdered sugar
Shake well with cracked ice; strain into 6 oz. sour glass. Fill with carbonated water and stir. Decorate with orange slices and cherry.

SCOTCH WHISKEY HIGHBALL

1 cube of ice
2 oz. Scotch
Fill 8 oz. highball glass with ginger ale or carbonated water. Add twist of lemon peel, if desired, and stir.

SCREWDRIVER

Put 2 or 3 cubes of ice into 6 oz. glass. Add 2 oz. Vodka. *Fill balance of glass with orange juice and stir.*

SEESAW

Pony of Cognac
3 or 4 dashes of Benedictine
3 or 4 dashes of French Vermouth
1 dash of bitters
Shake well.

SENSATION COCKTAIL

Juice of ¼ lemon
1½ oz. Dry Gin
1 teaspoon Maraschino Liqueur
3 sprigs fresh mint
Shake well with cracked ice and strain into 3 oz. cocktail glass.

SEPTEMBER MORN COCKTAIL

White of 1 egg
1½ oz. Rum
Juice of ½ lime
1 teaspoon Grenadine
Shake well with cracked ice and strain into 4 oz. cocktail glass.

SEVENTH HEAVEN COCKTAIL

2 teaspoons grapefruit juice
½ oz. Maraschino Liqueur
1¼ oz. Dry Gin
Shake well with cracked ice and strain into 3 oz. cocktail glass. Decorate with sprig of fresh mint.

SEVILLA COCKTAIL

½ teaspoon powdered sugar
1 egg
1 oz. Port Wine
1 oz. Rum
Shake well with cracked ice and strain into 4 oz. cocktail glass.

SHAMROCK COCKTAIL

1½ oz. Irish Whiskey
½ oz. Dry Vermouth
1 teaspoon Crème de Menthe (Green)
Stir well with cracked ice and strain into 3 oz. cocktail glass. Serve with an olive.

SHANDY GAFF

5 oz. Beer
5 oz. Ginger Ale
Use 12 oz. Tom Collins glass and stir very gently.

SHANDY TANG

One half English beer or ale
One half lemon soda
Serve cold, no ice.

SHANGHAI COCKTAIL

Juice of ¼ lemon
1 teaspoon Anisette
1 oz. Jamaica Rum
½ teaspoon Grenadine
Shake well with cracked ice and strain into 3 oz. cocktail glass.

SHERRY AND EGG COCKTAIL

Place an egg in a glass, being careful not to break the yolk. Fill glass with Sherry. Use 4 oz. cocktail glass.

SHERRY COBBLER

Dissolve:
1 teaspoon powdered sugar
2 oz. carbonated water
Fill goblet with shaved ice; add
3 oz. Sherry Wine
Stir well and decorate with fruits in season. Serve with straws.

SHERRY COCKTAIL

2½ oz. Sherry Wine
1 dash bitters
Stir well with cracked ice and strain into 3 oz. cocktail glass. Twist of orange peel and drop in glass.

SHERRY EGGNOG

1 egg
1 teaspoon powdered sugar
3 oz. Sherry Wine
Fill glass with milk. Shake well with cracked ice and strain into 12 oz. Tom Collins glass. Grate nutmeg on top.

SHERRY FLIP

1 egg
1 teaspoon powdered sugar
1¼ oz. Sherry Wine
2 teaspoons sweet cream (if desired)
Shake well with cracked ice and strain into 5 oz. flip glass. Grate a little nutmeg on top.

SHERRY SANGAREE

Dissolve ½ teaspoon powdered sugar in 1 teaspoon of water. Add
2 oz. Sherry Wine
Serve in 8 oz. highball glass with 2 cubes of ice. Fill balance with soda water. Stir, leaving enough room on which to float a tablespoon of Port Wine. Sprinkle lightly with nutmeg.

SIDEBOARD TODDY

Muddle 1 lump of sugar with 1 pinch of nutmeg in an old fashioned glass.
Pour 1 oz. carbonated water and 2 oz. Bourbon over two ice cubes. Serve with silver spoon.

SIDECAR COCKTAIL

Juice of ¼ lemon
½ oz. Triple Sec
1 oz. Brandy
Shake well with cracked ice and strain into 3 oz. cocktail glass.

SILVER COCKTAIL

1 oz. Dry Vermouth
1 oz. Dry Gin
2 dashes orange bitters
¼ teaspoon simple syrup
½ teaspoon Maraschino Liqueur
Stir well with cracked ice and strain into 3 oz. cocktail glass. Twist of lemon peel and drop into glass.

SILVER FIZZ

Juice of ½ lemon
1 teaspoon powdered sugar
2 oz. Dry Gin
White of 1 egg
Shake well with cracked ice and strain into 8 oz. highball glass. Fill with carbonated water and stir.

SINGAPORE SLING

Juice of ½ lemon
1 teaspoon powdered sugar
2 oz. Dry Gin
½ oz. Wild Cherry Flavored Brandy
Shake well with cracked ice and strain into 12 oz. Tom Collins glass. Add ice cubes and fill with carbonated water; stir. Decorate with fruits in season and serve with straws.

SIR WALTER COCKTAIL

¾ oz. Rum
¾ oz. Brandy
1 teaspoon Grenadine
1 teaspoon Curaçao
1 teaspoon lemon juice
Shake well with cracked ice and strain into 3 oz. cocktail glass.

SKIDMORE '54 COCKTAIL

¼ oz. orange juice
¼ oz. Dubonnet
¾ oz. Dry Vermouth
¾ oz. Whiskey
Shake well with cracked ice and strain into 3 oz. cocktail glass.

SLING

1 jigger Liquor
Lump of sugar
Nutmeg
1 teaspoon water
1 twist lemon peel
Use preferred liquor. Serve in whiskey glass. Dissolve sugar in water, add liquor and lemon peel, grated nutmeg on top.

SLOE GIN COLLINS

Juice of ½ lemon
2 oz. Sloe Gin
Shake well with cracked ice and strain into 12 oz. Tom Collins glass. Add several cubes of ice, fill with carbonated water and stir. Decorate with slice of lemon, orange and a cherry. Serve with straws.

SLOE GIN FIZZ

Juice of ½ lemon
1 teaspoon powdered sugar
2 oz. Sloe Gin
Shake well with cracked ice and strain into 8 oz. highball glass. Fill with carbonated water and stir. Decorate with slice of lemon.

SLOE GIN FLIP

1 egg
1 teaspoon powdered sugar
½ oz. Sloe Gin
2 teaspoons sweet cream (if desired)
Shake well with cracked ice and strain into 5 oz. flip glass. Grate a little nutmeg on top.

SLOE GIN RICKEY

1 cube of ice
Juice of ½ lime
2 oz. Sloe Gin
Fill 8 oz. highball glass with carbonated water and stir. Leave lime in glass.

SLOPPY JOE'S COCKTAIL NO. 1

Juice of 1 lime
¼ teaspoon Curaçao
¼ teaspoon Grenadine
¾ oz. Rum
¾ oz. Dry Vermouth
*Shake well with cracked ice and strain into 3 oz.
cocktail glass.*

SLOPPY JOE'S COCKTAIL NO. 2

¾ oz. pineapple juice
¾ oz. Cognac
¾ oz. Port Wine
¼ teaspoon Curaçao
¼ teaspoon Grenadine
*Shake well with cracked ice and strain into 3 oz.
cocktail glass.*

SMASH (A Miniature Julep)

1 jigger Liquor
Few mint leaves
1 teaspoon water
1 lump of sugar
*Serve in old fashioned glass. Muddle sugar, water,
mint leaves in bottom of glass. Add liquor and 1 cube
of ice. Stir. Smashes are also made with Bourbon,
Applejack, Brandy, etc.*

SNOOTY FOX DAIQUIRI

Juice of half lemon and half orange
Dash of Falernum and a dash of banana liqueur
2 oz. light rum
Shake well and serve.

SOUTH SIDE COCKTAIL

Juice of ½ lemon
1 teaspoon powdered sugar
2 sprigs fresh mint
1½ oz. Dry Gin
*Shake well with cracked ice and strain into 3 oz. cock-
tail glass.*

SOUTH SIDE FIZZ

Juice of ½ lemon
1 teaspoon powdered sugar
2 oz. Dry Gin
*Shake well with cracked ice and strain into 7 oz.
highball glass. Fill with carbonated water and stir.
Add fresh mint leaves.*

SOUTHERN BEAUTY (Non-alcoholic)

Juice of ½ lime
1 egg white
2 dashes bitters
*Shake vigorously with crushed ice and pour into cock-
tail glass.*

SOUTHERN GIN COCKTAIL

2 oz. Dry Gin
2 dashes orange bitters
½ teaspoon Curaçao
*Stir well with cracked ice and strain into 3 oz. cock-
tail glass. Twist of lemon peel and drop into glass.*

SPRITZER HIGHBALL

Pour 3 oz. chilled Rhine Wine *or* Sauterne *into 8 oz.
highball glass with ice cubes. Fill balance with carbonated water and stir gently.*

STINGER

1 oz. Crème de Menthe (White)
1 oz. Brandy
*Shake well with cracked ice and strain into 3 oz.
cocktail glass.*

STINGERING

1 part Bourbon
1 part Green Chartreuse
Shaved ice
*Stir Bourbon, Chartreuse and shaved ice. Strain into
saucer champagne glass and serve.*

TEMPTATION COCKTAIL

1½ oz. Whiskey
½ teaspoon Curaçao
½ teaspoon Pernod
½ teaspoon Dubonnet
1 twist orange peel
1 twist lemon peel
Shake well with cracked ice and strain into 3 oz. cocktail glass.

TEQUILA STRAIGHT

½ lemon
Pinch of salt
1 jigger Tequila
First suck lemon, place salt on tongue, then swallow Tequila.

TEQUILA COCKTAIL

1½ oz. Tequila
½ oz. Dry Vermouth
1 dash bitters may be added
Stir well with cracked ice and strain into 3 oz. cocktail glass. Twist lemon peel and drop into glass.

TEQUINI

A Martini made with Tequila instead of Gin. Serve with a twist of lemon peel.

THIRD RAIL COCKTAIL

¾ oz. Rum
¾ oz. Apple Brandy
¾ oz. Brandy
¼ teaspoon Pernod
Stir well with cracked ice and strain into 3 oz. cocktail glass.

TIGER SPECIAL

2 oz. Light Rum
½ oz. Cointreau
Juice of ½ lime
Ice
Shake well, and strain into cocktail glass.

T. N. T. COCKTAIL

1¼ oz. Whiskey
1¼ oz. Pernod
Stir well with cracked ice and strain into 3 oz. cocktail glass.

TODDIES

1 oz. sugar syrup
3 oz. Liquor
2 or 3 cloves
1 dash ground cinnamon or small stick cinnamon bark
1 dash ground nutmeg
1 thin slice lemon
Combine all ingredients except the nutmeg in a highball glass or goblet. Fill glass with hot or cold water and sprinkle nutmeg over the top.
Popular toddies include Applejack, Brandy, Gin, Irish, Rum, Scotch or Whiskey.

Jerry Thomas, the world's greatest bartender

A LONG the wall of the El Dorado in San Francisco, across
from the private booths, was a bar and here worked Jerry
Thomas, who eventually became known as the Professor and
in later years received the accolade "Michelangelo of all Bartenders" from visiting bon vivants. In front of an audience of
prospectors one bitter afternoon, Jerry decided to put on a little
show. He took down two silver mugs and poured a jigger of
Scotch into one, along with an equal amount of boiling water.
Then he struck a match and set fire to the contents. As the
curious crowd grew larger, he tossed the flaming contents from
one silver mug to the other, then smothered the flames, stirred
in some sugar, added a twist of lemon peel and set the drink
down before one of his audience. A husky miner grabbed the
mug and swallowed the contents in a series of quick gulps.
He slammed the container down on the bar, shuddered violently, and bellowed, "M-a-a-n-n ! That wuz good!

In later years, Jerry Thomas went into vaudeville, eventually
forming a partnership with the famed Lew Dockstader in a
touring minstrel show. Whenever show business slowed down,
he'd return to his bartending and one day, at the Planter's
House in St. Louis, he concocted the popular Tom and Jerry.
San Francisco was Thomas' chosen home, however, and he
eventually returned to the city to take a job at the bar of the
Occidental Hotel. He was a bigger attraction than nearly any
vaudeville entertainer of the day, and at least once or twice a
night, at the insistence of the Occidental clientele, would pause
in his duties to make a few new mixed drinks for an appre-
ciative audience.

*From "On the House" by Matty and Don Simmons.
Published by Coward-McCann, 1955.*

TOM AND JERRY

First prepare batter, using mixing bowl. Separate the yolk and white of 1 egg, beating each separately and thoroughly. Then combine both, adding enough superfine powdered sugar to stiffen. Add to this 1 pinch of baking soda and ¼ oz. Rum to preserve the batter. Then add a little more sugar to stiffen. To serve, use hot Tom and Jerry mug, using 1 tablespoon of above batter, dissolved in 3 tablespoons hot milk. Add 1½ oz. Rum. Then fill mug with hot milk within ¼ inch of top of mug and stir gently. Then top with ½ oz. Brandy and grate a little nutmeg on top.
The secret of a Tom and Jerry is to have a stiff batter and a warm mug.

TOM COLLINS

Juice of ½ lemon
1 teaspoon powdered sugar
2 oz. Dry Gin
Shake well with cracked ice and strain into 12 oz. Tom Collins glass. Add several cubes of ice, fill with carbonated water and stir. Decorate with slice of lemon, orange and a cherry. Serve with straws.

TOVARICH COCKTAIL

1½ oz. Vodka
¾ oz. Kümmel
Juice of ½ lime
Shake well with cracked ice and strain into 3 oz. cocktail glass.

TRANQUILIZER

Jigger of Bourbon with dash of sweetened lime juice. Stir and serve on the rocks.

TRILBY COCKTAIL

1½ oz. Whiskey
¾ oz. Sweet Vermouth
2 dashes orange bitters
Stir well with cracked ice and strain into 3 oz. cocktail glass.

TRINITY COCKTAIL

¾ oz. Sweet Vermouth
¾ oz. Dry Vermouth
¾ oz. Dry Gin
Stir well with cracked ice and strain into 3 oz. cocktail glass.

TROPICAL COCKTAIL

¾ oz. Crème de Cacao
¾ oz. Maraschino Liqueur
¾ oz. Dry Vermouth
1 dash bitters
Stir well with cracked ice and strain into 3 oz. cocktail glass.

TULIP COCKTAIL

¼ oz. lemon juice
¼ oz. Apricot Flavored Brandy
¾ oz. Sweet Vermouth
¾ oz. Apple Brandy
Shake well with cracked ice and strain into 3 oz. cocktail glass.

TURF COCKTAIL

¼ teaspoon Pernod
2 dashes bitters
1 oz. Dry Vermouth
1 oz. Dry Gin
Stir well with cracked ice and strain into 3 oz. cocktail glass. Twist of orange peel and drop in glass.

TUXEDO COCKTAIL

*The Living Room
Chicago, Ill.*

1¼ oz. Dry Gin
1¼ oz. Dry Vermouth
¼ teaspoon Maraschino Liqueur
¼ teaspoon Pernod
2 dashes orange bitters
Stir well with cracked ice and strain into 3 oz. cocktail glass. Serve with a cherry.

TWIN SIX COCKTAIL

1 oz. Dry Gin
½ oz. Sweet Vermouth
¼ teaspoon Grenadine
½ orange juice
White of 1 egg
Stir well with cracked ice and strain into 4 oz. cocktail glass.

TWISTER

2 oz. Vodka
Juice of ⅓ lime
Pour into 12 oz. Tom Collins glass. Add several cubes of ice, drop rind into glass. Fill with Seven-Up and stir well.

TWO RUTHS

1 jigger Light Rum
Juice of ½ lemon
½ jigger pineapple juice
½ jigger Apricot Brandy
Shaved ice
Mix in electric mixer, and serve frappéd in cocktail glass.

UNION JACK COCKTAIL

¾ oz. Crème de Yvette
1½ oz. Dry Gin
½ teaspoon Grenadine
Shake well with cracked ice and strain into 3 oz. cocktail glass.

VALENCIA COCKTAIL

½ oz. orange juice
1½ oz. Apricot Flavored Brandy
2 dashes orange bitters
Shake well with cracked ice and strain into 3 oz. cocktail glass.

VANDERBILT COCKTAIL

¾ oz. Wild Cherry Flavored Brandy
1½ oz. Brandy
1 teaspoon simple syrup
2 dashes bitters
Stir well with cracked ice and strain into 3 oz. cocktail glass.

VERMOUTH CASSIS

¾ oz. Crème de Cassis
1½ oz. Dry Vermouth
1 cube of ice
Fill 8 oz. highball glass with carbonated water and stir.

VERMOUTH COCKTAIL

1 oz. Dry Vermouth
1 oz. Sweet Vermouth
1 dash orange bitters
Stir well with cracked ice and strain into 3 oz. cocktail glass. Serve with a cherry.

VIRGIN

½ jigger Gin
½ jigger Crème de Menthe
½ jigger Forbidden Fruit Liqueur
Ice
Shake well. Strain into cocktail glass. Decorate with maraschino cherry.

VODKA AND APPLE JUICE

Put in 2 or 3 cubes of ice into 6 oz. glass. Add 2 oz. Vodka. Fill balance of glass with apple juice and stir.

VODKA AND TONIC

2 oz. Vodka
Cube of ice
Lemon or lime
Use Tom Collins glass and fill balance with quinine water, squeeze in lemon or lime and stir. Drop slice of lemon in glass.

VODKA COOLER

Same as GIN COOLER except use Vodka instead of Gin.

VODKA DAISY

Juice of ½ lemon
½ teaspoon powdered sugar
1 teaspoon Grenadine
2 oz. Vodka
Shake well with cracked ice and strain into stein or 8 oz. metal cup. Add cube of ice and decorate with fruit.

VODKA GIMLET

1½ oz. Vodka
Juice of ½ lime
Stir well with cracked ice and strain into 3 oz. cocktail glass.

VODKA GRASSHOPPER COCKTAIL

¾ oz. Vodka
¾ oz. Crème de Menthe (Green)
¾ oz. Crème de Cacao (White)
Shake well with cracked ice and strain into 3 oz. cocktail glass.

VODKA GYPSY COCKTAIL

1½ oz. Vodka
¾ oz. Benedictine
1 dash bitters
Stir well with cracked ice and strain into 3 oz. cocktail glass.

VODKA SOUR

Juice of ½ lemon
½ teaspoon powdered sugar
2 oz. Vodka
Shake well with cracked ice and strain into 6 oz. sour glass. Fill with carbonated water and stir. Decorate with half-slice of lemon and a cherry.

VODKA STINGER

1 oz. Vodka
1 oz. Crème de Menthe (White)
Shake well with cracked ice and strain into 3 oz. cocktail glass.

the drink
you cannot see
... or taste

By ANDREW BARTON

NOT long ago, a pretty young thing with a tumbling cascade of golden curls ordered a drink in the Colony. She said to the waiter, "Give me a Vodka Martini, very dry. Don't put any water in it."

This story may not be true, but it wouldn't surprise anybody if it were. Vodka is the restaurant industry's Barbra Streisand —or more so. Its rise in popularity is so astonishing that leaders of the restaurant and liquor industry are still gaping in wonderment. Twenty years ago, Vodka was listed in the industry's annual sales in total anonymity, as part of the 2.3% sales of "miscellaneous liqueurs." Today, Vodka accounts for roughly 14% of the entire alcoholic beverage sales in the United States.

The liquor industry's experts, although they may try to disguise it, are in some confusion as to why Vodka has become so popular, but there are some general observations—and rather interesting ones—which can be made.

Vodka tastes good because it doesn't taste at all. Vodka is (no matter what your bartender tells you) nothing but alcohol diluted with water. Brandy has flavor which is inherent in the grapes from which it is pressed. Whiskey derives its flavor from the character of the grains used in its manufacture.

Vodka, on the other hand, is not only produced as a flavorless liquor—it is also colorless—but it is then subjected to a further purifying process in which it is drained through charcoal, which would take away any telltale flavor it might have had. Vodka is almost surgically pure. For a manufacturer of Vodka to be able to sell his product is just as contradictory as it would be for a man selling orange juice to boast that his product had no taste. Contradictory as this state of affairs may appear, it is none the less the fact and Vodka manufacturers are highly amused when writers on the subject of Vodka speak of its flavor.

This is not to decry Vodka in any sense of the word. The very fact that Vodka is bland is the thing which makes it so palatable to so many people. Bread is bland too, and lots of people seem to spend lots of time eating bread.

Vodka is superbly suited for blending with almost anything, whereas drinks of heavier body are not so adaptable. There is no kind of fruit juice or mix into which Vodka doesn't fit like a dream. You can put it into orange juice, thus making the now-celebrated Screw Driver. You can put it into tomato juice, thus producing the even more celebrated Bloody Mary. You can mix it with Vermouth to make a Dry Martini ("Please don't put any water in it"), or it can be served by itself on the rocks, or El Rocco, as they say in Mexico City.

Vodka, as an American phenomenon, began where many another American phenomena began, i.e., Hollywood. (One Vodka manufacturer, at a recent convention remarked wryly, "The only really American thing in America is Vodka," a remark previously attributed to Coca Cola). A Hollywood restaurant called The Cock 'N Bull, which was built to resemble an English pub, decided to feature ginger beer, which is an English version of our familiar ginger ale. The owner experimented with various alcoholic ingredients and discovered that the most pleasing was Vodka. At that point, the Vodka supply in the United States consisted of maybe enough to satisfy a few white Russian immigrants and perhaps a Pole or two. However, The Cock 'N Bull proceeded with its innovation and it caught on. People liked the ginger beer and Vodka mixture. The Cock 'N Bull christened it the Moscow Mule. In a short time, the state of California was consuming what in those days were mountainous quantities of Vodka. People began buying Vodka for home use. They rapidly discovered that it could be mixed with things other than ginger beer. People in the liquor industry thought that this Vodka craze, then confined almost entirely to California, would pass as so many previous California crazes had passed. But as it turned out, it didn't—and as of now, most of the major distillers in the country make Vodka.

Vodka is a unique beverage in other respects than its lack of flavor. For one thing, it can be made from almost any kind of base. In Russia, it is made from potatoes, and in Poland from a combination of potatoes and grain, and in this country from grain alone. Khrushchev may not like to hear this, but American Vodka is infinitely superior to Russian Vodka. It is also infinitely cheaper, since Russian Vodka, being a state monopoly and therefore, subject to brutally heavy taxes, costs about $9 a bottle. Vodka is unique also, in that it comes, unlike other drinks, in two strengths—80 proof and 100 proof. All the Scottish whisky in this country is 86 proof. (In Scotland it is 80 proof, for some reason probably obscured in the mists of Highland history.) Gin varies sometimes from 90 proof to 94 proof, but only Vodka comes in two types. If you order Vodka in a restaurant, you will invariably get the 80 proof because this is cheaper, since taxes on alcoholic beverages are based upon alcoholic content and thus the 100 proof is more costly.

Leaders in the liquor industry, in observing the Vodka sky-rocket, discovered something which most surprised them, and that is that lots of people don't like the taste of whiskey or Gin or any of the traditional form of drink. This particularly applied to some who are quite pleased with the glow of satis-faction that the drink could give them but weren't at all inter-ested in the somewhat heavy flavor of the traditional drinks. Secondly, since we vaguely regard orange juice as full of nut-brown goodness and health, the Vodka Screwdriver, a drink of which orange juice is an ingredient, seems less wicked to many people than a highball or a conventional cocktail.

It is an interesting question which nobody in the business seems to be able to answer: What ever happened to the man who now orders a Vodka Martini rather than a Gin Martini? Did the people who make Gin lose a Gin drinker? The answer seems to be that they did not; but the Vodka people gained a man who perhaps didn't drink at all before; and this applies particularly to women, who love Vodka, and to lower age groups, especially those in their twenties who regard Vodka as chic which, in most fashionable restaurants today, it most certainly is. Actually, although Vodka has a reputation for laying strong men out in the manner of a tornado, it is not a particularly lethal drink. It couldn't be, obviously, because most Vodka at 80 proof is weaker in alcohol content than other drinks. This is another reason why women drinkers and younger people like it. You can drink Vodka and survive, whereas a drink of 100 proof Bourbon can be about as gentle as a hurricane.

For those who care, Vodka may be one of the most historic of mankind's alcoholic beverages. It is so old that nobody knows how old it is, but it may be said to antedate even poteen, which was the ancient Gaelic distilled drink now grown up to what we call Scottish whisky. Vodka, since its birth, probably in Poland, but perhaps in Russia, always was an aristocratic drink, although in its various forms it was part of the life of the less weathy people.

It took a long time for Vodka to travel from the steppes of Eastern Europe to the steps of the Copacabana, but it made the journey with some glory. It seems inescapable that Vodka is here to stay.

VOLCANO

Stampler's Filet Mignon
New York, N. Y.

1 part lemon juice
1 part Vodka
1 part Southern Comfort
1 dash Grenadine
Stir well with cracked ice and strain into cocktail glass.

WAIKIKI

1 jigger Gin
1 oz. orange juice
1 oz. pineapple juice
Dash lemon juice
Dash bitters
Powdered sugar
Ice
Shake and strain into cocktail glass. Serve with fresh pineapple stick.

WALLICK COCKTAIL

1¼ oz. Dry Vermouth
1¼ oz. Dry Gin
1 teaspoon Curaçao
Stir well with cracked ice and strain into 3 oz. cocktail glass.

WARD EIGHT

Juice of ½ lemon
1 teaspoon powdered sugar
1 teaspoon Grenadine
2 oz. Whiskey
Shake well with cracked ice and strain into 8 oz. stem glass previously prepared with 2 cubes of ice, slice of orange, lemon and a cherry. Serve with straws.

WASHINGTON COCKTAIL

1½ oz. Dry Vermouth
¾ oz. Brandy
2 dashes bitters
½ teaspoon simple syrup
Stir well with cracked ice and strain into 3 oz. cocktail glass.

WHISKEY COBBLER

1 teaspoon powdered sugar
2 oz. carbonated water
Fill goblet with shaved ice; add
2 oz. Whiskey
Stir well and decorate with fruits in season. Serve with straws.

WHISKEY COCKTAIL

1 dash bitters
1 teaspoon simple syrup
2 oz. Whiskey
Stir well with cracked ice and strain into 3 oz. cocktail glass. Serve with a cherry.

WHISKEY COLLINS

Juice of ½ lemon
1 teaspoon powdered sugar
2 oz. Whiskey
Shake well with cracked ice and strain into 12 oz. Tom Collins glass. Add several cubes of ice, fill with carbonated water and stir. Decorate with slice of lemon, orange and a cherry. Serve with straws.

WHISKEY DAISY

Juice of ½ lemon
½ teaspoon powdered sugar
1 teaspoon raspberry syrup or Grenadine
2 oz. Whiskey
Shake well with cracked ice and strain into stein or 8 oz. metal cup. Add cube of ice and decorate with fruit.

WHISKEY EGGNOG

1 egg
1 teaspoon powdered sugar
2 oz. Whiskey
Fill glass with milk. Shake well with cracked ice and strain into 12 oz. Tom Collins glass. Grate nutmeg on top.

WHISKEY FIX

Juice of ½ lemon
1 teaspoon powdered sugar
1 teaspoon water and stir
Fill glass with shaved ice and add
2½ oz. Whiskey
Use 8 oz. highball glass. Stir well. Add slice of lemon. Serve with straws.

WHISKEY FLIP

1 egg
1 teaspoon powdered sugar
1½ oz. Whiskey
2 teaspoons sweet cream (if desired)
Shake well with cracked ice and strain into 5 oz. flip glass. Grate a little nutmeg on top.

WHISKEY HIGHBALL

1 cube of ice
2 oz. Whiskey
Fill 8 oz. highball glass with ginger ale or carbonated water. Add twist of lemon peel, if desired, and stir.

WHISKEY MILK PUNCH

1 teaspoon powdered sugar
2 oz. Whiskey
½ pt. milk
Shake well with cracked ice and strain into 12 oz. Tom Collins glass and grate nutmeg on top.

WHISKEY ORANGE

Juice of ½ orange
1 teaspoon powdered sugar
½ teaspoon Pernod
1½ oz. Whiskey
Shake well with cracked ice and strain into 8 oz. highball glass. Decorate with slice of orange and lemon.

WHISKEY RICKEY

1 cube of ice
Juice of ½ lime
1½ oz. Whiskey
Fill 8 oz. highball glass with carbonated water and stir. Leave in glass.

WHISKEY SANGAREE

Dissolve ½ teaspoon powdered sugar in 1 teaspoon of water. Add
2 oz. Whiskey
2 cubes of ice
Serve in 8 oz. highball glass. Fill balance with soda water. Stir, leaving enough room on which to float a tablespoon of Port Wine. Sprinkle lightly with nutmeg.

WHISKEY SOUR

Juice of ½ lemon
½ teaspoon powdered sugar
2 oz. Whiskey
Shake well with cracked ice and strain into 6 oz. sour glass. Fill with carbonated water and stir. Decorate with a half-slice of lemon and a cherry.

WHITE LADY COCKTAIL

White of 1 egg
1 teaspoon powdered sugar
1 teaspoon sweet cream
1½ oz. Dry Gin
Shake well with cracked ice and strain into 4 oz. cocktail glass.

WHITE ROSE COCKTAIL

¾ oz. Dry Gin
½ oz. orange juice
Juice of 1 lime
½ oz. Maraschino Liqueur
Shake well with cracked ice and strain into 4 oz. cocktail glass.

WIDOW'S DREAM COCKTAIL

1½ oz. Benedictine
1 whole egg
Shake well with cracked ice and strain into 4 oz. cocktail glass. Float 1 teaspoon of cream on top.

WIDOW'S KISS COCKTAIL

½ oz. Yellow Chartreuse
½ oz. Benedictine
1 oz. Apple Brandy
1 dash bitters
Shake well with cracked ice and strain into 3 oz. cocktail glass. Strawberry may be served on top.

YALE COCKTAIL

1½ oz. Dry Gin
½ oz. Dry Vermouth
1 dash bitters
1 teaspoon Crème de Yvette
Stir well with cracked ice and strain into 3 oz. cocktail glass.

YANUCK FEVER

½ oz. Dry Vermouth
½ oz. Sweet Vermouth
1¼ oz. Brandy
¼ teaspoon Pernod
1 teaspoon Curaçao
Stir well with cracked ice and strain into 3 oz. cocktail glass.

ZERO MINT

For each serving desired, chill 2 oz. Crème de Menthe (Green) mixed with 1 oz. water in freezing compartment of refrigerator for 2 hours or longer if desired. (Does not have to be frozen). Serve in 3 oz. cocktail glasses.

the day
the beachcomber
invented the Zombie

DON the Beachcomber's is a typically Los Angeles kind of dining place. It is typical because it is unusual. This is the trademark of most restaurants in this city. Here neo-Oriental foods were originated and drinks were born out of experiment and were promptly called Oriental drinks.

One night, a customer complained to Don about a severe hangover. Mr. E. R. Beachcomber told him he had exactly the correct remedy. He walked behind his bar, reached haphazardly for just about every kind of Rum in sight, added a few other ingredients and passed it on to the customer. The gentleman drank it and just sat there staring. "How was it?" Don asked anxiously. "Fine," moaned the customer, "except for one thing: I feel like I'm dead." Naturally the alert proprietor promptly named the drink "The Zombie."

ZOMBIE

> 1 oz. Passion Fruit Nectar
> 1 oz. unsweetened pineapple juice
> Juice of 1 lime
> Juice of 1 small orange
> 1 teaspoon powdered sugar
> ½ oz. Apricot Flavored Brandy
> 2½ oz. Rum
> 1 oz. Jamaica Rum
> *Add cracked ice and agitate for full minute in electric mixing machine (if none available, shake very well in cocktail shaker), and strain into 14 oz. frosted zombie glass. Decorate with square of pineapple and and 1 green and 1 red cherry.*
> *Carefully float ½ oz. 151 proof Demerara Rum and then top with sprig of fresh mint dipped in powdered sugar. Serve with straws.*

NON-ALCOHOLIC "LEGAL" RECIPES AS PREPARED BY WEIGHT WATCHERS® MAGAZINE

BLOODY SHAME

6 oz. tomato juice
Dash of Worcestershire sauce
Dash of pepper
Combine all ingredients; mix well.
Pour over ice cubes in glass.

BENT NAIL

1 quart beef bouillon
2 tablespoons vanilla extract
Vanilla beans to garnish
Combine bouillon and vanilla extract. Let stand at least 1 hour. Serve over ice cubes, garnish with vanilla beans. Makes about 8 servings.

BULL ON THE ROCKS

6 oz. beef bouillon
Dash of Tabasco sauce
Pour bouillon over ice cubes in glass.
Add Tabasco sauce.

CALYPSO COLA

1 teaspoon rum extract
1 pint low-calorie cola-flavored beverage
Lime slices to garnish
Add rum extract to low-calorie beverage. Stir. Pour over ice cubes in glass. Garnish with lime slice. Makes 2 servings.

DOLPHIN'S DELIGHT

4 oz. clam juice
2 oz. tomato juice
1/8 teaspoon celery salt
Pour juices over ice cubes in glass.
Add celery salt.

GRAPEFRUIT JUICE HIGHBALL

1 oz. unsweetened grapefruit juice
4 oz. low-calorie citrus-flavored beverage
Lemon wedge
Pour grapefruit over ice cubes in glass. Add low-calorie beverage. Serve with lemon wedge.

MINT TULIP

2 tablespoons mint leaves
Non-caloric sweetener to equal ¾ cup sugar
24 oz. low-calorie ginger ale
Combine mint leaves and sweetener. Add ginger ale. Let stand at least 30 minutes. Pour over ice cubes in glass. Makes 4 servings.

RHUBARB PUNCH

1½ lbs. rhubarb
1 quart water
Non-caloric sweetener to equal 2 cups sugar
½ cup lemon juice
Few grains of salt
1 quart low-calorie ginger ale
Cut rhubarb in small pieces. Add water and cook until fruit is soft. Add sweetener. Strain through double thickness of cheesecloth. Add lemon juice and salt. Chill. Add ginger ale. Pour into large pitcher or bowl over ice cubes or block of ice. Makes 12 servings.

SAUERKRAUT JUICE COCKTAIL

1 tablespoon lemon juice
⅛ teaspoon caraway seeds
4 oz. sauerkraut juice
Combine lemon juice and caraway seeds in glass. Add ice cubes, then sauerkraut juice. Stir well.

THIN 'N TONIC

6 oz. low-calorie quinine water
Lime slice
Pour quinine water over ice cubes in glass. Squeeze juice from lime slice into drink, then add slice.

snack
recipes

THE recipes on the following pages should brighten nearly any party or gathering and also make for some interesting midnight raids on the refrigerator. They are by no means a complete selection, but there are some unusual offerings here; some so unusual that they have never been published before.

It has been said elsewhere in this book that food along with drink will make drinking more pleasurable and less volatile. We recommend that you try some of these dishes.

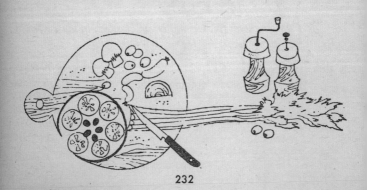

AVOCADO SPEARS

1 Avocado
Lemon juice
Garlic salt
¼ cup Soy Sauce

Halve and peel avocado. Sprinkle with lemon juice. Cut in cubes. Place on platter around small bowl in center containing soy sauce. Sprinkle avocado with garlic salt. Serve with toothpicks to dip cubes in soy sauce.

BEAN APPETIZER

*Omar Khayyam Restaurant
Washington, D.C.*

1 lb. dry Chick Peas
1 cup Sesame Seed or Peanut Oil
1 clove Garlic, minced
1 teaspoon Salt
⅛ teaspoon Cayenne Pepper
4 tablespoons Lemon Juice

Wash the chick peas, cover with water and bring to a boil. Let soak 1 hour. Drain and add fresh water to cover. Cook until very soft, about 2 hours. Drain. Combine the chick peas with the oil, garlic, salt cayenne pepper and lemon juice. Mash until very smooth. Taste for seasoning and chill. Serve with crisp crackers as a spread.
Makes about 3½ cups.

CANAPÉS BACCARA

Baccara Restaurant
New York, N. Y.

2 Tomatoes, peeled and chopped
2 hard-cooked Eggs
2 Green Peppers, chopped
2 Anchovy Fillets
4 Sardines
¼ cup Tuna Fish
1 teaspoon Salt
¼ teaspoon freshly ground Black Pepper
6 slices White Bread, trimmed
4 tablespoons Butter
½ cup Russian dressing
Worcestershire Sauce

*Drain the tomatoes very well and mix with the eggs,
green peppers, anchovies, sardines, tuna fish, salt and
pepper until very smooth. Heat in a double boiler.
Sauté the bread in the butter until lightly browned on
both sides. Heap the mixture on the toast and spread
with the Russian dressing. Sprinkle with a few drops
of Worcestershire sauce and serve hot. Serves 6.*

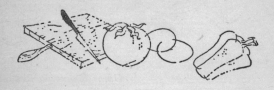

CANAPÉS MARGUERY

4 pieces of Toast
1 hard-boiled Egg
6 Anchovy Fillets
½ Green Pepper
1 peeled Tomato
Tuna fish
1 teaspoon Russian dressing
Worcestershire Sauce

*Make toast with sweet butter in oven until crisp. Mix
and chop other ingredients together and spread on
toast. Add Russian Dressing (or mayonnaise and chili
sauce) .Garnish with a dash of Worcestershire sauce,
serve immediately. Serves two.*

CAVIAR RADISHES

12 large Radishes
1 tablespoon Lemon Juice
1 jar Black Caviar

Wash and hollow out center of large radishes. Fill each one with caviar and sprinkle with lemon juice.

CHEESE SPEARS

8 ¾" cubes Swiss Cheese
8 tiny Gherkin Pickles
8 Walnut halves

Spear cheese cube, walnut and pickle on sturdy toothpicks.

CHICKEN RAJAH FRICASSEE

Two 14 oz. cans of Chicken Fricassee
1 drained 8 oz. can small white Onions
¾ cup drained canned whole kernel Corn
¼ teaspoon Curry Powder
¼ teaspoon Salt
⅛ teaspoon Pepper
1 can refrigerated pan-ready biscuits
Snipped Parsley

In skillet or saucepan with tight-fitting cover, heat chicken fricassee with onions, corn, curry powder, salt, pepper, stirring gently occasionally. When mixture is bubbling hot, place biscuits on top (don't push down into gravy). Cover tightly; simmer 25 min. until biscuits are done. Top with parsley. Serve six.

CHILI CON QUESO

Robin Hood Inn
Albuquerque, New Mexico

(Chili with Cheese)
½ cup finely Chopped Onions
2 tablespoons Butter
1 29-oz. can Tomatoes, well drained
1 can Green Chili, drained and chopped fine
1 lb. Velveeta Cheese

Sauté the onions in the butter for 10 minutes. Add the tomatoes and chili; cook over low heat 15 minutes. Place over hot water and add small amounts of the cheese at a time. Cook until melted and smooth. Serve as a dip with potato or corn chips or fried tortillas. Makes about 4 cups.

CIOFALO'S CAVIAR RITZ

2 oz. Caviar, Black or Red
¼ cup chopped Scallions
½ cup Sour Cream

Serve each ingredient in separate bowls set in ice. Surround with assorted crackers. Each cracker should be spread with caviar, cream and topped with scallions.

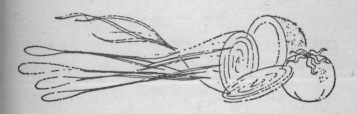

COCONUT CHEESE

3 oz. pkg. Cream Cheese
2 tablespoons Milk
2 tablespoons Shredded Coconut
½ teaspoon Soy Sauce

Thin cheese with milk. Add coconut and soy sauce. Serve with crisp crackers.

CREAMED HERRING

8 oz. jar Herring Fillets
1 sliced Onion
1 pt. Sour Cream
¼ small chopped Apple

Wash brine off fish. Cover with sour cream and freshly sliced onion. Add chopped apple. Serve in large bowl with cream.

CRÊPES

1 cup sifted Flour
1 teaspoon Salt
2 Eggs, beaten
1 cup Milk
2 tablespoons Salad Oil
4 tablespoons Butter

Sift the flour and salt into a bowl. Beat in the eggs, milk and oil until smooth. Chill 1 hour. Heat a little butter in a 7-inch skillet and pour just enough batter in to cover the bottom thinly. Cook until delicately browned on both sides. Stack while preparing the balance.

237

CRÊPES FILLINGS

(See crêpes recipe page 237)   *Colony Restaurant*
                                    New York, N. Y.

Filling #1   2 tablespoons Curry Powder
                  2½ cups Medium White Sauce
                  1 tablespoon Prepared Mustard
                  3 tablespoons Butter
                  16 Shrimp, cooked and diced
                  ¼ lb. lump Crabmeat, diced

*Add curry powder to 1½ cups white sauce. Blend
the mustard into the other cup of white sauce. Keep
hot. Melt butter in a skillet; sauté the shrimp and
crabmeat for 2 minutes. Add half the curry sauce
and cook 3 minutes. Place 2 heaping tablespoons on
each pancake, then fold over 2 sides and roll up in
a tabular shape. Trim the outer edges and place 2
pancakes on each plate with some curry sauce on the
side and mustard sauce on other side. Serves 4.*

Filling #2   3 tablespoons Butter
                  2 tablespoons minced Onion
                  2 tablespoons Flour
                  1½ teaspoons Salt
                  ¼ teaspoon White Pepper
                  1½ cups Light Cream
                  ½ cup grated Gruyère or Parmesan
                  1 lb. lump Crabmeat
                  2 tablespoons Cognac
                  2 teaspoons Curry Powder
                  ¼ teaspoon Pernod
                  ½ cup Whipped Cream

*Melt the butter in a saucepan; sauté the onion 3
minutes. Blend in the flour, salt and pepper. Gradually add the cream, stirring steadily to boiling point.
Cook over low heat 5 minutes. Remove ½ cup sauce.
Add cheese to balance and let melt. Reserve.*
*Mix together the crabmeat, Cognac, curry powder,
Pernod, and the ½ cup sauce. Place 2 tablespoons
of the mixture in the center of each pancake; roll up.
Put a pancake in the center of a dinner plate or individual baking dish. Cover with the cheese sauce and
place a dab of whipped cream over it. Broil for 2
minutes or until declicately browned. Serves 4.*

CUCUMBER DILL

2 Cucumbers
1 cup Sour Cream
Salt and Pepper
1 clove Garlic, crushed
2 tablespoons Salad Oil
1 tablespoon Powdered Dill

Slice cucumbers. Combine remaining ingredients and pour over cucumbers. Serve with toothpicks.

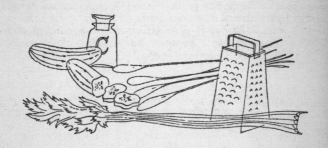

CUCUMBER DIP

8 oz. pkg. Cream Cheese
4 tablespoons Sour Cream
2 tablespoons grated Cucumber
½ cup slivered Almonds

Thin cheese with cream. Add cucumber and almonds. Serve with potato or cheese chips.

CURRIED EGGS

¼ cup Onion
1 tablespoon Oil
1 tablespoon Curry Powder
4 tablespoons Mayonnaise
3 hard boiled Eggs, chopped
3 tablespoons chopped Scallions
2 Celery stalks, chopped
Salt and Pepper

Sauté onion and curry in oil. Strain and add onion to eggs, scallions, celery and mayonnaise. Season to taste.

EGGS ALLA FLORENTINE

Italian Garden
Kansas City, Missouri

3 tablespoons Olive Oil
¼ cup diced Onions
1½ teaspoons Salt
¼ teaspoon freshly ground Black Pepper
1 20-oz. can Tomatoes, strained
1 can (#2) Green Peas
6 Eggs
3 tablespoons grated Romano or Parmesan Cheese
1 tablespoon minced Parsley

Heat the oil in a deep skillet; sauté the onions 10 minutes. Add the salt, pepper and tomatoes. Cook over low heat 20 minutes. Stir in the peas and cook 10 minutes. Carefully break the eggs into the sauce (as for poached eggs). Cook over low heat 20 minutes without stirring. Sprinkle with the cheese and parsley. Serves 6.

FONDUE

1½ lbs. grated Emmental Swiss Cheese
1 clove Garlic
½ pt. White Wine
1 small glass Kirsch
1 teaspoon Cornflour
1 pinch Bicarbonate of Soda
Basketful of bread crusts

Heat the white wine in an earthen chafing dish previously rubbed with garlic. Then add the grated cheese, stirring constantly. As soon as the mixture bubbles add the cornflour (which has been mixed into a paste with Kirsch) and allow to cook for 2 or 3 minutes longer. Add bicarbonate of soda and pepper, nutmeg or paprika for taste. This is better when cooked on a stove and then kept warm at the table as guests eat. Serve each guest with a fork, a plate, a glass and bread crusts. The bread crust is impaled on a fork and used as a stirrer until sopped with Fondue. The Fondue must be kept well stirred to prevent bottom of dish from turning brown. When meal is half-way through serve a small glass of Kirsch. Serves 6-8.

GUACAMOLITOS

El Poche Cafe
San Gabriel, California

3 Avocados
3 Scallions, finely chopped
1 Tomato, peeled and chopped
½ teaspoon minced Garlic
1 tablespoon Salad Oil
1½ tablespoons Lemon Juice
1 teaspoon Salt
1 teaspoon Pepper
1½ teaspoons Chili Powder

Scoop out all the pulp from the avocados (reserve one pit) and mash fine. Add all the remaining ingredients and beat until smooth. Place the pit in the center (to keep avocado from turning color) and chill until needed. Serve with tortillas (available in cans) that have been fried in deep fat. Makes about 2½ cups.

HAM AND CHEESE ROLL

Thin slices of Ham
Roquefort Cheese
Cream Cheese
Tomatoes, fresh
Bread

Mix Roquefort and cream cheese and spread over ham slices. Roll, fasten with toothpicks, place in icebox to chill firm enough to slice. Slice tomatoes, cut bread circles same size as the slices. Toast bread discs, butter, spread thinly with mayonnaise and place a tomato slice on top of each toast disc. Cut ham and cheese roll in thin slices and place one on top of each tomato slice.

HERRING SALAD, SWEDISH STYLE

The Stockholm
Detroit, Michigan

2 Salt Herring Fillets (Iceland, if available)
2 Apples, peeled and diced
3 Potatoes, cooked and diced
1½ cups diced Pickled Beets
⅓ cup diced Onions
2 tablespoons sugar
¼ teaspoon White Pepper
½ cup Cider Vinegar

Soak the herring overnight in water to cover. Drain well and dice. Add apples, potatoes, beets and onions. Mix well. Blend together the sugar, pepper and vinegar. Add to the mixture and toss lightly. Chill. Garnish with chopped hard-cooked eggs and sour cream. Serves 6-8.

HERRING SNACK

1 Cucumber
1 jar Herring Tidbits
Capers

Wash and score cucumbers with fork tines. Cut in ¼ inch slices. Spear 2 capers, herring tidbit on toothpick and secure on cucumber slice.

MASSOLETTI'S CHEESE FONDUE

1 cup scalded Milk
1 cup soft stale Breadcrumbs
1 cup mild Cheese (cut in pieces)
1 tablespoon Butter
½ teaspoon Salt
3 Eggs

Beat together the milk (scalded), breadcrumbs, cheese, butter, salt and the egg yolks. Fold in egg whites beaten until stiff. Pour into a buttered baking dish and bake forty minutes in a moderate oven. Serves 4.

MEAT BALLS, ITALIAN STYLE

*Country House
Minneapolis, Minn.*

1 lb. ground Beef
¼ lb. ground Pork
½ cup diced Bread Crumbs
½ cup minced Parsley
1½ teaspoons Salt
¼ teaspoon freshly ground Black Pepper
⅛ teaspoon Tabasco
1 teaspoon Basil
½ teaspoon minced Garlic
3 Eggs
2 tablespoons grated Parmesan Cheese

Mix all ingredients together until well blended. Shape into walnut-sized balls. Arrange on a greased baking pan. Bake in a 400° oven 30 minutes. Serve hot or cold, on cocktail picks, with cocktail sauce if desired. Makes about 42.

MOZZARELLA SKEWERED WITH CANADIAN BACON

4 12" Skewers
12 ozs. Mozzarella Cheese
12 slices long French Bread, ½" thick
12 ozs. sliced Canadian Bacon (28 slices)
12 slices Tomato, ½" thick
⅓ cup Salad Oil
2 8-oz. cans Tomato Sauce
Grated Parmesan Cheese
Paprika

*Cut 28 slices of cheese into 1" squares about ¼"
thick. Wrap a bacon slice around each piece. Cut
each piece of tomato and bread in half. Heat oil in
a large skillet. Brown bread lightly on both sides.
Put alternate pieces of bacon-wrapped mozzarella,
bread and tomato, starting and ending with the bacon,
on to skewers. Place skewers in a shallow baking pan
or shallow earthenware casserole. Pour tomato sauce
over skewers. Sprinkle with cheese, paprika and oil.
Preheat oven to 400°. Bake until brown on top, and
serve piping hot. Twelve slices.*

OYSTER FRITTERS

6½ oz. can Oysters, well drained
1 packet instant Chicken Bouillon
1 cup cold Water
⅛ teaspoon Salt
⅛ teaspoon Pepper
Dash Cayenne Pepper
3 tablespoons Butter
3 Eggs
1 cup all-purpose Flour
½ teaspoon Baking Powder
2 tablespoons minced Onion
2 tablespoons Green Pepper, minced
Salad Oil

Put water, chicken bouillon and condiments in a small heavy saucepan over a low flame and bring to a boil. Add butter and let melt. Remove pan from flame. Add sifted flour and baking powder mixture. Stir well until smooth. Add eggs, unbeaten and blend into the batter by stirring. Add oysters, green pepper and onion, mixing well. Cover mixture and place in refrigerator until serving time. When ready to make fritters, heat oil to a depth of ¼" in a heavy frying pan. Drop large tablespoons of the mixture into pan. Sauté until browned on both sides. Drain on absorbent paper. Serve with cold Rémoulade Sauce (see page 248).

OYSTERS AND CELERY

2 dozen Oysters
3 Celery stalks
1 glass White Wine

Chop celery and sauté in butter. When tender add oysters and simmer until the edges of the oysters curl. Add wine, season and serve in its own sauce.

OYSTERS AND MUSHROOMS

Fresh Oysters
Large Mushrooms, peeled
Olive Oil or Butter

Take each oyster and place in a peeled mushroom. Dip in olive oil or butter, sprinkle with salt, pepper, paprika and a dash of celery salt. Place under a hot grill. Serve on half shell or a piece of thin toast.

PÂTÉ

1 lb. Butter
1 Onion, chopped
¼ lb. Lard
1 jigger Sherry
1 Laurel Leaf
Salt and Pepper
Dash of Red Pepper
1 jigger Brandy
½ lb. Calf's Liver, diced (soak liver 24 hrs. in cold
   water)

*Brown meat in fat; remove, and sauté onions with
½ lb. butter, lard and sherry. Combine meat, laurel
leaf and seasonings. Mix thoroughly all together and
let simmer slowly for ten minutes. Strain through
cheese cloth or fine wire strainer. Mix in Brandy and
remaining butter.*

*Place in a mold and cover top with a few table-
spoons of clear, dissolved gelatin. Put into refrigerator
and chill until firm. Serve on hot toasted squares, or
crackers. Serves eight.*

PETITE RAREBITS

½ lb. Swiss Cheese, grated
½ lb. American Yellow Cheese, grated
2 Egg Yolks
1 cup rich Cream

*Mix ingredients together. Spread on crackers or toast
cut in rounds. Boil under quick flame and sprinkle
with paprika before serving. Serves four.*

PICKLE DILLIES

Dill Pickles
Grated Cheese

*Use a small-mouthed glass to cut circular pieces of
bread. Put one or two slices of dill pickle on each
bread circle, sprinkle with grated cheese. Bake in
oven until cheese melts. Serve hot.*

PIGS IN CLOVER

Lean Bacon
Large Oysters

Wrap oyster in bacon, sprinkle with salt, pepper, paprika and garlic salt. Secure with toothpick and place under a hot grill. Serve when bacon is done.

PUFFS

1 cup French Dressing (spicy)
Crisp Crackers
1 Egg White

Beat egg white until stiff. Fold in dressing and pile lightly on to crackers. Toast under broiler until lightly browned.

RAMEQUINS DE GRUYÈRE

Swiss Pavilion Restaurant
New York

Pastry for 2-crust pie
1½ cups grated Swiss Gruyère or Swiss Cheese
2 teaspoons Flour
2 Eggs
⅔ cup Milk
⅔ cup Light Cream
1½ teaspoons Salt
¼ teaspoon freshly ground Black Pepper
⅛ teaspoon Nutmeg

Preheat oven to 425°. Line 6 3½" pie plates with the pastry, fluting the edges. (Or a 9" pie plate— and bake 30 minutes longer.) Dredge (toss) the cheese with the flour and divide evenly among the pie plates. Beat the eggs well and add the milk, cream, salt, pepper and nutmeg. Pour over the cheese in even amounts. Bake 10 minutes, then reduce heat to 375° and bake 10 minutes longer or until browned and set. Serve hot as soon as possible.

RAREBIT WITH BEER

  1 lb. American Cheese
  1 cup light Beer
  1 Egg
  Dash of Cayenne
  1 tablespoon English Mustard
  ½ teaspoon Worcestershire Sauce
  Salt
  2 tablespoons Butter

Melt butter in chafing dish, add grated cheese stirring into a paste. Mix seasonings in a cup with a tablespoon of beer; add egg and beat together. Add the beer to the melting cheese a little at a time, stirring for about ½ hour until mixture is thick. When smooth, stir in egg. Egg will thicken slightly. Serve over toasted crackers or toast. Serves 6.

RÉMOULADE SAUCE

  1 cup Mayonnaise
  ¼ cup Sour Cream
  2 tablespoons finely minced Sour Pickle
  2 teaspoons finely chopped Capers
  1 tablespoon finely minced Parsley
  1 teaspoon finely chopped fresh Chervil (or ½ teaspoon dried Chervil)
  2 teaspoons Anchovy Paste
  1 teaspoon Dijon Mustard

Mix ingredients together in a large bowl. Keep chilled. Excellent as a dip for chilled shrimp, lobster chunks, crabmeat, etc.

ROQUEFORT STUFFED SHRIMP

Black Caesar's Forge
Miami, Florida

1½ teaspoon Salt
1 stalk Celery
½ teaspoon Pickling Spice
3 cups Water
2 lbs. large Raw Shrimp
¼ lb. Roquefort Cheese
¼ lb. Cream Cheese
1½ tablespoons Mayonnaise
¾ cup finely chopped Parsley

Buy very large shrimp, about 15 to the pound. Combine the salt, celery, pickling spice and water in a saucepan. Bring to a boil and add the shrimp. Cook over low heat 6 minutes. Drain and cool. Shell the shrimp and remove the black vein. Split halfway through the deveined side and force open slightly. Cream together the Roquefort, cream cheese and mayonnaise. Stuff the shrimp and roll in the parsley. Arrange on a serving dish and pierce with cocktail picks. Makes about 30.

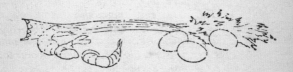

SALMON PLATTER

2 lb. Poached Salmon, cubed
2 Eggs
2 tablespoons Olive or Salad Oil
Salt and Pepper
½ cup Cream
½ teaspoon Worcestershire Sauce
1 tablespoon chopped fresh Dill

Beat eggs and add remaining ingredients, except salmon, beating constantly until well mixed. Place in bowl on platter surrounded with salmon cubes. Serve with toothpicks.

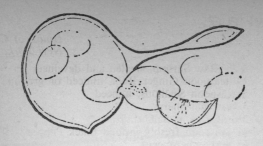

SCRAMBLED EGGS WITH ANCHOVY TOAST

8 Eggs
Salt
White Pepper
8 slices white Bread
6 oz. sweet Butter
2 teaspoons Anchovy Paste
2 teaspoons minced Chives
¼ teaspoon Lemon Juice

Allow 3 oz. butter to stand at room temperature until soft enough to spread easily. Mix with anchovy paste, lemon juice and chives. Put in refrigerator until needed. Beat eggs thoroughly. Add salt and pepper. Melt the remaining butter in a large skillet over a low flame. Add the eggs. Stir frequently until eggs begin to set. Slowly add the remainder of the butter. Continue to cook until eggs are done. Toast the bread in preheated broiler. Spread each piece with anchovy butter. Serve with eggs. Serves 4-6.

SHRIMP MADRID

1 lb. cooked, cleaned Shrimp
1 cup Chicken Stock
½ clove Garlic, minced
Salt and Pepper
4 tablespoons Minced Parsley
1 teaspoon Dry White Wine

Mix all ingredients except shrimp. Serve cold with cold boiled shrimp.

SHRIMP PUFFS

House of Chan
New York, N. Y.

1 lb. Raw Shrimp, shelled and deveined
¼ teaspoon Ginger Root, minced or ground
1 teaspoon Scallions, minced
1 teaspoon Sherry
1¼ teaspoons Salt
⅛ teaspoon freshly ground Black Pepper
⅛ teaspoon Aćcent
30 thin slices White Bread
Fat for deep frying

Grind the shrimp in a food chopper and blend in the ginger, scallions, Sherry, salt, pepper and Aćcent. Mix well, then pick up mixture and slap it down hard on the table several times. Taste for seasoning.

Cut bread in 3-inch rounds with a biscuit cutter. Make sandwiches with the shrimp mixture and press down the edges well. (Mixture will be sticky enough to seal bread.)

Heat the fat to 360° and fry a few sandwiches at a time until browned. Drain and serve hot. Makes about 15.

SHRIMP SIMON

1½ lb. cleaned Shrimp, boiled
½ cup Mayonnaise
½ cup Sour Cream
½ teaspoon Horseradish
2 tablespoons Ketchup
1 tablespoon Durkee's Dressing
1 teaspoon Lemon Juice
⅛ teaspoon Prepared Mustard

Combine all ingredients except shrimp in order indicated. Add chopped parsley, dill, celery or capers, if desired. Chill and serve over shrimp, cooked lobster chunks or crabmeat.

SIMMONS' CAESAR SALAD

(This is not just a Caesar Salad, but our own special Caesar Salad. If you're a nut for salads, like we are, you can make a double portion and consider it a whole meal.)

1 head of Lettuce, (thoroughly washed and chilled)
½ Green Pepper, diced
1 Cucumber, sliced and quartered
½ large Onion, chopped
1 clove Garlic, chopped
2 large Tomatoes, eighthed
2 raw Eggs
1 can flat Anchovies
½ cup oil
¼ cup Vinegar
Salt
Pepper
Grated Parmesan Cheese

Tear lettuce into small pieces. Add other ingredients and toss. Quarter strips of anchovies and toss into mixing bowl. Add vinegar, oil, salt and pepper. Drop in the yolks of two eggs and toss again. Sprinkle cheese on top, mix, add more cheese and mix. Garnish again with cheese. Serves 6 to 8.

SIMMONS' SPECIAL OMELET

(Here's an omelet that's Western, Spanish and Simmons.)

3 Eggs
1 tablespoon Milk
½ rind of Green Pepper
½ Onion
½ Tomato (outside peel only)
1 slice of Baloney or Salami (about 5″ square)
2 slices boiled Ham (about 5″ square each)
Dash of Salt
Dash of Pepper
1 tablespoon Butter

Beat eggs vigorously, adding milk, pepper and salt. Melt butter in 10″ frying pan, making sure to cover entire surface of pan. Cut all other ingredients into one inch squares. Brown meat on both sides. Add green pepper, onion, and tomato to egg mixture and continue beating. Pour mixture slowly into pan and cook until ready.

SLICED STURGEON

Sprinkle white pepper and put a few chopped chives on thin slices of smoked sturgeon (or smoked salmon).

SOUP SANDWICHES

1½ cups Grated Cheese
¾ cup Ham, finely ground
1 can condensed Tomato Soup
1½ teaspoon Prepared Mustard
1½ teaspoon grated Horse Radish

Combine and mix thoroughly. Spread generously on slices of bread or toast. Grill open sandwiches under broiler until lightly browned. Garnish with parsley.

SPREAD SUGGESTIONS

1. Put equal parts of Bermuda onion on Swiss cheese through a meat grinder; spread on buttered bread, cut into small pieces.
2. Fry bacon crisp, let it dry out, then chop it into fine pieces. Mix with peanut butter and spread on crackers.
3. Mix chopped ham, hard-boiled egg and mayonnaise for another good spread.
4. Mix red or black cavair with cottage cheese and a dash of garlic.
5. Mix chopped lobster and crabmeat with mayonnaise and anchovy paste. Spread on unsalted crackers.

STEAK SANDWICHES, SMOTHERED ONIONS

4 8 oz. boneless Shell Steaks
2 large Spanish Onions
3 tablespoons Butter
1 medium-sized Green Pepper
2 teaspoons Meat Extract
¼ cup Dry Red Wine
2 tablespoons Brandy
Salt, pepper, cayenne pepper
4 center slices round Italian Bread

Cut green pepper into long thin strips, removing stem and seeds. Cut onion in half through stem end and then cut crosswise into thinnest possible slices. Melt butter in heavy saucepan over low flame. Add green pepper and onion. Sauté, stirring slowly and frequently until onions are deep yellow. Add meat extract and mix well. Add wine and simmer until wine is reduced to half original amount. Add brandy and seasoning.

Heat a heavy frying pan. Panbroil the steaks (with no added fat) until medium brown on both sides. Dust with salt and pepper. Meanwhile, toast the bread in a preheated broiler. Brush with butter if desired. Place steaks on toast and top wtih smothered onions. Serves 4.

STUFFED CELERY

Celery Hearts
Cream Cheese
Blue Cheese, Crushed Pineapple or Anchovy Paste

Wash and thoroughly dry celery hearts. Leave some green on top. Mix cream cheese with blue cheese or crushed pineapple or anchovy paste to taste. Stuff celery stalks.

STUFFED SHRIMP

Pelican Restaurant
Clearwater, Florida

½ cup Lobster, minced
42 large raw Shrimp, shelled and deveined
¼ lb. Red Snapper or White-meat Fish
¼ cup minced Onion
¼ teaspoon minced Garlic
6 tablespoons Butter
2 tablespoons Lemon Juice
½ cup Flour
1½ teaspoon Salt
⅛ teaspoon Pepper
1 dash Cayenne Pepper
⅛ teaspoon Celery Salt
⅛ teaspoon Nutmeg
¼ cup Light Cream
2 Egg Yolks, beaten
Fat for deep frying

Chop the lobster, 8 shrimp and snapper in very fine pieces. Sauté with the onion and garlic in 3 tablespoons of the butter for 10 minutes, stirring frequently. Melt the remaining butter in a saucepan; stir in 2 tablespoons flour, the salt, pepper, cayenne, celery salt and nutmeg. Gradually add the cream, stirring steadily to the boiling point. Cook over low heat 5 minutes. Add to the egg yolks, stirring steadily to prevent curdling. Blend in the fish mixture and chill. Split the remaining shrimp and stuff with the mixture. Press together firmly. Roll in the remaining flour. Heat the fat to 370° and fry the shrimp in it until browned. Drain and serve at once. Makes about 34 as an hors d'oeuvre, or serves 6-8 as a main course.

TIDBITS

1 large can Pineapple wedges
½ lb. Bacon
1 lb. cooked Shrimp

Wrap ⅓ slice of bacon around each shrimp and pineapple wedge and fasten with a toothpick. Bake in 300° oven until bacon is crisp. Can also be done with lobster and liver.

TOASTED ALMONDS

6 oz. Almonds, unblanched
Salt
Butter

Drop almonds into boiling water for 1 minute. Slip off brown skins and dry almonds. Place in pan with butter and salt in slow oven. Toast until golden, tossing in butter frequently.

TOASTED CRAB MEAT

Crab Meat (fresh or canned)
Chili Sauce
Celery Salt
Pimiento

Mix together and spread on crackers, toast strips, or in pastry shells and bake under the grill for several minutes.

TONGUE TIDBITS

Sliced Tongue
English Mustard
Red Pepper
Olive Oil

Spread mustard, pepper and oil on tongue. Pack the slices together and put in icebox. When ready to serve, separate slices of tongue and fry in butter. Serve hot, on thin slices of bread.

WELSH RABBIT

1 tablespoon Butter
1 cup Ale or Beer
1 lb. Cheddar Cheese, chopped or grated
2 Eggs
¼ cup Milk
1 dash of Salt
2 teaspoons Worcestershire Sauce

Warm the butter and ale in a chafing dish, then add the cheese, stirring over the fire until smooth. Add egg yolks which have been mixed with milk, salt, and Worcestershire Sauce. Stir a few minutes till thickened. Serve on toasted bread. Sprinkle with paprika. Serves six.

WHIPPED DIP

½ cup Heavy Cream, whipped
Crisp Rye Crackers
1 jar Roquefort Cheese spread
Seasoned Salt
Cayenne Pepper

Fold whipped cream into cheese which has been creamed. Add seasonings, chill and serve surrounded by crisp rye crackers.

glossary of drink terms

Absinthe—A green liquor containing oils of wormwood and other aromatics. Absinthe in its original form is contraband in the United States as well as in Switzerland, where it was created, and in France. Its preparation and sale was prohibited because it was believed to be habit-forming, and the cause of nervous disorders as well as sterility. Many drinks contain Absinthe, but it is an absinthe substitute, usually Herbsaint or Pernod.

Advokaat (ahd-vo-kaht)—A blend of egg and Brandy, similar to eggnog; 40 proof.

Alcohol—Usually this means ethyl or beverage alcohol. Pure alcohol (200 proof) is generally man-made and is used only in the laboratory for scientific purposes. Almost-pure alcohol (190 proof) is ordinarily sold as "grain neutral spirits," and can be bought in liquor stores as easily as Gin, whiskey, and other alcoholic drinks in many states.

Aleatico (ah-lay-ah-tee′-co)—This wine is fermented from, and has the spicy, fruity taste of, the Italian Aleatico grape. It is served both as a medium-sweet red table wine and a sweet red dessert wine. It is especially good during or after dessert, or with snacks between meals. Aleatico table wine is also occasionally served with meals. It is equally good chilled or at room temperature.

Amer—A bitter aperitif compounded of Wine and Brandy with additional flavorings. It is served in mixed drinks, or taken with soda, sometimes sweetened with some Grenadine; 78 proof. The first Amer was prepared in France, and is called Amer-Picon.

Amontillado (ah-mon-tee-ya′-do)—A variety of Spanish sherry, ordinarily dry, but occasionally slightly sweet.

Angelica—A white dessert wine of the cordial type. It is sweet; straw or amber-colored; and mild or fruity in flavor. Among the numerous varieties or grapes from which Angelica is made are Mission and Grenache. It is suitable with dessert or at the end of the meal, and with snacks in-between meals. It tastes fine either chilled or at room temperature.

Anisette—A colorless, licorice tasting liqueur flavored with anise seed. It comes in a variety of strengths, from 48 to 92 proof. Some of them are dry, and these include the 92 proof Greek anisette named Ouzo.

Aperitif or Dessert Wine—In this category are all wines which contain over 14% but not more than 21% alcohol. The majority of them are sweet, but the "dessert" group also embraces the "appetizer" wines. These are the Sherries, Madeiras, Marsalas, and the aperitifs like Vermouth and the wines which are new in flavor.

Applejack—An American Brandy distilled from Cider.

Apple Wine, or Cider—Unfermented apple juice. "Hard Cider" stands for fermented Cider, which usually contains from 7 to 11% alcohol. Abroad, Cider (which is sometimes spelled cyder and cidre) indicates that the beverage is fermented. According to law, homemade Hard Cider must not contain more than 7% alcoholic content. In Colonial times, Cider was usually drunk with raisins, other flavorings and sugar added. When Apple Brandy is combined with Hard Cider, it is known as Apple Wine, which is usually 20% in alcohol content.

Apricot Liqueur—Apricot flavored Liqueur combined with a Brandy base. Ordinarily 60 to 80 proof. Some manufacturers give their products proprietary names, like Abricotine or Abry. There are other types of Apricot Brandies, which as a rule are 70 proof.

Aquavit (ak'va-veet) (Nor., Dan., & Sw.—"Water of Life")—A clear Scandinavian brandy made by redistilling neutral spirits, with caraway flavoring.

Aroma—The winy fragrance which stems from the grapes used.

Asti Spumante—A sparkling white Italian wine, like Champagne, but with a spicy flavor.

B & B Liqueur—A blend of Brandy and Benedictine, 86 proof.

Bacchus—A full-bodied fine quality red table wine made from a native small, shiny black grape called Bacchus. It first appeared at Newburgh, New York, during the 1870's. In good years, this wine has little of the "grapey" flavor which is associated, most of the time, with Concord.

Banyuls—A sweet appetizer wine which comes from an area near Banyuls in France.

Barbera (bar-bair'a)—A dry, tart, heavy-bodied red table wine which derives its flavor and fragrance from the Italian Barbera grape. It is especially good with well seasoned foods, and in particular with red meat. This wine tastes best when rather young. Drink it at room temperature, or mildly chilled. This is a Burgundy wine.

Barberone (bar-bair-o'-nay)—A red table wine, similar to Barbera, though not necessarily manufactured from the Barbera grape.

Barolo—A dry, tart red Italian table wine.

Barsac—Similar to Sweet Sauterne. A French white table wine, sweet in flavor.

Beaujolais (bo-zho-lay)—A French dry red Burgundy.

Benedictine—A spicy, golden liqueur which contains a base of angelica oil, blended with dozens of herbs and spices, as well as seeds, honey and brandy; 86 proof. Benedictine is a French proprietary name.

Black Muscat—A spicy red dessert wine made from the Black Muscat grape.

Bordeaux Blanc—French white table wine, either dry or somewhat sweet.

Bordeaux Rouge—A tart, dry French red table wine.

Branch Water—Cold water combined with liquor. This is a southern term, which actually means the water of a small stream.

Burgundy—Red table wine. A rich, dark ruby-red wine with a more definite flavor, body and bouquet than Claret. Medium heavy-bodied. It is made from one or perhaps more of several types of grapes. Among them are Pinot Noir, Carignane, Mondeuse, Refosco, and Petite Sirah. It is particularly popular with red meats, especially game. Serve either somewhat chilled or at room temperature.

Cabernet (kab-er-nay')—Red table wine, made of the best of the Claret wine grapes, Cabernet Sauvignon, from which all of the splendid French Bordeaux wines are fermented. It has an easily recognizable fruity flavor. California Cabernet has a more intense flavor than Claret, but is less strong than Burgundy. Medium bodied. Serve at room temperature.

Calvados—An Apple Brandy made only in Normandy. The Calvados sold in the U.S. generally runs from 90-100 proof, but you can obtain a higher proof Calvados on the Continent.

Campari—An ingredient of highballs, and such cocktails as the Negroni. Italian red bitters.

Caramel—Burnt sugar used as a coloring agent for Rums, Brandies and Blended whiskies. No taste, except that it is mildly bitter.

Carignane (Car-een-yahn')—Claret-type red table wine, fermented from Carignane grapes. It is the principal grape of the Pyrenees in Southern France. It is exceeded in acreage only by Zinfandel in the California wine-growing area.

Catawba—Named after the Catawba River in North Carolina. Very dry, white wine made from the home-grown American Catawba grape. Somewhat tart, the grape yielded the first American Champagne, produced by Nicholas Longworth during the nineteenth century. It was called "Sparkling Catawba."

Chablis (shah-blee')—White table wine. A pale wine, somewhat like Rhine wine, but not so tart. Fruity flavor and body. Derived from one or more types of grape, including Pinot Blanc, Chardonnay, Burger, Golden Chasselas, and Green Hungarian. Particularly delightful with seafood and white meats. Serve chilled.

Champagne (sham-pain)—White table wine. The Champagne process produces the sparkle by means of an additional fermentation of finished wine, which results in a natural effervescence. Champagne is dry, and the label usually says *Brut* (broo); semi-dry, ordinarily called *dry* or *sec;* and sweet, usually marketed with the description *Doux* (doo). Blended of one or several types of grape. These customarily include Pinot Noir, Chardonnay, and Pinot Blanc. Also favored are Folle Blanche, Burger and other light wines. A versatile wine for all occasion. Serve chilled. In addition, there is a pink champagne, often called Oeil de Pehdrix (eul-d' pair-dree').

Charbono (shar-bo'no)—Red table wine. Fermented from the Charbono grape which grows in Italy. It is sometimes mistaken for the hard-to-recognize Barbera, to which Charbono is much superior for wine. Burgundy type.

'Charcoal Mellowed"—When pertaining to whiskey, this phrase means that the liquor has been percolated through charcoal to produce a smoother flavor. However, whiskey so treated may no longer be called "Bourbon" or "Rye."

Chardonnay—Chablis produced from the Pinot Chardonnay grape.

Chartreuse (shar-truz)—A French liqueur prepared from a secret formula which is rumored to call for 130 herbs and spices. Green Chartreuse is 110 proof; yellow Chartreuse is 86 proof.

Chassagne—A French white burgundy.

"Château" Sauterne—Sweet Sauterne.

Chateauneuf-du-Pape (sha-toe-nuf du pap)—A dry, tart red wine which originates in the Rhone Valley of France.

Chenin Blanc (sheh-nan blahnk)—Sweet white table wine produced from the Chenin Blanc grape.

Cherry Liqueur—A variety of cherry-colored, cherry-flavored liqueurs with a base of sweetened Brandy, 49 to 60 proof. The best known is the Danish liqueur Cherry Heering. This is distinctly different from the colorless Cherry Brandy called Kirsch or Kirschwasser, and from Cherry Flavored 70 proof Brandies.

Chianti (kee-ahn-tee)—Dry, tart, red table wine, ordinarily marketed in bottles covered with straw. White Chiantis are also available.

Cider—See Apple Wine.

Claret—Red table wine. Dry, medium-bodied red wine, pleasantly sharp. Claret type wines are the favorite mealtime wines of nearly every country. They are made from one or more of several types of grapes, including Cabernet, Carignane, Mataro, Zinfandel, Mondeuse, Beclan and Charbono. Particularly good with white meats. Serve slightly chilled or at room temperature.

Clos de Vougeot (clo der-voo-zho')—A French red Burgundy.

Cobbler—A warm-weather drink prepared from iced wine and sugar, served in a wine glass, and ornamented with fresh fruit after the ingredients are blended.

Cocktail Sherry—Slightly sweet Sherry.

Coffee Liqueurs—Mainly 53 to 60 proof. Favorites are Kahlua and Tia Maria.

Cointreau Liqueur (kwan-tro)—A colorless, sweet, orange-peel liqueur, known also as Triple Sec. It is 80 proof. Cointreau is a proprietary name and this label is also affixed to other drinks.

Collins—A tall iced drink prepared from spirits, sugar and lime or lemon juice, and served in a 14 oz. glass over ice cubes. Soda water and garnishment is then added.

Cologne spirits—Neutral spirits.

Concord—The most common of all U.S. grapes, since it is very strong and can survive in a cold climate. It is used for a rather ordinary wine, and is often combined with other homegrown grapes to produce Burgundy, Claret, or red table wine. The Concord grape is also used for almost all grape juice in the United States.

Cooler—A tall drink which originally came from Boston. Prepared with lemon juice, sugar, spirits, ice and soda water, and served in a Collins glass.

Cordial—See Liqueur.

Crackling wines—Slightly effervescent wines. Also known as pétillant (French) and frizzante (Italian).

Cream Sherry—Sweet sherry.

Crème d'Ananas—Pineapple liqueur.

Crème de Bananes—Banana liqueur, 56 proof.

Crème de Chocolate—Chocolate liqueur, 52 proof.

Crème de Cacao—A white or brown liqueur, 50 to 60 proof, flavored with cacao and vanilla beans. It is the base of the Alexander cocktail.

Crème de Cassis—A liqueur flavored with black currants, 35 to 50 proof.

Crème de Fraises—Strawberry liqueur.

Crème de Framboises—Raspberry liqueur.

Crème de Mandarine—Liqueur flavored with dried peel of tangerine oranges; 60 proof.

Crème de Menthe—A white, green, or gold liqueur with oil of mint leaves added for flavor. 60 proof. Combined with brandy, it is used in the Stinger Cocktail.

Crème de Noyaux (no-yo)—A liqueur with an almond taste, prepared from crushed apricot, cherry, peach and plum seeds, and containing orange-peel flavoring and a Brandy base. 60 proof.

Crème de Rose—Liqueur flavored with rose petals and vanilla.

Crème de Vanille—Liqueur flavored with rose petals and vanilla flavoring.

Crème de Yvette—A liqueur which has the color and flavor of violets. Sometimes blue.

Cups—Wine drinks, somewhat like punches, prepared with fruits and liqueurs.

Curaçao (cure'-a-so)—An orange-peel liqueur with an intense flavor; yellow-orange, green, blue, or colorless. It is somewhat similar to colorless Cointreau and Triple Sec, except that it is 60 proof, while they are 80 proof.

Dash—⅛ teaspoon, or 1/48 of a fluid ounce.

Decanting—Transferring wine from its original bottle, into a new container, to free the wine from the sediment.

Delaware—America's top quality native white wine grape. It is a tiny, red, extremely sweet grape, and provides clean, fresh and fruity wine, with a spicy and pleasing bouquet. The finest types of Delaware Wine for commercial use originate in the Lake Erie Islands section of Ohio and the Lake Canandaigua area of New York.

Demijohn—A large wine bottle, covered with wicker, and ordinarily containing 4.9 gallons.

Dessert wines—(See Aperitif).

Diamond—An excellent white American wine grape which has been a favorite with vintners in New York state for over fifty years. Similar to Alsatian wine. The finest Diamond grape comes from the Lake Canandaigua region of the Finger Lakes.

Diana—A first rate wine, at its best. Fermented from one of the three highest quality home-grown grapes for white wines (the others are Iona and Dutchess). Grown extensively in the Finger and Sandusky (Lake Erie Islands) areas. Since Diana is sensitive to cold, the flavor and bouquet of this wine may vary a great deal from one year to another.

D.O.M.—A section of the trade mark of Benedictine Liqueur.

Stands for Deo Optimo, Maximo ("To God, Most Good, Most Great.").

Drambuie—A golden beverage, with a base of Scotch malt whisky combined with spices and honey. 80 proof.

Duriff (doo'riff)—Also known as Petite Sirah. Burgundy dry red table wine fermented from Duriff grapes. Excellent varieties grow in the Sonoma County and Napa Valley areas of California, where the grape yields a clean beautifully-colored substantial wine. Wine from these sections is almost invariably good. Next to the Zinfandel, the Duriff is the most extensively grown quality wine grape in California. It is the chief ingredient of the majority of the finer Burgundy wines of that state.

Dutchess—Extremely light, dry wine with distinctive characteristics. One of the three top U.S. white wine grapes (the others are Diana and Iona), the offspring of a white Concord plant and the Delaware.

Elvira—A home grown, white wine grape which comes originally from Missouri and is now widely planted in the Finger Lakes area of New York State, where it is used in large quantities for producing Champagne. At its best, its still wine is second to none on the East coast.

Falernum—A mildly alcoholic colorless spiced syrup which adds flavor to Rum beverages.

Fermentation—The transformation of sugars, through the action of yeast, into ethyl alcohol and carbon dioxide; the method by which beer and wine are made into grains and fruits.

"Fifth"—Four-fifth quart bottle: 25.6 fluid ounces; 1/5 gallon.

Fino (fee-no)—A dry, "nutty" variety of Spanish Sherry.

Fior Alpini—92 proof Italian yellow liqueur marketed in big bottles containing rock-sugar crystals shaped into a tree.

Fizz—A sparkling drink ordinarily containing the juice of ½ a lemon; ½ teaspoon of sugar, fruit syrup, spirits, charged water and ice.

Flavored Brandies—Sweet grape Brandies flavored with such fruits as cherry, ginger, peach, apricot, and blackberry. Often 70 proof. Known abroad as "Blackberry Brandy," "Cherry Brandy," etc., but it is illegal in the United States to label the Brandy in this way unless it is actually made from the fruit mentioned on the label. When they are less than 70 proof, they are known as liqueurs or cordials.

Flip—Drinks prepared with egg, wine and liquor, with sugar and cracked ice added.

Forbidden Fruit—A citrus liqueur.

"Fortified"—It is now illegal to apply this word to any wine in the U.S. However, at one time it meant that Brandy had been added to dessert wines, while they were being fermented, to control the action of the yeast and maintain the sweetness of the wine.

"Foxy"—A term describing the typical grape flavor of most commercially sold grape juice. It is characteristic of the bouquet of the Concord and related grapes.

Franken Riesling (franken reezling)—See Sylvaner.

Frappé—An after-dinner liqueur, served in a cocktail glass over shaved ice.

French-type Vermouth—Dry Vermouth.

Galliano—A Yellow Italian 90 proof liqueur.

Gallon—In the U.S., the gallon is 128 fluid ounces; in Great Britain, it is 1.2 American gallons.

Gamay (gam-ay)—Red table wine, a product of Gamay grapes, the chief red wine grape of the Beaujolais area of France. In the mountainous section of California the Gamay grape can yield wines which are a delight even to the connoisseur. Burgundy type.

Gevrey-Chambertin (zhevray sham-bair-tan')—A red French Burgundy.

Gewürz Traminer (geh-wurtz trah-mee-ner)—Spicy white table wine produced by the Gewürztraminer grape. Medium-sweet or dry.

Glögg—A hot, spiced Scandinavian drink like mulled wine, but with spirits such as Aquavit added.

Golden Chasselas (shah-sal-ah)—White table wine made from Golden Chasselas grapes, also known as Gutedel.

Goldwasser—A spicy liqueur, with a citrus flavor, and actual grains of real gold leaf. Also known as Liqueur d'Or, it was originally concocted as a result of the legend that gold was a remedy for various illnesses.

Grand Marnier—A French Curaçao liqueur, 80 proof, with a Cognac base.

Graves (grahv)—A dry or medium-sweet French white table wine. In addition, there are also some red Graves wines.

Green Hungarian—A grape which leaves a slightly bitter taste, used mainly to give body to white table wines.

Grenadine—Syrup of pomegranates or red currants, used as a flavoring. Non-alcoholic. There are some Grenadine liqueurs, too.

Grey Riesling (reezling)—White table wine, a product of Grey Riesling grapes. At its best, this is a light, clean wine. Not the same as the famous Johannisberger Riesling. Rhine Wine type.

Grignolino (green-yo-leen'oh)—Red table wine made from the Grignolino grape, source of one of the best Northern Italian red wines. Also produces acceptable, though not outstanding, wines in the south of California. Claret type.

Grog—A heavy-bodied Rum drink, rationed to the crews of British and Canadian naval ships every morning at eleven. The recipe calls for one third Rum and two thirds water. Sometimes on Canadian boats, cola is used instead of water. Grog calls for full-bodied Rum. Men who prefer money instead of liquor are given their preference.

Gutedel (goot-aydle)—See Golden Chasselas.

Half and Half—In this country, a commercial blend of Sherry and Port. In England, a widely used drink composed of Ale and Stout in equal parts.

Haut sauterne (oh so-tairn)—Medium-sweet Sauterne.

Hermitage (air'me-taj)—Dry white or red table wine produced in France's Rhone Valley.

Highball—A tall drink, for which a large highball glass is used, prepared with one jigger of a particular spirit, carbonated water and cracked ice.

Hock—See Rhine Wine.

Iona—Grown in a favorable environment, it yields a wine second to none, most of which is produced by amateur vintners. Rarely sold commercially, it is one of the three best native white wines (the other top quality wine grapes in this country are Diana and Dutchess).

Irish Mist—80 proof liqueur with an Irish Whiskey base.

Isabella—Frequently used for Champagnes in the Finger Lakes district. One of the first U.S. red wine grapes.

Italian-type vermouth—Sweet Vermouth.

Ives—Frequently used, in combination with Norton, for preparing good day-in-day-out table wines. The matured wine is far better than the young variety.

Jeroboam—Large wine bottle, equal to four bottles of usual size.

Johannisberger Riesling (yo-hahn-is bear-ger reezling)—The foremost of all Rhine Wine grapes, also known as White Riesling. The most commonly grown grape in the northern wine sections of the Rhine and the Moselle, it is not planted very widely in California, although the climate in some areas of the state brings this grape to wine-producing perfection. Varietal wines bearing this name are a buy not to be missed. Rhine Wine type.

Julep—A mixed drink compounded of fresh mint, Rye or Bourbon, chipped or crushed ice, and poured into a frosted glass.

Kahlua—Coffee liqueur.

Kijafa—A Danish Wine fortified with Brandy. 35 proof. The best known here is Cherry Kijafa.

Kirsch—A Cherry Brandy that is non-aged. Unlike the American Cherry Brandies available, Kirsch is not sweet and heavy; rather it is dry, light and colorless. Made primarily in Germany and Switzerland. Also known as Kirschwasser.

Kümmel (kim-mel)—Colorless liqueur with caraway and other seeds added for flavor. 80 proof.

Light Muscat—Dry or sweet spicy white table wine of the Muscat grape.

Liqueur—Liquors made by redistilling neutral spirits with fruits, flowers, herbs, seeds, roots, plants or juices with sweetening added. Most Liqueurs are sweet and colorful, with a highly concentrated flavor. Many are known by trade or proprietary brand names.

"Liqueur, Scotch," "Liqueur, Brandy"—Either of these terms on the label implies that the spirits are sufficiently aged and smooth enough to be taken straight.

Madeira (mah-day'rah)—Appetizer, dessert or between-meal wine resembling Sherry, but sweeter and deeper in color. Medium-bodied. Prepared from one or more of several types of grapes. Among them are Palomino and Mission. Serve at room temperature or chilled. Sweet Sherry type.

Magnum—Large wine bottle, the size of two fifth bottles.

Malaga—Heavy-bodied amber dessert wine.

Maraschino Liqueur—A colorless liqueur made from Marasca cherries, with rose petals and spices added for flavor. 60 and 64 proof. Used primarily for cocktails and fruit dishes.

Marsala (mar-sah'la)—Appetizer, dessert, or between-meals wine. Definite amber color. Resembles Sherry, but is sweeter. Medium-bodied. Prepared from Grenadine, Mission, or other types of grape, either alone or in combination. Serve either chilled or at room temperature.

Mavrodaphne—A sweet red Greek dessert wine, resembling Port.

May Wine—Sweet white table wine flavored with woodruff.

Methusaleh—Large wine bottle, which holds as much as eight bottles of regular size.

Mezcal—A Mexican drink, with a more pronounced flavor than Tequila. Prepared from fermented maguey cactus juice.

Montilla (mon-tee-ya)—A dry, bitter Spanish Sherry.

Montrachet (mohn-ra-shay)—A French white Burgundy.

Moselle (mozle)—See Rhine Wine.

Mourestel (moor-ess-tell')—Red table wine prepared from Mourestel grapes. A good, but not outstanding, table wine of satisfying flavor. Claret type.

Muddle—The process of pulverizing or dissolving an ingredient, usually powdered sugar, in the bottom of a glass. Done by adding small amount of liquid to the property to be dissolved and by stirring vigorously with a spoon. A barspoon used for this purpose is called a muddler.

Mulled wine—Spiced wine served hot.

Muscat de Frontignan (moo-skah, or mooskaht fron'tee-yawn)—A sweet dessert wine prepared from Muscat de Frontignan grapes.

Muscat, Light—White table wine, either dry or semi-sweet. Sometimes known as "Dry Muscat." A light wine prepared from Muscat grapes with the distinctive Muscat taste and bouquet. The dry Muscat is served with white meat or seafood. Semi-sweet Muscat is suitable with or after dessert or in-between meals.

Muscatel—A white dessert wine, spicy and sweet, prepared from the Muscat grape.

Nebbiolo—Dry, tart Italian red table wine.

Nebuchadnezzar—A big wine bottle, twenty times the size of a regular bottle.

Neuchâtel—Dry, tart white Swiss table wine.

Niagara—A widely grown U.S. white wine grape.

Norton—One of the top quality home grown red wine grapes which is cultivated with far better results in the south than in the north. This is a substantial wine with an agreeable flavor.

O. F. C.—Old Fine Canadian.

Oloroso—A Spanish Sherry of varied degrees of sweetness.

Orvieto—A white Italian table wine, ordinarily dry.

Peppermint Schnapps—60 proof liqueur; mint flavored; lighter than Crème de Menthe.

Pernod—Most famous of the drinks used instead of Absinthe. 90 and 100 proof.

Perry—Pear Wine.

Petite Sirah (p'teet sir-rah) See Duriff.

Piesporter—A dry or medium-sweet German Rhine wine.

Pinot Blanc (pea-no blawnk)—White table wine prepared from the Pinot Blanc grape, one of the foremost of the California grapes, nearly equal in quality to the first-rate Pinot Chardonnay. However, Blanc is not widely cultivated and its wine is rare. Chablis type.

Pinot Chardonnay (pea-no′ shar-doe-nay′)—White table wine obtained from the Pinot Chardonnay grape. These are the brightest stars in the grape constellation for producing excellent Chablis wines, and are used for all the celebrated White Burgundies. These grapes are also an ingredient of some of the best French Champagnes. Chablis type.

Pinot Noir (pea-no nwahr′)—Red table wine produced by the Pinot Noir grape, the finest Red Burgundy grape. Also a source of most of the white wine used in the production of French Champagne. In California, this grape, as well as the Pinot Blanc, yields the best white wine available. Chablis type.

Pomerol—Dry, tart French red table wine.

Pommard (po-mar′)—French Red Burgundy.

Port—A rich, sweet red dessert wine, prepared from one or more of several types of grape, including Trousseau, Carignane, and Petite Sirah. Particularly good with cheese; also popular with dessert, and in-between or at the end of meals. Served at room temperature or chilled.

Punch—A drink usually prepared in large measure in a bowl and served, buffet-style, in cups or glasses. Can also be prepared in individual glasses. Ingredients should be well blended so that no particular flavor predominates.

Red Pinot—See Pinot Noir.

Rehoboam—A large wine bottle, the size of six ordinary-size bottles.

Rhine Wine—Also known as Hock or Moselle. White table wine. A light dry, tart wine. Prepared from one or more types of grape, including Folle Blanche, Traminer, and one or several of the Riesling grapes. A favorite with white meats and seafood. Served chilled.

Rickey—Drinks containing spirits or liqueurs, lime or lemon, sweetening and ginger ale or soda, served over cracked ice.

Riesling (reezling)—Rhine Wine prepared from Riesling grapes, usually from White Riesling. Compare with *Johannisberger Riesling.*

Rioja (Ree-oh′-ha)—Spanish tart, dry red table wine.

Rock and Rye—A former cold remedy now served as a drink. Contains Rye whiskey, neutral spirits, rock candy syrup, and, as a rule, pieces of fruit, such as cherries or orange.

Rosé (roe-say′)—Pink table wine, noted for its lightness; prepared from such grapes as Gamay, Grenache, and Grignolino. Served chilled or at room temperature, they are excellent for luncheons or picnics.

Saint-Émilion (san tay-mi-yon′)—French red table wine. Dry and tart.

Sainte-Estèphe (san tes-tef′)—French red table wine. Dry and tart.

Saint-Julien—French red table wine. Dry and tart.

Salmanazar—An extra-large wine bottle, which holds 12 times as much as regular wine bottles.

Sangaree—A wine-and-sugar drink served with ice and grated nutmeg. Use a small bar glass. Also red wine and water, with sugar and spice.

Sauterne (so-tairn' or so-turn' or saw-turn')—A full-bodied white table wine. Sometimes dry, but more often semi-sweet.

Sauterne, Château—A very sweet type of Sauterne. Excellent with dessert or at the end of the meal, or with mid-afternoon or mid-evening snacks. Also enjoyable with a meal.

Sauterne, Sweet—Also known as Haut (oh) or Haute (ohte) Sauterne. An unusually sweet Sauterne. Ordinarily a dessert or between-meal wine; also served with white meat and seafood. Drink chilled.

Sauvignon Blanc (so'veen-yawn blawnk)—White table wine, prepared from the Sauvignon grape. This is the foremost grape for the production of the famous white wines from the Graves area of France. In California, this grape yields a topflight wine which runs from dry to sweet in flavor. Sauterne type.

Schnapps—Holland gin. (In Germany and Holland, any distilled drink.)

Scuppernong—One of the southern Muscadine grapes, which has been a consistent wine-producer for about four centuries. This wine is usually over-sweet and therefore not too desirable with meals.

Sediment—Solid fragments of grape which form a deposit on the bottle.

Semillon—A white table wine, a product of the Semillon grape.

Setup—All the "fixin's" for a particular drink, with the exception of the spirits.

Sherry—Appetizer or dessert wine. A white wine with a "nutty" flavor. Comes in a variety of colors and flavors, from light to deep amber; and from dry to sweet. Dry Sherry is the favorite among appetizer wines. It is a versatile wine, suitable for any occasion which calls for appetizer or dessert wines. Among the grapes which are used to produce Sherry are Carignane, Mondeuse, Zinfandel, and Petite Sirah. Fine with meals, or by itself. Serve chilled.

Sling—A Brandy or Gin drink, with sugar and nutmeg.

Sloe Gin—A sweet reddish liqueur, flavored with the sloe berry. As a rule, 60 to 70 proof.

Smash—A julep-like drink prepared from liquor and mint, water, sugar and ice.

Soave (so-ah-vay)—Dry white Italian table wine.

Solera (so-lay-ra)—A term referring to the Spanish process of aging wines, little by little, in small casks, blending new wine with old from time to time.

Sommelier (so-mal-yay')—The restaurant "captain" in charge of serving wine.

Sour—An alcoholic beverage calling for lemon or lime juice with sugar.

Southern Comfort—A blend of old Bourbon whiskey and peach cordial, aged together. 86 and 100 proof.

Sparkling Burgundy—Red wine treated in the same manner as Champagne, to produce effervescence. Among the grapes which yield Sparkling Burgundy are Carignane, Mondeuse, Zinfandel, and Petite Sirah. Fine either with or without meals. Serve chilled.

Sparkling Wines—In addition to Champagne and Sparkling Burgundy, there are a few other wines made effervescent by the same method used to produce Champagne. The principal ones are Sparkling Moselle, Sparkling Muscat, and Sparkling Sauterne.

Spirits—In general use, the word refers to any strong alcoholic liquor produced by distillation.

"Split"—A 2/5 pint wine bottle (6.4 fluid ounces) for table wines; 8 ounces for Champagne.

Spritzer—White wine and seltzer.

Still Wine—Term used to describe non-sparkling type of wine in contrast to those that sparkle.

Strega—An 85 proof yellow, orange-flavored Italian liqueur.

Swedish Punch—A yellow liqueur which includes lemon, tea and herbs.

Swizzle—To prepare this drink, combine the ingredients in a glass pitcher with lots of shaved ice; stir forcefully with a swizzle stick held between the palms of the hands until the pitcher becomes frosted. You can also use a cocktail shaker.

Slyvaner (seel-wah′ner)—Next to Johannisberger Riesling, this is possibly the best of the white wines in this country. The Sylvaner is famous in the German Rhineland, as well as in Alsace. It is widely grown here with fine results. Rhine Wine type.

"Table" Wines—Refers to any grape wine with 14% alcohol or less. Also known as "light" wines.

Tavel—A Rosé wine originating in the French Rhone Valley.

"Tenth"—Four-fifth pint bottle; or 1/10 of a gallon. Occasionally referred to as a half-bottle.

Toddy—This drink is composed of sugar, water and Spirits, with other ingredients such as cinnamon sticks and lemon added. Hot water is most often used as a base.

Tokay—A combination of sweet wines (ordinarily Angelica, Port and Sherry) served with or after dessert or in-between meals. Taken chilled or at room temperature.

Traminer (trah-mee′-ner)—Dry or medium-sweet white table wine produced from the Traminer grape.

Ugni Blanc (oon-ye blawnk)—White table wine produced from the Ugni Blanc grape. A topflight grape which yields some of the best Italian white Chianti, and some renowned white French wines in the Rhone area. Chablis type.

Valpolicella (vahl pol-ee-chel′-la)—Dry, tart red Italian table wine.

Verdicchio—Dry white Italian table wine.

Vergennes—A fine, but infrequently grown, American white wine grape which someone came upon in Vergennes, Vermont in 1874. In favorable years, it yields a most agreeable wine with an easily recognizable fragrance.

Vino (vee-no)—Italian and Spanish for wine.

V.F.C.—Very Fine Cognac.

V.O.—Very Old.

Vodka, Flavored—Vodka flavored with orange, grape, mint, cherry, etc. are marketed in some parts of the U. S. Ordinarily 70 proof.

V.O.P.—Very Old Pale.

Vosne-Romanée (Vone ro-ma-nay')—French red Burgundy.

Vouvray—Dry or medium-sweet white French table wine.

V.S.O.P.—Very Special Old Pale.

V.S.Q.—Very Special Quality.

V.V.O.—Very, Very Old.

V.V.S.O.P.—Very, Very Superior Old Pale.

White Chianti (kee-ahn'tee)—Trebbiano and Muscat-flavored grapes are combined to produce this medium-bodied white table wine. Goes well with white meat and seafood. Taken chilled.

White Pinot (pea-no)—See Pinot Blanc.

White Port—A sweet, substantial white dessert wine. Prepared from one or more types of grape. Served with or after dessert, or in-between meals. Taken chilled or at room temperature.

Zinfandel (zin-fon'dle)—Red table wine with the characteristic flavor and bouquet of the Zinfandel grape. One of the most enjoyable of all table wines when grown under favorable conditions, in cool vineyards. This wine, when cultivated in too warm an area, however, may be altogether without distinction. Produced in California. Claret type.

King Edward's liquor laws are still with us

By DON SIMMONS

DURING the middle of the Sixteenth Century, England's good King Edward the Sixth took to donning the robes of a peasant and circulating among his subjects. During one of these journeys he visited a prominent London alehouse and was dismayed to discover that, not looking like a particularly desirable customer, he was given watered ale. Being no mean fancier of the brewer's art he returned to his palace and set down a group of ordinances governing all taverns, tippling places and ale houses. In this manner, civilization's first liquor laws were established.

Many of King Edward's laws are still in effect today not only in England but in the United States and other countries all over the world. Minors, for example, were not allowed to be served intoxicating liquors nor could a drinking establishment serve an habitual drunk or a feeble minded person. Drinks could not be watered and, in a move to raise the price of these imbibings as well as to enrich the treasury, stiff liquor taxes were imposed.

During the Colonial days of early America, liquor laws were rigidly enforced. It was in this era that opening and closing hours were given to taverns and to any other property at which drinks were served to the public. Drunks were treated in a stern manner. An overly ambitious drinker would be whipped and locked in the stocks for a day. In certain parts of New England, the offender was made to carry a large card with the letter "D" for "Drunk" on his chest for weeks after being found guilty of intoxication. On the other hand, the Colonials felt that the tavern also played a very important part in the community and in 1656, the General Court of Massachusetts enacted a law making a town liable to a fine for not sustaining a house at which liquor was sold.

Nowadays, liquor laws are almost entirely state controlled. In many ways the states agree completely on the yesses and noes of drinking. Some years ago, for example, the well known Miss Pat Ward of the famed Jelke trials had her ambitions as a cafe singer cut short by the State Liquor Boards of New Jersey, New York and the local board controlling the District of Columbia. Most states ban felons in cafes although, oddly enough, Kentucky makes an exception. They allow the employment of a person who was convicted of forgery.

There are other exceptions that might very well startle those outside of the liquor trade. All were set for good reason even though this reasoning often applies to only the particular state in which they have been enacted.

Indiana forbids the cashing of checks. Illinois will not allow sidewalk cafes. In New York, a bar must be visible from the street and a barroom must be lit well enough for a patron to be able to read a newspaper without eye strain. In Alabama, you can't get a free drink from the proprietor while Connecticut forbids the sale of liquor to any person receiving civil aid. In California, wine can be mixed only if it is done in front of the patron; therefore, technically, a Martini should be devised before the orderer's eyes.

In 1959, Oklahoma repealed its Prohibition law, thus leaving Mississippi as the only completely dry state. Many states have dry counties. In Oregon, liquor and beer companies can do no radio and television advertising except between the hours of one a.m. and midnight on Sunday. In Michigan, you can't mention Santa Claus in an ad selling an alcoholic product. Advertising men in Iowa often run short of selling ideas for here they cannot make use of the words "saloon," "bar" or "nightclubs." New Yorkers and natives of most other states are used to the familiar beer schooner with its advertisement of a well known brew but in the state of Washington this is not allowed nor can a beer or liquor company print calendars or posters.

Most any big liquor company is publicly against overimbibing. So are the people hired and elected to protect the citizenry. There's almost always a good reason for a law.

index

The following is an index to the drink and food recipes published on these pages. A number of the drinks are repeated here because while each drink is listed under the primary liquid ingredient(s) involved in its preparation, many drinks involve a combination of ingredients.

BOURBON

Admiral's Toddy	31
Beehive	42
Blinker Cocktail	53
Bourbon Collins	58
Bourbon Crème	58
Bourbon Egg Nog	59
Bourbon Fruit	59
Bourbon Highball	59
Bourbon Old Fashioned	59
Bourbon Shake	59
Bourbon Sour	59
Bourbon and Coke	60
Bourbon and Egg	60
Bourbon and Iced Tea	60
Bourbon and Soda	60
Caracas	71
Commando	88
Continental	89
Dixie Julep	97
Georgian	112
Hawaiian Sour	128
Highhat	128
Honest John	130
Jailai	143
Kentucky Cocktail	146
Kentucky Colonel Cocktail	146
Kentucky Horse's Neck	147
Little Colonel	151
Manhattan Perfect	156
Manhattan Sweet	157
Merry-Go-Round	158
Mike's Muddler	159
Mint Julep	161
Mint Julep (Southern Style)	161
New Orleans Mint Julep	168
New Orleans Punch	168
Old Charter	169
Sideboard Toddy	205
Stingering	209
Tranquilizer	213

BRANDY

After Dinner Cocktail	31
After Supper Cocktail	31
Alabama Cocktail	31
Alexander Cocktail No. 2	32
American Beauty Cocktail	34
Angel's Kiss	34
Angel's Wing	34
Apple Blow Fizz	35
Apple Brandy Cocktail	35
Apple Brandy Highball	35
Apple Brandy Rickey	32
Apple Brandy Sour	36
Applejack Cocktail	36
Applejack Collins	36
Applejack Daisy	37
Applejack Flip	37
Applejack Old Fashioned	37
Applejack On The Rocks	37
Applejack Rickey	37

Applejack Sling	37	Button Hook Cocktail	68
Applejack Smash	38	Café Royale	70
Applejack Sour	38	Cardinal Punch	71
Applejack Toddy	38	Carrol Cocktail	72
Apricot Brandy Rickey	38	Champagne Cup	73
Apricot Cocktail	38	Charles Cocktail	74
Apricot Cooler	39	Charlie Chaplin	74
Apricot Fizz	39	Cherry Blossom Cocktail	75
Aunt Emily	39	Cherry Fizz	75
Baltimore Bracer Cocktail	40	Cherry Flip	75
Baltimore Eggnog	40	Cherry Sling	75
Bermuda Bouquet	43	Chicago Cocktail	76
Bermuda Highball	44	Chocolate Daisy	77
Bermuda Rose Cocktail	44	Chocolate Flip	77
Between the Sheets Cocktail	44	Cider Cup	84
Big Apple	44	Claret Cup	84
Blackberry Julep	46	Claret Punch	85
Blood & Sand Cocktail	53	Claridge Cocktail	85
Bolero Cocktail	56	Classic Cocktail	85
Bombay Cocktail	56	Coffee Cocktail	87
Bombay Punch	56	Coffee Flip	87
Booster Cocktail	57	Cold Deck Cocktail	88
Boston Cocktail	57	Country Cocktail	90
Boston Side Car Cocktail	58	Créme de Menthe Frappe	91
Brandy and Soda	60	Cuban Cocktail No. 2	92
Brandy Blazer	60	Darb Cocktail	94
Brandy Cobbler	60	Deauville Cocktail	94
Brandy Cocktail	61	Dempsey Cocktail	94
Brandy Collins	61	Derby	94
Brandy Daisy	61	Diana Cocktail	95
Brandy Eggnog	62	Douglas Fairbanks	98
Brandy Fix	62	Dream Cocktail	98
Brandy Fizz	62	East India Cocktail No. 1	99
Brandy Flip	62	Egg Sour	102
Brandy Gump Cocktail	62	English Highball	103
Brandy Highball	63	English Rose Cocktail	103
Brandy Julep	63	Ethel Duffy Cocktail	104
Brandy Milk Punch	63	Fairy Belle Cocktail	104
Brandy Punch	63	Fancy Brandy Cocktail	105
Brandy Sangaree	64	Fantasio Cocktail	106
Brandy Sling	64	Favourite Cocktail	106
Brandy Smash	64	Fifth Avenue	106
Brandy Sour	64	Fish House Punch	107
Brandy Squirt	64	Flamingo Cocktail	108
Brandy Toddy	65	Frankenjack Cocktail	109
Brandy Toddy (Hot)	65	Froupe Cocktail	110
Brandy Vermouth Cocktail	65	Gilroy Cocktail	112
Breakfast Eggnog	65	Golden Slipper Cocktail	123
Bulldog Cocktail	67	Grand Slam	124
Bullfrog	67	Harvard Cocktail	126
Bull's Eye	67	Harvard Cooler	127
Bull's Milk	68	Honeymoon Cocktail	130

Hop Toad Cocktail	131	Bucks Fizz	67
Hot Brandy Flip	131	Cardinal Punch	71
Jack-in-the-Box Cocktail	142	Champagne Cocktail	72
Jack Rose Cocktail	143	Champagne Cup	73
Jamaica Granito	143	Champagne Punch	73
Jersey Lightning Cocktail	144	Diamond Fizz	95
Judgette Cocktail	146	Dinermo	96
Kiss-in-the-Dark Cocktail	147	Duke Cocktail	99
Kopman Caprice	148	French "75"	110
Leave It To Me Cocktail No. 1	149	London Special Cocktail	151
Loving Cup	154	Luxury Cocktail	154
Luxury Cocktail	154	Monte Carlo Imperial Highball	165
Merry Widow Cocktail No. 2	159	Ponce de Leon	179
Morning Cocktail	166		
Olympic Cocktail	170	**COGNAC**	
Panama Cocktail	173	Adam & Eve	30
Paradise Cocktail	173	Alpine Glow	33
Peach Sangaree	174	Ambrosia	33
Phoebe Snow Cocktail	175	B & B	39
Pink Whiskers Cocktail	178	Brighton Punch	66
Pisco Sour	178	Champs Élysées Cocktail	73
Polonaise Cocktail	179	Classic	85
Polynesian Cocktail	179	Club No. 4	86
Poop Deck Cocktail	179	Cognac Highball	87
Pousse Café	181	Epicurean	104
Pousse L'Amour	182	Hot Apple Toddy	131
Quaker's Cocktail	183	Kahlualexander	146
Rhine Wine Cup	184	Lover's Delight	154
Roman Punch	187	Ponce De Leon	180
Rose Cocktail (English)	187	Prairie Oyster Cocktail	182
Rose Cocktail (French)	187	Seesaw	202
Saratoga Cocktail	198	Sloppy Joe's Cocktail No. 2	208
Saucy Sue Cocktail	199		
Sauterne Cup	199	**GENERAL**	
Sidecar Cocktail	205	(This category refers to special	
Singapore Sling	206	varieties of drinks which can be	
Sir Walter Cocktail	206	made with any one of a number	
Stinger Cocktail	209	of different spirits.)	
Third Rail Cocktail	211	Champarelle	73
Tom and Jerry	213	Cobbler	87
Tulip Cocktail	214	Collins	88
Two Ruths	215	Coolers	89
Valencia Cocktail	215	Crustas	91
Vanderbilt Cocktail	216	Cup	93
Washington Cocktail	223	Daisy	93
Widow's Kiss Cocktail	226	Fix	107
Yanuck Fever	227	Fizz	107
		Flip	108
CHAMPAGNE		Highball	129
		Sangaree	198
Ambrosia	33	Smash	208
Black Velvet	53	Swizzle (see Green Swizzle)	125
Bombay Punch	55		

Toddies	211	Chelsea Side Car Cocktail	75
Toddy (Hot)	132	Chocolate Flip	77
		Chocolate Soldier Cocktail	77
GIN		Circus Rickey	84
Abbey Cocktail	30	Claridge Cocktail	85
Acacia	30	Clove Cocktail	85
Adam & Eve	30	Clover Club Cocktail	86
Alabama Fizz	32	Clover Leaf Cocktail	86
Alaska Cocktail	32	Club No. 2	86
Albemarle Fizz	32	Club Cocktail	86
Alexander Cocktail No. 1	32	Colonial Cocktail	88
Alexander's Sister Cocktail	32	Cooperstown Cocktail	89
Allen Cocktail	33	Cornell Cocktail	89
Allies Cocktail	33	Coronation Cocktail	89
Angler's	35	Cream Fizz	90
Appetizer	35	Crème de Gin Cocktail	90
Aunt Emily	39	Crimson Cocktail	91
Bachelor's Bait Cocktail	40	Crystal Slipper Cocktail	91
Barbary Coast Cocktail	41	Damn-The-Weather Cocktail	93
Baron Cocktail	42	Darb Cocktail	94
Beauty Spot Cocktail	42	Deep Sea Cocktail	94
Bees' Knees	43	Dempsey Cocktail	94
Belmont Cocktail	43	Derby	94-95
Bennett Cocktail	43	Diamond Fizz	95
Bermuda Bouquet	43	Dickens' Martini Cocktail	95
Bermuda Highball	44	Dinermite	96
Bermuda Rose Cocktail	44	Dixie Cocktail	97
Biffy Cocktail	44	Double Standard Sour	98
Bijou Cocktail	45	Douglas Fairbanks	98
Billy Taylor	45	Du Barry Cocktail	98
Bird of Paradise Fizz	45	Dubonnet Cocktail	98
Black Hawk Cocktail	46	Eclipse	100
Blackthorn Cocktail	53	Emerald Isle Cocktail	103
Blood Bronx Cocktail	54	English Highball	103
Bloodhound Cocktail	54	English Rose Cocktail	103
Blue Devil Cocktail	55	Fairy Belle Cocktail	104
Blue Moon Cocktail	55	Falernum Tom Collins	105
Boomerang	57	Fallen Angel Cocktail	105
Boston Cocktail	57	Fancy Gin Cocktail	105
Bronx Cocktail	66	Farmer's Cocktail	106
Bronx Cocktail (Dry)	66	Favourite Cocktail	106
Bronx Silver Cocktail	66	Fifty-Fifty Cocktail	106
Bronx Terrace Cocktail	67	Fine & Dandy Cocktail	106
Brown Cocktail	67	Flamingo Cocktail	108
Bulldog Cocktail	67	Floradora Cooler	108
Bulldog Highball	67	Fog Horn	109
Bull Shot	68	Frankenjack Cocktail	109
Cabaret Cocktail	68	French "75"	110
Café de Paris Cocktail	69	Froth Blower Cocktail	110
Casino Cocktail	72	Futurity	111
Charlie Chaplin	74	Gaslight	112
Charlotte Russe	74	Gatsby's Collins	112

Gibson	112	Jockey Club Cocktail	145
Gilroy Cocktail	113	John Collins	145
Gimlet	113	Johnnie Cocktail	145
Gin and Bitters	113	Journalist Cocktail	145
Gin and It	113	Judge Jr. Cocktail	146
Gin and Tonic	113	Judgette Cocktail	146
Gin Buck	119	Kahlualexander	146
Gin Cobbler	119	Kiss-in-the-Dark Cocktail	147
Gin Cocktail	119	Knickerbocker Cocktail	147
Gin Cooler	119	Kopman Caprice	148
Gin Daisy	120	Lady Alexander	148
Gin Fix	120	Lady Love Fizz	148
Gin Fizz	120	Leave It To Me Cocktail No. 1	149
Gin Highball	120	Leave It To Me Cocktail No. 2	149
Gin Milk Punch	120	Lemonade (Modern)	150
Gin Rickey	120	London Cocktail	151
Gin Sangaree	121	Lone Tree Cocktail	151
Gin Sling	121	Lone Tree Cooler	152
Gin Smash	121	Love Cocktail	154
Gin Sour	121	Maiden's Blush Cocktail No. 1	155
Gin Squirt	121	Maiden's Blush Cocktail No. 2	155
Gin Swizzle	122	Maiden's Prayer Cocktail	155
Gin Toddy	122	Mainbrace Cocktail	155
Gin Toddy (Hot)	122	Major Bailey	156
Golden Fizz	123	Martini	157-158
Golden Gate Cocktail	123	Merry Widow Cocktail No. 1	158
Golf Cocktail	123	Merry Widow Fizz	159
Gourmet Cocktail	124	Mint Collins	160
Grand Passion	124	Monkey Gland	166
Grand Royal Fizz	124	Monte Carlo Imperial Highball	166
Grapefruit Cocktail	124	Montmartre Cocktail	166
Green Dragon Cocktail	125	Moulin Rouge Cocktail	167
Green Fizz	125	Napoleon Cocktail	167
Green Swizzle	125	New Orleans Gin Fizz	168
Gypsy Cocktail	126	Opal Cocktail	170
Harlem Cocktail	126	Opera Cocktail	170
Hasty Cocktail	127	Orange Bloom Cocktail	170
Hawaiian Cocktail	127	Orange Blossom Cocktail	171
Hi-De-Ho Special	128	Orange Gin Collins	171
Hoffman House Cocktail	129	Orange Gin Fizz	171
Homestead Cocktail	130	Orange Gin Highball	171
Honolulu Cocktail No. 1	130	Orange Milk Fizz	171
Honolulu Cocktail No. 2	130	Palisades	172
H.P.W. Cocktail	132	Palm Beach Cocktail	172
Hula-Hula Cocktail	132	Paradise Cocktail	173
Ideal Cocktail	140	Peach Blossom	174
Imperial Cocktail	141	Peach Blow Fizz	174
Income Tax Cocktail	141	Peking Express	174
Irish Shillelagh	142	Perfect Cocktail	175
Jamaica Glow Cocktail	143	Peter Pan Cocktail	175
Jewel Cocktail	144	Piccadilly Cocktail	175
Jeyplak Cocktail	144	Ping-Pong Cocktail	176

Pink Lady Cocktail	177	Irish Whiskey Cocktail	142
Pink Rose Fizz	177	Irish Whiskey Highball	142
Poppy Cocktail	180	Paddy Cocktail	172
Princeton Cocktail	182	St. Patrick's Day Cocktail	197
Queen Elizabeth Cocktail	183	Shamrock Cocktail	203
Racquet Club Cocktail	183		
Ramos Fizz	184	**LIQUEUR**	
Robert E. Lee Cooler	184	Absinthe Cocktail	30
Rose Cocktail (English)	187	Acacia	30
Rose Cocktail (French)	187	Adam and Eve	30
Royal Cocktail	187	After Dinner Cocktail	31
Royal Fizz	188	After Supper Cocktail	31
Russian Cocktail	196	Alaska Cocktail	32
Salty Dog	197	Alexander Cocktail No. 1	32
San Francisco Cocktail	197	Alexander Cocktail No. 2	32
Sands-Martin Cocktail	197	Alexander's Sister Cocktail	32
Sangaree	197	Allen Cocktail	33
Sapphire	198	Alpine Glow	33
Savannah	199	Amer Picon Cocktail	33
Sensation Cocktail	203	Angel's Delight	34
Seventh Heaven Cocktail	203	Angel's Kiss	34
Silver Cocktail	206	Angel's Tip	34
Silver Fizz	206	Angel's Wing	34
Singapore Sling	206	B & B	39
Sloe Gin Collins	207	Baltimore Bracer Cocktail	40
Sloe Gin Fizz	207	Barbados Cocktail	41
Sloe Gin Flip	207	Barbary Coast Cocktail	41
Sloe Gin Rickey	207	Between the Sheets Cocktail	44
South Side Cocktail	208	Bijou Cocktail	45
South Side Fizz	209	Black Russian	46
Southern Gin Cocktail	209	Blue Devil Cocktail	55
Tom Collins	213	Blue Monday Cocktail	55
Trinity Cocktail	214	Blue Moon Cocktail	55
Turf Cocktail	214	Boston Side Car Cocktail	58
Tuxedo Cocktail	214	Brandy Punch	63
Twin Six Cocktail	215	Brighton Punch	66
Union Jack Cocktail	215	Button Hook Cocktail	68
Virgin	216	Caracas	71
Waikiki	222	Champagne Cup	73
Wallick Cocktail	222	Champarelle	73
White Lady Cocktail	226	Champs Élysées Cocktail	73
White Rose Cocktail	226	Chelsea Side Car Cocktail	75
Yale Cocktail	226	Chez Asch	76
		Cider Cup	84
IRISH WHISKEY		Claret Cup	84
Blarney Stone Cocktail	53	Claret Punch	85
Cameron's Kick Cocktail	70	Claridge Cocktail	85
Everybody's Irish Cocktail	104	Cold Deck Cocktail	88
Gloom Lifter	122	Commando	88
Irish Coffee	141	Crème de Gin Cocktail	90
Irish Rickey	141	Crème de Menthe Frappe	91
Irish Shillelagh	142	Crystal Slipper Cocktail	91

Deauville Cocktail	94	Pousse Café	181
Diana Cocktail	95	Pousse l'Amour	182
Dixie Cocktail	97	Rhine Wine Cup	184
Dream Cocktail	98	Russian Bear Cocktail	195
Duke Cocktail	99	Russian Cocktail	196
Epicurean	104	Sapphire	198
Ethel Duffy Cocktail	104	St. Patrick's Day Cocktail	197
Fifth Avenue	106	Sauterne Cup	199
Fine and Dandy Cocktail	106	Sidecar Cocktail	205
Flying Grasshopper Cocktail	108	Stinger	209
Fox River Cocktail	109	Stingering	209
Georgian	113	T.N.T. Cocktail	211
Gloom Chaser	122	Tiger Special	211
Golden Slipper Cocktail	123	Tovarich Cocktail	213
Grand Passion	124	Tropical Cocktail	214
Grand Slam	124	Union Jack Cocktail	215
Grasshopper Cocktail	125	Vermouth Cassis	216
Green Dragon Cocktail	125	Virgin	216
Hawaiian Cocktail	127	Vodka Grasshopper Cocktail	217
High Hat	128	Vodka Gypsy Cocktail	217
High Life	128	Vodka Stinger	217
Honeymoon Cocktail	130	Widow's Dream Cocktail	226
Honolulu Cocktail No. 2	130	Widow's Kiss Cocktail	226
Ice Cream Flip	133	Zero Mint	227
Jailai	143		
Jamaica Granito	143	**MISCELLANEOUS**	
Jewel Cocktail	144	Absinthe Cocktail	30
Johnnie Cocktail	145	Absinthe Drip Cocktail	30
Kahlualexander	146	Absinthe Special Cocktail	30
Lady Alexander	148	Black Velvet	53
Leatherneck	148	Bloody Dagmar Cocktail	54
Lover's Delight	154	Bull's Eye	67
Loving Cup	154	Buttonhook Cocktail	68
Mainbrace Cocktail	155	Duchess Cocktail	99
Margarita Cocktail	157	Green Eye Opener	125
Merry Widow Cocktail No. 2	159	Maiden's Blush Cocktail No. 2	155
Mike's Muddler	159	Margarita Cocktail	157
Mint Highball	160	Mimosa	159
Mint on Rocks	165	Palisades	172
Mogel's Millions	166	Pike's Peak Cooler	175
Montmartre Cocktail	166	Shandy Gaff	204
Ninotchka Cocktail	169	Shandy Tang	204
Olympic Cocktail	170	Tequila Straight	210
Opal Cocktail	170	Tequila Cocktail	210
Opera Cocktail	170	Tequini	210
Orange Bloom Cocktail	170		
Oriental Cocktail	171	**NON-ALCOHOLIC**	
Panama Cocktail	173	(see also WEIGHT WATCHERS®	
Parisian Blonde Cocktail	173	RECIPES)	
Ping-Pong Cocktail	177	Cider Eggnog	84
Ponce de Leon	180	Egg Nog	102
Port and Starboard	180	Fruit Cup	111

General Harrison's Eggnog 112
Grenadine Rickey 126
Hick's Hangover Recipe 128
Horse's Neck 131
Lemon Squash 149
Lemonade (Carbonated) 149
Lemonade (Egg) 150
Lemonade (Fruit) 150
Lemonade (Golden) 150
Lemonade (Plain) 150
Limeade 151
Orange Smile 171
Orangeade 172
Pussyfoot 183
Saratoga Cooler 198
Southern Beauty 209

RUM

Alpine Glow 33
American Grog 34
Apple Pie Cocktail 36
Bacardi Cocktail 39
Baltimore Eggnog 40
Barbados Cocktail 41
Barbados Rum Swizzle 41
Barbary Coast Cocktail 41
Between the Sheets Cocktail 44
Bitters Highball 45
Black Stripe Cocktail 46
Blossom 55
Bolero Cocktail 56
Bolo Cocktail 56
Boomerang 57
Boston Cooler 57
Boston Side Car Cocktail 58
Brown Cocktail 67
Bull's Milk 68
Burgundy Bishop 68
Captain's Blood 71
Cardinal Punch 71
Carioca 72
Carioca Collins 72
Carioca Eggnog 72
Chicago Fizz 76
Chinese Cocktail 76
Christmas Yule Eggnog 77
Cream Puff 90
Cuba Libre 92
Cuban Cocktail No. 1 92
Cuban Special Cocktail 92
Daiquiri Cocktail 93
El Presidente Cocktail No. 1 102

El Presidente Cocktail No. 2 102
Eye-Opener Cocktail 104
Fair and Warmer Cocktail 104
Falernum Rum Collins 105
Fireman's Sour 107
Fish House Punch 107
Four W 109
Fresco 110
Frozen Daiquiri 110
Frozen Daiquiri Cocktail 111
Grand Slam 124
Green Tree 126
Havana Cocktail 127
Havana Daiquiri 127
Hawaiian Collins 127
Hop Toad Cocktail 131
Hot Apple Toddy 131
Hot Buttered Rum 132
Huntsman Cocktail 133
Imperial Fizz 141
Irish Shillelagh 142
Isle of Pines 143
Jamaica Rum Cobbler 143
Jamaica Rum Collins 143
Jamaica Rum Sour 144
Judge Jr. Cocktail 146
Mary Pickford Cocktail 158
Nevada Cocktail 167
Night Cap 169
Palmetto Cocktail 173
Pals Tropical Punch 173
Parisian Blonde Cocktail 173
Passion Daiquiri Cocktail 174
Pineapple Cocktail 176
Pineapple Dream Cocktail 177
Pineapple Fizz 177
Plantation Punch 178
Planter's Punch No. 1 178
Planter's Punch No. 2 179
Planter's Punch No. 3 179
Ponce de Leon 180
Puerto Rican Cocktail 182
Quakers' Cocktail 183
Quarter Deck Cocktail 183
Roman Punch 187
Rum Cooler 188
Rum Cobbler 188
Rum Collins 188
Rum Daisy 189
Rum Eggnog 189
Rum Fix 194
Rum Highball 194

Rum Milk Punch	194	Klondike Cooler	147
Rum Old Fashioned	194	Ladies' Cocktail	148
Rum Rickey	195	Leatherneck	148
Rum Sour	195	Mad Hatter	154
Rum Swizzle	195	Manhattan Cocktail	156
Rum Toddy	195	Manhattan Cocktail (Dry)	156
Rum Toddy (Hot)	195	Milk Punch	159
Santiago Cocktail	198	Mogel's Millions	166
September Morn Cocktail	203	New York Cocktail	168
Sevilla Cocktail	203	New York Sour	168
Shanghai Cocktail	203	Old Fashioned Cocktail	169
Sir Walter Cocktail	206	Oriental Cocktail	172
Sloppy Joe's Cocktail No. 1	208	Palmer Cocktail	172
Snooty Fox Daiquiri	208	Pineapple Blossom	175
Third Rail Cocktail	211	Preakness Cocktail	182
Tiger Special	211	Rock and Rye	185
Tom and Jerry	213	Rye Eggnog	196
Two Ruths	215	Rye Highball	196
Zombie	228	Rye Old Fashioned	196
		Rye Rickey	196
RYE & BLENDED		Rye Whiskey Cocktail	196
Bittersweet	45	Sazerac Cocktail	200
Black Hawk Cocktail	46	Skidmore '54 Cocktail	206
Blinker Cocktail	53	Smash	208
Blue Blazer	55	Temptation Cocktail	210
Boston Sour	59	TNT Cocktail	211
Brighton Punch	66	Trilby Cocktail	213
Cablegram Highball	69	Ward Eight	223
California Lemonade	70	Whiskey Cobbler	223
Canadian Cocktail	70	Whiskey Cocktail	223
Christmas Yule Eggnog	77	Whiskey Collins	223
Club No. 3	86	Whiskey Daisy	224
Commodore Cocktail	88	Whiskey Eggnog	224
Cowboy Cocktail	90	Whiskey Fix	224
Creole Lady Cocktail	91	Whiskey Flip	224
Dinah Cocktail	95	Whiskey Highball	224
Divan	96	Whiskey Milk Punch	225
Dixie Whiskey Cocktail	97	Whiskey Orange	225
Double Standard Sour	98	Whiskey Rickey	225
Elk's Own Cocktail	103	Whiskey Sangaree	225
Fancy Whiskey Cocktail	105	Whiskey Sour	225
Flip	108		
Fox River Cocktail	109	**SCOTCH**	
Frisco Sour	110	Affinity Cocktail	31
Highball	129	Barbary Coast Cocktail	41
High Life	128	Beadlestone Cocktail	42
Horse's Neck	131	Beals Cocktail	42
Hot Brick Toddy	131	Blood and Sand Cocktail	53
Hot Toddy	132	Bobby Burns Cocktail	56
Imperial Fizz	141	Cameron's Kick Cocktail	70
Japanese Fizz	144	Derby Fizz	95
King Cole Cocktail	147	Flying Scotchman Cocktail	109

Frozen Scotch El Borracho	111	Broken Spur Cocktail	66
Gaslight	112	Bronx Cocktail	66
High Life	128	Bronx Cocktail (Dry)	66
Highland Cooler	129	Bronx Silver Cocktail	66
Highland Fling Cocktail	129	Bronx Terrace Cocktail	67
Hole-In-One Cocktail	129	Brown Cocktail	67
Hoot Mon Cocktail	130	Carrol Cocktail	72
Leviathan 477	151	Charles Cocktail	74
Mamie Gilroy	156	Claridge Cocktail	85
Mamie Taylor	156	Clove Cocktail	85
Miami Beach Cocktail	159	Club Cocktail	86
Morning Glory Fizz	167	Cold Deck Cocktail	88
Rob Roy Cocktail	184	Cooperstown Cocktail	89
Scotch Bishop Cocktail	200	Coronation Cocktail	89
Scotch Cooler	201	Country Club Cooler	90
Scotch Milk Punch	201	Damn-the-Weather Cocktail	93
Scotch Mist	201	Darb Cocktail	94
Scotch Old Fashioned	201	Deep Sea Cocktail	94
Scotch Rickey	201	Devil's Cocktail	95
Scotch Sour	202	Dickens' Martini Cocktail	95
Scotch Whiskey Highball	202	Dinerflo	96
		Diplomat Cocktail	96
SOUTHERN COMFORT		Dixie Cocktail	96
Canasta	70	Du Barry Cocktail	98
Dinerflo	96	Duchess Cocktail	99
Little Colonel	151	East India Cocktail No. 2	99
Missouri Mule	165	El Presidente Cocktail No. 2	102
Omar's Delight	170	English Highball	103
Scarlett O'Hara	200	English Rose Cocktail	103
Volcano	222	Epicurean	104
		Fair and Warmer Cocktail	104
VERMOUTH		Fantasio Cocktail	106
Adonis Cocktail	31	Farmer's Cocktail	106
Affinity Cocktail	31	Favourite Cocktail	106
Allies Cocktail	33	Fifty-Fifty Cocktail	106
American Beauty Cocktail	34	Flying Scotchman Cocktail	109
Apple Pie Cocktail	36	Frankenjack Cocktail	109
Bamboo Cocktail	41	Froupe Cocktail	110
Baron Cocktail	42	Futurity	111
Beadlestone	42	Gaslight	112
Beals Cocktail	42	Gilroy Cocktail	112
Beauty Spot Cocktail	42	Gin & It	113
Bermuda Highball	44	Golf Cocktail	123
Bijou Cocktail	45	Gourmet Cocktail	124
Blackthorn Cocktail	53	Gypsy Cocktail	126
Blood and Sand Cocktail	53	Harvard Cocktail	126
Blood Bronx Cocktail	54	Highland Fling Cocktail	129
Bloodhound Cocktail	54	Hoffman House Cocktail	129
Bobby Burns Cocktail	56	Hole-in-One Cocktail	129
Bombay Cocktail	56	Homestead Cocktail	130
Brandy Vermouth Cocktail	65	Hoot Mon Cocktail	130
Brazil Cocktail	65	H.P.W. Cocktail	132

Ideal Cocktail	140	Turf Cocktail	214
Imperial Cocktail	141	Tuxedo Cocktail	214
Income Tax Cocktail	141	Twin Six Cocktail	215
Jersey Lightning Cocktail	144	Vermouth Cassis	216
Jewel Cocktail	144	Vermouth Cocktail	216
Jeyplak Cocktail	144	Wallick Cocktail	222
Journalist Cocktail	145	Washington Cocktail	223
Judgette Cocktail	146	Yale Cocktail	226
Katz' Meow	146	Yanuck Fever	227
Kiss-In-The-Dark Cocktail	147		
Knickerbocker Cocktail	147	**VODKA**	
Leave It To Me Cocktail No. 1	149	Banana Punch	41
Lone Tree Cocktail	151	Black Russian	46
Lone Tree Cooler	152	Bloody Bloody Mary Cocktail	54
Manhattan	156-157	Bloody Mary Cocktail	54
Martini	157-158	Blue Monday Cocktail	55
Mary Garden Cocktail	158	Bull Shot	68
Merry Widow Cocktail No. 1	158	Chez Asch	76
Miami Beach Cocktail	159	Dinermite	96
Montmartre Cocktail	166	Dinermo	96
Morning Cocktail	166	Flying Grasshopper Cocktail	108
Moulin Rouge Cocktail	167	Gibson	112
Orange Bloom Cocktail	170	Gimlet	113
Oriental Cocktail	172	Huntsman Cocktail	134
Paddy Cocktail	172	Katz' Meow	146
Palmetto Cocktail	173	Moscow Mule	170
Perfect Cocktail	175	Ninotchka Cocktail	169
Peter Pan Cocktail	175	Polonaise Cocktail	179
Piccadilly Cocktail	175	Polynesian Cocktail	179
Pink Whiskers Cocktail	178	The Rockette	185
Preakness Cocktail	182	Russian Bear Cocktail	195
Princeton Cocktail	182	Russian Cocktail	196
Queen Elizabeth Cocktail	183	Screwdriver	202
Racquet Club Cocktail	183	Tovarich Cocktail	213
Rob Roy Cocktail	184	Twister	215
Rose Cocktail (English)	187	Vodka & Apple Juice	216
Rose Cocktail (French)	187	Vodka & Tonic	216
Salome	197	Vodka Cooler	216
San Francisco Cocktail	197	Vodka Daisy	217
Sands-Martin Cocktail	197	Vodka Gimlet	217
Sangaree	198	Vodka Grasshopper Cocktail	217
Scotch Bishop Cocktail	200	Vodka Gypsy Cocktail	217
Shamrock Cocktail	203	Vodka Sour	217
Silver Cocktail	206	Vodka Stinger	217
Skidmore '54 Cocktail	206	Volcano	222
Sloppy Joe's Cocktail No. 1	208		
Tequila Cocktail	210	**WEIGHT WATCHERS® MAGAZINE'S**	
Tequini	210	**NON-ALCOHOLIC RECIPES**	
Trilby Cocktail	213		
Trinity Cocktail	214	Bloody Shame	230
Tropical Cocktail	214	Bent Nail	230
Tulip Cocktail	214	Bull on the Rocks	230
		Calypso Cola	230

Dolphin's Delight	230	Madeira Eggnog	155
Grapefruit Juice Highball	231	Mary Garden Cocktail	158
Mint Tulip	231	Mimosa	159
Rhubarb Punch	231	Opera Cocktail	170
Sauerkraut Juice Cocktail	231	Phoebe Snow Cocktail	175
Thin 'n Tonic	231	Pineapple Cooler	176
		Poop Deck Cocktail	180
WINE		Port Milk Punch	180
Adonis Cocktail	31	Port Wine Cobbler	180
Alfonso XIII	33	Port Wine Cocktail	181
Appetizer	35	Port Wine Eggnog	181
Baltimore Eggnog	40	Port Wine Flip	181
Bamboo Cocktail	41	Port Wine Negus	181
Biffy Cocktail	44	Port Wine Sangaree	181
Bishop	45	Quarter Deck Cocktail	183
Bombay Punch	56	Queen Charlotte	183
Brazil Cocktail	65	Rhine Wine Cup	184
Broken Spur Cocktail	66	Roman Punch	187
Burgundy Bishop	68	Salome	197
Cardinal Punch	71	Saterne Cobbler	199
Champagne Punch	73	Sauterne Cup	199
Chicago Fizz	76	Sevilla Cocktail	203
Chocolate Cocktail	76	Sherry and Egg Cocktail	204
Chocolate Daisy	77	Sherry Cobbler	204
Chocolate Soldier Cocktail	77	Sherry Cocktail	204
Claret Cobbler	84	Sherry Eggnog	205
Claret Cup	84	Sherry Flip	205
Claret Punch	85	Sherry Sangaree	205
Club No. 1	86	Skidmore '54 Cocktail	206
Coffee Cocktail	87	Sloppy Joe's Cocktail No. 2	208
Coffee Flip	87	Spritzer Highball	209
Coronation Cocktail	89		
Country Cocktail	90	**SNACK INDEX**	
Creole Lady Cocktail	91	Almonds, Toasted	256
Crimson Cocktail	91	Avocado Spears	233
Cup	93	Bean Appetizer	233
Devil's Cocktail	95	Caesar Salad, Simmons'	252
Dinermite	96	Canapés Baccara	234
Dubonnet Cocktail	98	Canapés Marguery	234
Dubonnet Fizz	99	Caviar Radishes	235
Dubonnet Highball	99	Caviar Ritz, Ciofalo's	236
East India Cocktail No. 2	99	Celery, Stuffed	254
Elk's Own Cocktail	103	Cheese Spears	235
General Harrison's Eggnog	112	Chicken Rajah Fricassee	235
Glüg	123	Chili Con Queso	236
Hollywood Cooler	129	Coconut Cheese	236
Hot Buttered Wine	129	Crab Meat, Toasted	256
Hot Springs Cocktail	132	Crêpes	237
Jamaica Glow Cocktail	143	Crêpes Fillings	238
Japanese Fizz	144	Cucumber Dill	239
Lemonade (Claret)	149	Cucumber Dip	239
Lemonade (Modern)	150	Eggs alla Florentine	240

Eggs, Curried	239	Rarebits, Petite	246
Fondue	241	Rarebit with Beer	248
Fondue (Massoletti's)	243	Rémoulade Sauce	248
Guacamolitos	241	Roquefort Stuffed Shrimp	249
Ham and Cheese Roll	242	Salmon Platter	249
Herring Creamed	237	Scrambled Eggs with	
Herring Salad, Swedish Style	242	Anchovy Toast	250
Herring Snack	243	Shrimp Madrid	250
Meat Balls, Italian Style	243	Shrimp Puffs	251
Mozzarella Skewered with		Shrimp Simon	251
Canadian Bacon	244	Shrimp, Stuffed	255
Omelet, Simmons' Special	255	Shrimp, Stuffed with Roquefort	249
Oyster Fritters	245	Soup Sandwiches	253
Oysters and Celery	245	Spread Suggestions	253
Oysters and Mushrooms	245	Steak Sandwiches,	
Pâté	246	Smothered Onions	254
Pickle Dillies	246	Sturgeon, Sliced	253
Pigs in Clover	247	Tidbits	255
Puffs	247	Tongue Tidbits	256
Rabbit, Welsh	257	Whipped Dip	257
Ramequins de Gruyère	247		

Current SIGNET Movie and Television Tie-In Titles